D0882257

THE

CIVIL WAR

INFANTRYMAN

IN CAMP, ON THE MARCH, AND IN BATTLE.

BY

GREGORY A. COCO

THOMAS PUBLICATIONS
Gettysburg, PA 17325

Copyright © 1996 Gregory A. Coco

Printed and bound in the United States of America

Published by   THOMAS PUBLICATIONS
             P.O. Box 3031
             Gettysburg, Pa. 17325

ISBN-1-57747-007-9 (softcover)
ISBN-1-57747-009-5 (hardcover)

LC# 96-60651

Front cover illustration, "Confederate Standard Bearer"
by Don Troiani. Back cover illustration, "Eagle of the
Eighth" by Don Troiani. Both paintings courtesy of
Historical Art Prints, Southbury, CT.

Cover design by Ryan C. Stouch

To my former
"Brothers in Arms"

Through these fields of destruction
Baptisms of fire
I've watched all your suffering
As the battles raged higher
And though they did hurt me so bad
In the fear and alarm
You did not desert me
My brothers in arms
                    c1984 Dire Straits

In memory of my friend
John Lawrence Andrews
1952-1996
"You did not desert me..."

CONTENTS

Foreword v

Preface vi

Introduction 1

PART I — THE MILITARY ORGANIZATION

The Men 5

The Regiment 9

Building the Armies 12

Training 17

PART II — FOOD AND EQUIPMENT

Rations 24

Uniforms and Clothing 33

Equipment 49

Weapons and Accouterments 61

PART III — CAMPAIGNING AND FIGHTING

The Veteran Infantryman 77

On the March 82

Fighting the Battles 90

Continuing Combat 98

Injury, Death, and Burial 130

Muster-Out 148

Epilogue 153

Notes 154

Index 160

FOREWORD

"The battle at that point was fought by the sturdy men who carried the guns." This is how Ellis Spear, second-in-command of the 20th Maine during their famous defense of Little Round Top at Gettysburg in 1863, described the fight. With these same words, Spear may have summed up nearly every land battle fought by major armies for centuries. Sooner or later, the bulk of the work falls on the backs of the men many know simply as "grunts."

One of the fascinations we may have with the Civil War is its stark simplicity in comparison to our modern concept of armed conflict. Central to this, the infantryman reminds us that even in an age of advanced technological warfare human beings making critical decisions "on the ground" are still an irreplaceable element of tactics and strategy. Today, a U.S. Army indoctrination film shown to all new recruits soon after they arrive at Fort Benning, Georgia's School of the Infantry reminds them that, even in our high-tech age, the infantryman is indispensible.

Indeed, any understanding of the Civil War must begin with a basic knowledge of the more than three million people who shouldered what we now consider primitive weapons, stood elbow to elbow in two rows twenty-eight inches apart, and in groups of tens of thousands. At its most fundamental level, one cannot truly understand any facet of the war without some understanding of a soldier's experience. In addition, it is important to grasp the mundane day-to-day life of the infantryman and not just the relative few moments of chaos they knew as battle.

Whether one seeks to know more about how their ancestors, North or South, lived as soldiers in the war, or to better understand how major battles began, developed, and ended, understanding the life of the common soldier is critical. So often, the answers to major Civil War questions come down to some facet of the private soldiers' experience.

In previous works, Greg Coco has unravelled the complexity of Civil War hospital care and the gruesome aftermath of the battle at Gettysburg. In this volume he offers the reader, whether novice or expert, a guide to the life and times of the combat infantryman—the basic tool of warfare in the 1860s. He explores here everything from the formation of army doctrine at the outbreak of war to the details of what the common soldier ate, how he slept, and how he felt about both killing and dying.

And well he should. A decorated combat veteran himself, the author has spent more than a decade researching, writing, and interpreting the Civil War in ten books, numerous articles, and as a Park Ranger on the Gettysburg battlefield. With all of this background, he brings a personal knowledge and empathy to his subject that greatly enhances the result.

Prior to this work, getting to know the life of an 1860s infantryman required the reading of a wide variety of sources to gain a full knowledge of army life. This work alleviates that task. Greg Coco has brought a vast array of useful information together into one succinct and well-organized book. Anyone who seriously considers the idea of getting to know the people who fought the Civil War and how they fought it would do well to begin here.

Tom Desjardin
Gettysburg, PA
August 1996

PREFACE

Oh War! Thou Son of Hell!

William Shakespeare

Among the odd assortment of collectibles in my office, which includes various fossils, meteorites and Indian arrowheads, are a few Civil War items that have been picked up on old battlefields and campsites, or obtained from the descendants of soldiers who served in that war. A pair of those mementos catches my eye at this very moment as I sit here at my desk working and keeping warm on an icy spring morning, just a few miles north of Gettysburg, Pennsylvania. The relics are rifle muskets. One, a U.S. Model 1861 Springfield, and the other a British Pattern 1853 Enfield. Both could have been carried in that great battle. A dull, pale, almost silvery light coming through the window beside them barely illuminates the weapons. If one cared to look more closely, it would be apparent that the guns could hardly excite for long the curiosity of a purist in the field of antique firearms. Truthfully, the pieces are in pretty rough condition, and this coarse appearance does little to enhance their value. What makes the muskets attractive to me, however, are their histories. Made in late 1861 or early 1862, the Springfield was issued to Private John A. Gilger of Company K, 46th Pennsylvania Infantry, who enlisted in that regiment on February 22, 1862 at Harrisburg, only 30 miles from where the rifle now collects dust. Just sixteen when he joined, Gilger carried the gun for three years, four months, and 25 days, and was present during the engagements at Winchester, Cedar Mountain, Antietam, Chancellorsville, Gettysburg, Resaca, New Hope Church, Pine Mountain, Lost Mountain, Kolb's Farm, Kennesaw Mountain, Peach Tree Creek, and the Siege of Atlanta, plus numerous smaller skirmishes and actions. Sometime after his second enlistment on February 13, 1864, John Gilger thought enough of his faithful weapon to have his name, company, and regiment stamped into the cold hard metal of the barrel. Upon discharge from the army on July 16, 1865, Gilger purchased the rifle for $6.00 and took it home, where it remained in his family for over 100 years. In all likelihood, it was treated as an esteemed and valuable eyewitness to his long and arduous service.

(Top) Enfield rifle musket carried by Pvt. William H. Beard, 13th Georgia.
(Bottom) Springfield rifle musket used by Pvt. John A. Gilger, 46th Pennsylvania.

(GAC)

The Enfield, on the other hand, was made in England in 1861 and bears the distinct markings of a weapon sold to the Confederate state of Georgia and shipped there through the Federal blockade. Eventually this particular weapon was issued to the 13th Georgia Infantry (which received Enfields in May 1862) then into the hands of Private William Harman Beard of Company E, a resident of Randolph County. Beard had enlisted at Griffin, Georgia on July 8, 1861 and was described as measuring 5' 6" tall, with fair complexion, dark hair and gray eyes. He served in the 13th, a part of General Gordon's Brigade, until captured at High Bridge, Virginia near Appomattox Court House on April 6, 1865, three days shy of Lee's surrender there on April 9. Since Beard's rifle was picked up after the Battle of Gettysburg as a trophy of that engagement, he would never, like Private Gilger, have been able to take it home as a souvenir of the war. No one can now know why Beard left his musket at Gettysburg. During the time it was in his possession, however, the weapon was in frequent combat. It was even "personalized" by Private Beard, who carved his name in the stock, altered the rear sight for an easier aim, and replaced the British hammer (which probably broke from use) with an American-made one. After receiving the Enfields, the 13th Georgia, as part of Stonewall Jackson's Corps, fought in the Seven Days' Battles around Richmond, and also at Cedar Mountain, Second Manassas, Harpers Ferry, Sharpsburg, Fredericksburg, Chancellorsville, Winchester and Gettysburg. William Beard was by all accounts a good infantryman. During the three years, eight months and 28 days he spent in the Confederate army, he was absent for only a few months in 1863 and 1864 due to typhoid fever, both times when his unit was on inactive duty between campaigns. After serving two months and twenty days as a prisoner of war in 1865, Beard returned to his home near Cuthbert, Georgia where he died on September 13, 1921.

Although years would pass before an army musket became the official emblem of the U.S. infantry, the weapon was already the symbol of the combat infantryman. No one can imagine, even today, a mental "picture" of a foot soldier without seeing a rifle somewhere on his person, either in his hands, or propped upon, or slung from his body. Whether a British "Brown Bess" carried by a Revolutionary private on the field of Germantown or an outdated Harpers Ferry musket balanced on the shoulder of a dusty Confederate marching through Vicksburg, or the black steel and plastic of an M-16 assault rifle hanging loosely in the sweaty grip of an American draftee in Cu Chi Province, Vietnam, the image is always the same. The infantryman, equipped with a hand-held weapon, has been, is, and will be the ultimate fighter. His business is death at close quarters, and his lot in wartime is a combination of fear, boredom, loneliness, exhaustion, danger, and excitement, plus the daily prospect of primitive living conditions consisting of poor food, worn and soiled clothing, and all too brief periods of sleep.

The infantryman is the theme of this book. By enhancing these pages with the infantryman's personal documentary, a more complete and honest evaluation of the man and his craft can be gleaned. The material presented covers a limited but varied set of subject matter, such as the character and makeup of the men who served, their recruitment and enlistment, the rigors of training and camplife, rations, uniforms and clothing, equipment, and weapons; also the hardships of marches and battles, and the inevitability of wounds, deaths and burials. Integrated within these major issues are subtle diversions; some deal with an infantryman's feelings before, during and after combat, "close calls," hand-to-hand fights, accidents, "friendly-fire" casualties, atrocities, the actions and antics of shells and bullets on and around the individual soldier, the filth and burdens of field campaigning, and the importance of, and loss of, friends and comrades.

Mundane facets also are examined. For instance, how "hard tack" was eaten, or a rifle was loaded and fired, and what was the accuracy of Civil War shooting; plus the difficulty of filling a canteen in a hurry, and the way a cartridge box was packed for and employed in battle, or how a veteran infantryman "looked" after months of army service; how tents were pitched, or beds were made while on the march, and a little of the humorous side of the private's life. These dimensions add to the total composite portrait of the fighting men, North and South, who were the meaning and essence of the era. No one can fully assimilate that war, which was the most important event in our country's history, without understanding and knowing the people involved, especially the men who risked and sometimes lost their lives in that supreme struggle. Within this book, the reader will gain useful insight and knowledge toward that end.

With the immense availability of published books documenting the experiences and memoirs of Civil War infantrymen, as well as the tremendous volume of unpublished letters, diaries, and memoirs residing in libraries, historical societies, archives, and private families, there was ample material for this study. Approximately 100 basic sources were studied and outlined. These were generally, but not entirely, books in print that have been published from shortly after the war ended, on up to and including one or two which came out less than a year ago. All books were either sets of surviving soldiers' correspondence, daily memoranda, or reminiscences penned immediately following the termination of the conflict, or in some cases even decades later. These works all described army infantry service, experiences, or observations, and anything deemed pertinent to the basic nature of that branch of the military was culled from the whole and used to bolster segments of the overall theme. Portions of the infantryman's life were skimmed over or bypassed completely, such as discipline and punishment, women in the ranks, religion, prison experiences, garrison duty, recreation, interaction with blacks and civilians, mail, pets, desertions, disease, gambling, drinking, prostitution, or the tactics used by their commanders in combat situations. These particular subjects are adequately covered in other more well known studies presently available. I have tried to hone in on the day-to-day existence of the infantryman as he survived the privations and hazards of active campaigning in a fighting regiment from the perspective of both the Union and Confederate side. I hope the results will satisfy the general reader and the specialists as well.

As in my other historical efforts, I have called on many kind and generous individuals for assistance in completing this book. It is my pleasure to mention the following good people.

First, is my most grateful acknowledgement to Cindy L. Small for her many hours of support in typing, editing, and in providing intelligent and thoughtful suggestions. Also my gratitude goes out to Dean S. Thomas, Don Troiani, David T. Hedrick, Len Rosa, D. Scott Hartwig, Lewis Leigh, Jr., Philip B. Ennis, Sarah C. Rodgers, James E. Thomas, Scott E. Wolf, William C. McKenna, Pat, Chet, Sam and Wes Small, Herbert O. Brown, Dwight V. Nitz, and especially Thomas A. Desjardin for the excellent foreword, Steven C. Hollingshead and Michael S. Brouse for photographic work and to Lynn W. Myers for several sketches. To all of you goes my deep thanks and sincere appreciation for your efforts and encouragement.

Gregory A. Coco
Bendersville, PA
March 29. 1996

PHOTO CREDITS

ACHS   Adams County Historical Society
ADK   A.D. Kirwan
BGP   Belle Grove Publishing Company
BL   *Battles and Leaders of the Civil War*
DST   Dean S. Thomas
EF   Edwin Forbes
ER   Emil Rosenblatt
GAC   Gregory A. Coco
GNMP   Gettysburg National Military Park
HAS   Harold A. Small
HC   *Hardtack and Coffee*
JIR   James I. Robertson, Jr.
NA   National Archives
NMHM   National Museum of Health and Medicine
PBE   Phillip B. Ennis
RGB   R.G. Barber
SCH   Steven C. Hollingshead
THS   The Horse Soldier Civil War Shop
USAMHI   U.S. Army Military History Institute, Carlisle Barracks
WCM   William C. McKenna
WRU   Western Reserve University

INTRODUCTION

I wondered whether the American people were civilized or not, to butcher one another in that manner; and I came to the conclusion that we were barbarians, North and South alike.

Pvt. John O. Casler
33rd Virginia Infantry

On Monday, August 20, 1866, President Andrew Johnson declared: "I...proclaim that the said insurrection is at an end and that peace, order, tranquility, and civil authority now exist in and throughout the whole of the United States of America."[1] With that proclamation, the War of the Rebellion, as it was officially called by the victors, was finally over. The cost had been enormous. Total deaths of soldiers from all causes were eventually placed at 623,026, the wounded at 471,427, all of which totalled 1,094,453, a figure considered by some to be probably too low. In dollars and cents, the very minimum price of the war would clearly top $10,000,000,000.[2]

The Civil War had begun on April 12, 1861 with the firing on Fort Sumter in Charleston Harbor, South Carolina. One former Confederate sergeant justified his war with these words:

> The Southern folk were always debaters, loving logic and taking off their hats to a syllogism. They had never been able to understand how any reasonable mind could doubt the right of secession, and they were in a chronic state of surprised incredulity, as the war began, that the North could indeed be about to wage a war that was manifestly forbidden by unimpeachable logic.[3]

Others saw it differently. General Grant was among them when he wrote:

> There was no time during the rebellion when I did not think...that the South was more to be benefited by defeat than the North. The latter had the people, the institutions, and the territory to make a great and prosperous nation. The former was burdened with an institution abhorent to all civilized peoples not brought up under it, and one which degraded labor, kept it in ignorance, and enervated the governing class. With the outside world at war with this institution, they could not have extended their territory. The labor of the country was not skilled, nor allowed to become so. The whites could not toil without becoming degraded, and those who did were denominated "poor white trash." The system of labor would have soon exhausted the soil and left the people poor. The non-slaveholders would have left the country, and the small slaveholder must have sold out to his more fortunate neighbors. Soon the slaves would have outnumbered the masters, and, not being in sympathy with them, would have risen in their might and exterminated them. The war was expensive to the South as well as to the North, both in blood and treasure; but it was worth all it cost.[4]

Even in the beginning, the sides were uneven. The population of the Southern states in 1860, from which it would draw its fighting men, was 12,315,373, of whom 3,953,696 were slaves. The North contained 19,127,948 people. Just nine cities in the entire United States had over 100,000 citizens. Only one, New Orleans, could be claimed by the Confederacy. As for "just plain manpower," or those of the ages available for war, the Federal states held around 10,500,000 while the eleven seceding states and those "pro-Confederate" in the five border states accounted for close to 3,500,000.

Improved farmland was a good indication of the disparity between North and South. A year before the start of the Civil War, the Southern states counted 57,089,633 acres, while Northerners could boast of 106,171,756 improved acres. The cash value of these farms was unequal also, with the North at over four billion dollars and the South at just under two billion. The value of machinery, animals, produce, and improvements was always in favor of the North, except in a few categories such as ginned cotton bales, pounds of rice, peanuts and peas.

Transportation and commerce showed major differences; here, the Confederates lagged far behind their Yankee counterparts. For instance, U.S. exports were $222,199,477 against $27,145,466 for eight Southern states. Ships entering the United States in the year before June, 1861 totaled 43,625, with a mere 1,975 of these going in and out of Confederate ports. Railroad miles were similarly imbalanced; 22,000 in the Union states and a bare 8,541 miles within the seceded states. Horseflesh, too, reared its dominant head in Yankeedom, with 6,115,458 animals to the South's nominal 1,698,328. Industrial establishments flourished up North, where there were 110,274 in operation in 1860, with only 18,026 below the Mason and Dixon Line. The "value of products" in the entire United States (including the would-be Confederacy) in 1860 totaled $1,900,000,000; only $145,350,000 were produced in the South.[5]

To win the war, the Confederacy would have to find some special component in its arsenal, one with which the North could not compete. Unfortunately for that new nation, it may have come close to the formula for victory, but in the end Southerners failed to locate what was needed.

At the very outset of the Rebellion the Federal government had little chance of subduing the Confederate populace with a Regular Army numbering only 1,108 officers and 15,254 enlisted men. Eventually however, the weight of the North's population would propel between 1,550,000 and 2,200,000 individuals into its armed forces. The Confederate States' military machine total is in dispute, but 750,000 men in arms is a reasonable number. So in the long run, the North had a three-to-one human advantage during the four years of conflict. As to potential, the Union factored in nearly 10,500,000 white males from which it could draw soldiers and sailors, while the South may have had about 3,500,000. In 1860, when the seceding Southern states were forming their Confederacy, all white males between the ages of eighteen and forty-five years of age who were available for service numbered approximately 2,000,000 for the South and 3,500,000 in the North.[6]

In time, many members of this "military age" population served in the various forces of the United States and Confederate States. Between 1861 and 1865 a total of 40 operational organizations or "field armies" were established: 23 in the Southern army and 16 under Federal command. These armies were usually named for the department in which they were located, and these same departments were often titled by the Union forces for nearby rivers, states or regions by the Confederates. Hence familiar names such as The Army of the Cumberland, or Army of the Mississippi were

Northern armies, while The Army of Mississippi, or The Army of Northern Virginia were Confederate organizations.

While the larger and more famous forces took part in what are familiar and grand battles including Chickamauga, Second Manassas, or Shiloh, there were in fact thousands of "fights" which took place that are unknown today, even by the most ardent historian of the Civil War. In total over 10,400 engagements of one kind or another were played out during the four years of unrelenting combat. These military actions can be further subdivided into 26 sieges, 76 battles, 6,337 skirmishes, 727 expeditions, 29 assaults, and so forth. Numbers varied from state to state as well. For example, there were 2,154 military events in Virginia (the leading area), during the course of the war, 1,462 in Tennessee, 336 in Alabama, 203 in Maryland, etc. The smallest summary was for the New Mexico Territory with only 75. Therefore, it is far more common to read of little known places, such as the Action at Lick Creek, Tennessee, the Expedition to Bear Wallow, Kentucky, and the Fight at Cowskin, Missouri, than the Battle of Fredericksburg, Virginia, or the Siege of Port Hudson, Louisiana. To the participant, however, one site could be as deadly as the other, and a mortal wound was equal in tragedy to the individual soldier near Gettysburg, Pennsylvania in 1863, as it was at Fort DeRussy, Louisiana, in 1864.

Sgt. Thomas Reed, 51st Pennsylvania, illustrates a typical Union infantryman. (GAC)

3

PART
I

(WCM)

The Military
Organization

The Men

Johnnie if a boy dies for his country the glory is his for ever isn't it?

Pvt. William Pope
9th Kentucky Infantry

Just what sort of humans were those who bore so much hardship, danger, and death in that relatively short period of time? Competent observers like Thomas Jefferson pointed out the general character of Americans from the two regions:

[Northerners] are cool, sober, laborious, perservering, independent, jealous of their own liberties, chicaning, superstitious, and hypocritical in their religion.... Southerners are fiery, voluptuary, indolent, unsteady, independent, zealous of their own liberties, but trampling on those of others, generous, candid, and without attachment or pretentious of any religion but that of the heart.

Much has been made about the individual Southerner being a better soldier than his Northern opponent. General Don C. Buell said it was all in the nature of the contest: "Individually, the Northern soldier was in no sense the inferior of the Southern.... Much was due to the character of the contest. Revolution is calculated to inspire bold and desperate action, and wars of sentiment, of the nature of which this partook more in the South than in the North, are always marked by unusual energy."

He related further that superior numbers, "were generally essential to Union victories due to the necessity of invasion against a hostile population." Buell also noted that the average Southerner had more implicit confidence in his leaders due to an inbred or produced subordination in his character, as well as being more contented with meager supplies and a simpler life. These and other factors helped the Rebels to accept hardship more readily than the Yankee soldiers. He ended by emphasizing that the women of the South exerted an important influence, as they, "in agony of heart girded the sword upon their loved ones and bade them go."

Southerner Henry W. Ravenal stated the Rebel case ominously:

I fear the Northern people have an impression that we are unable to cope with them, from inferiority in numbers, want of necessary means; & that our slave population is an element of weakness. It may be necessary therefore that they should be disabused of such impressions, & learn to appreciate & understand us better. If we must pass through the terrible ordeal of War to teach them this lesson, so be it. It may be the best in the end.[7]

Other historians over the years have found that Union and Confederate soldiers had countless corresponding characteristics, while still assuming many apparent and even major contrasts. In short and contradictorily, they were "very much alike, with great differences." Historian Bill I. Wiley, known for his monumental work on the common soldier in both armies, argued too, that in general they were alike and diverse at the same time. He noted in his studies that one-fourth to one-fifth of the Union army was foreign-born, while only one-twentieth to one-twenty-fifth of Confederates were born outside the U.S. Illiteracy was much more typical among Southerners. In an average regiment up to 200 men probably could not read and write, whereas in a Northern regiment only about six men were likely to be uneducated. Yankee soldiers came from a mixture of occupations including a variety of highly skilled positions, while Confederates were nearly always farmers. He characterized both sides as being comparable on morality issues such as the use of profanity, gambling, drunkenness, recreational fornication and so forth. Northerners, he said, were "practical and prosaic," with a deeper interest in political and intellectual affairs. Rebels appeared more emotionally religious in their letters and diaries and were on the whole more "fanciful" and "poetic" and humorous in their writings. Wiley found that the majority of Union men fought to save the Union or destroy slavery, but the average Confederate went to war to protect his family, home, self-government, states' rights, and the Southern way of life, including slavery. They displayed more "dash, elan, individual aggressiveness, and a devil-may-care-quality" in battle, but the Yankee showed "greater seriousness" and an intense "group consciousness and team spirit," and fighting for them required the "earnest and coordinated exertion of all those involved."

The infantrymen had their own thoughts on the subject of motivation. One Southern soldier, George Eggleston, remembered that a number of the volunteers on both sides soon acquired the steadiness and order of regulars and, "never lost their personal interest in the contest or their personal pride or manhood as a sustaining force under trying conditions."[8] Thousands of Confederate and Northern infantrymen soon, however, lost all civilian-bred attitudes toward the war, and subjects like patriotism, slavery, unionism, nationhood, and glory began to take a back seat as the fighting and suffering armies pounded each other relentlessly through the long years of civil war. It was not that the good and steady soldiers forgot or totally abandoned these concepts; it was merely that for them the war became a contest of survival. Comrades became their new families and the regiment was their only country. Captain James Williams, 21st Alabama, described it all: "What a pleasant thing to be a soldier! Rain, mud—want—sickness exposure—danger—death—and oblivion—are his portion! And Glory—I forgot that— Glory! yes it is a glorious thing to be a soldier of the Confederacy—fighting and suffering all that I have named for the cause of liberty—."[9]

Private Wilbur Fisk, 2nd Vermont, looking for reasons to fight called slavery "a relic of the darkest age and [even] the poorest government on earth is better in principle than that." Fisk was ready to go to any lengths to break the South and force it into submission, yet he experienced moments of doubt, demoralization and shameless selfishness. At times he had to put "Uncle Sam's Constitution" aside and pay attention to his own needs.[10]

Even tried and true "old soldiers" grew fatalistic. According to Captain Henry S. Nourse, 55th Illinois, sometimes solid veterans on the approach of yet another fight, "seem to be out of heart, and save for their pride almost willing to own that their courage had all but left them."[11] Hermon Clarke of the 117th New York went further, and declared:

> I would like to have those men who are so anxious for a vigorous prosecution of the war [to] witness such scenes as we did on the 29th of September and the 27th of October. [1864—at New Market Heights—Chaffin's Farm, Va.] Men wounded in every manner imaginable. Some dead, others dying, giving their last message to some comrade.

Some cursing the war that deprived them of a leg or an arm and made them cripples for life.... I am not in favor of withdrawing our armies and giving up everything, but think every honorable means that can be used to put an end to the war should be, and soon, too.[12]

Several historians have found that a lack of discipline was common in the Southern forces, making the average Confederate "an admirable fighting man but a poor soldier," and that this devil-may-care, reckless self-confidence may have finally destroyed them as a fighting force. For in the long run "the Rebel" could not compete against the "highly disciplined northern armies."[13]

In a purely physical comparison of the infantryman, the average height of Americans between 1860 and 1865 was 5 feet 8-1/4 inches. Colonel William Fox noted that out of 1,000,000 soldiers' heights recorded there were 3,613 over 6 feet 3 inches tall and some who were over 7 feet. One officer was measured at 82 1/2 inches, Captain David Van Buskirk of the 27th Indiana. By contrast, a 21-year-old in the 192nd Ohio was only 40 inches in height, and he was said to be able to "endure a greater amount of fatigue and exposure" than almost any man in the unit. Short, wiry men or "ponies" as they were called, proved to be more able to withstand the hard marches and general outdoor camp life of Civil War campaigns than the large, "strapping" fellows we often visualize as making good soldiers. Weight records were never completely studied by Colonel Fox but he indicated that the average was 143-1/2 pounds. Color of hair, complexion, and eyes varied, but the most common was a "light" complexion, blue eyes, and brown to light hair.

The median soldier was 25.8 years old during the war, but there were extremes on either end of the spectrum. A prospective recruit had to lie or obtain parental or a guardian's permission to enlist under the age of 18; therefore, many exceptions to the minimum age can be found. One private named E. Pollard in the 5th North Carolina, joined that regiment in 1862 at 62 years of age. A sample of 11,000 Confederate descriptive rolls turned up one soldier who was 13, three who were 14, and 31 who were 15. In a group of 14,000 Federals the rosters included three who were 12 when they enlisted, twelve who were 13, four who were 14, and five who had attained the age of 15. Charles C. Hay of Alabama claimed in 1901 that he had joined his regiment when he was all of 11 years old. But these very young or very old men and boys were definitely the exception, not the rule. On the whole, however, the Union recruited somewhat older men than the South, although Southerners often expressed surprise at how youthful some of their northern opponents appeared to be.[14]

The roster of Company H, 72nd Ohio gives some credence to Colonel Fox's findings. This regiment was not state or local militia, but a regular "fighting force," an ordinary field infantry unit. Out of over 100 men listed on its rolls, 42 were over the age of 30. The oldest in the company was 49, and the youngest 18 at the time of enlistment. The "old timer" was Jacob Steitz who was mortally wounded at Shiloh, Tennessee in April, 1862, four months after entering service.

After the war, many units claimed they held the youngest or oldest men on record in their ranks. Cases in point: the 58th Pennsylvania with an 8-year-old named Brady; the 66th Ohio recruited a 9-year-old; the 47th Pennsylvania had a 67-year-old color sergeant; there was a 9-year-old in the 14th New York Cavalry; a 13-year-old in the 10th Illinois Cavalry; and a 9-year-old musician in the 22nd Michigan named John Clem.

Occupations differed somewhat by region. In general, Union troops listed approximately 48% farmers in the ranks, 24% mechanics, 16% laborers, 5% in commercial pursuits, 3% classified as professional men, and 4% were of miscellaneous vocations. In this last category "gentleman," "gambler," "loafer," and "jack-of-all-trades" appeared. In the Southern ranks a sample of 107 company rolls containing 9,000 names, discloses 5,600 farmers, 474 students, 472 laborers, 321 clerks, 318 mechanics, 222 carpenters, 138 merchants, and some sailors, doctors, painters, teachers, lawyers, overseers, masons, tailors, bakers, and even a "rogue," a "convict" and several "gentlemen." Some less common occupations in U.S. rolls were "paper hanger," "optician," "house mover," "chemist," "gold beater," and "speculator."[15]

Fundamentally, these soldiers were simply plain American citizens. As humans they were a mixture of seriously flawed individuals and even some few godlike heroes, living, marching and fighting alongside each other in all their shared misery, excitement and boredom.

Private Fisk, 2nd Vermont, described the infantrymen he knew as young men "of every grade of character." He pointed out that a typical regiment was composed of men who were quiet and thoughtful; others were boisterous and overflowed with an animal spirit. A few could be found, "to whom you would have to listen long before you would hear a single manly thought expressed, or a single ennobling sentiment uttered," while others were, "sober, thoughtful young men who have come here for the sole purpose of putting down the rebellion...." There were those, too, who were rough, "but at heart honorable," and had seen hardship in every clime, on land and water. Fisk saw many as mere boys in experience, innocent and unsuspecting, and ever ready "to yield to the seductive flatteries of vice."[16]

Lieutenant Galwey, 8th Ohio, believed that, in truth, the "mass of soldiers like better to eat, drink, and be merry, than to march and fight." He heard men "growl incessantly" and without cause, but Galwey never heard even the best soldier growl for want of fighting. He accused most men of being malingerers at one time or another, saying, "A few brave men do all the fighting and a few industrious ones all the work, whilst the rest go off behind the clumps of bushes or into deep ravines and grow fat and save their bodies. They boil coffee, sleep, or play cards. It requires tact to get any labor at all out of them."[17]

Henry W. Prince, 127th New York, called soldiering, "a rough coarse life, calculated to corrupt good morals & harden a man's heart."[18] Robert Stiles underlined the great degree to which he came to understand other men, especially his comrades. "All the little shams, insencerities, and concealments of ordinary society disappeared; until, for the first time in our lives, we seemed to be stripped bare of the disguises under which we had theretofore been accustomed to hide our real characters; not only from the world in general and from our most intimate associates and companies, but even from ourselves."[19]

THE REGIMENT

If any more of the boys are going to enlist, advise them to join the infantry. Its the best arm of the service.

Pvt. Perry Mayo
2nd Michigan Infantry

Unlike our contemporary national volunteer army, the majority of Civil War operational organizations were composed of infantry units. While the cavalry and artillery of an 1860s force played an important role, it was the infantry or the "foot soldiers" and their officers who were relied upon to do the heaviest and hardest fighting, and to secure or defend most objectives or positions. Just as today, the infantry division was the main combat arm employed in the larger Civil War battles. It was the striking mechanism which hammered the opposing forces, for it was usually large enough to accomplish its mission, but small enough to be adequately handled by its officers, either as a single entity or in conjunction with other divisions.

In turn, the infantry regiment was the backbone of all military units from brigade through corps levels. In the main field armies, such as The Army of the Potomac, there could be several hundred regiments always present. For example, in the summer of 1863 this same army had over 340 cavalry, artillery, and infantry regiments and batteries on its rolls, with the average infantry regiment then numbering around 335 officers and enlisted men. Normally, however, an infantry regiment consisted of 1,025 officers and men, (slightly larger in Confederate service, with an authorized strength up to 49 officers and 1,340 men), divided into ten companies of 101 men and three officers, plus fifteen individuals on the "field and staff" of the regiment itself. Therefore, a typical company at full strength appeared "on paper" in this manner:

Company Formation

1 Captain	8 Corporals
1 First Lieutenant	2 Musicians
1 Second Lieutenant	1 Wagoner
1 First Sergeant	82 Privates
4 Sergeants	

Total 101

The ten companies of the regiment were lettered as A, B, C, D, through K. "J" was not used due to its resemblance to the letter I. The Field and Staff of the regiment often employed up to fifteen additional members:

Field and Staff

1 Colonel	1 Sergeant-Major
1 Lieutenant Colonel	1 Quartermaster's Sergeant
1 Major	1 Commissary-Sergeant

1 Adjutant	1 Hospital Steward
1 Quartermaster	2 Principal Musicians
1 Surgeon (rank of Major)	2 Assistant Surgeons
1 Chaplain[20]	

Regiments were enlisted or conscripted throughout the war by either the central government or individual states. There were regular regiments on both sides, i.e., units formed by the governments themselves, not the states. For instance, these were named "14th United States Infantry Regiment" in the Union Army, or "1st Confederate Regiment" in the South. Most infantry regiments, though, were raised by the states under the auspices of the national government and then transferred to that central government. These units kept their state identities, such as "56th Pennsylvania Volunteer Infantry Regiment" or "13th Georgia Volunteer Infantry Regiment."

During the war the U.S. organized 3,559 combat units which included regiments, separate battalions and companies, and batteries; of this total 2,144 were infantry regiments. The Confederacy fielded approximately 1,526 regiments, legions, separate companies, battalions and batteries. Their infantry regiments numbered 642. This figure includes home guards, state militia, local defense, and the like.

Within a typical army organization, several regiments, primarily between three and six in number, were combined into a brigade, and in turn, three to five brigades were grouped into a division. Divisions, usually two, three or four in number, would be known collectively as a corps. Army corps were the largest combat unit, and were generally commanded by a major general, or sometimes by a lieutenant general in the Confederate army. Southern regiments, brigades, divisions, and corps normally had higher numerical strength than their Union counterparts. This is often attributed (wrongly in some cases) to the fact that the United States authorized many more new regiments during the war than the South, therefore dooming their older veteran regiments to continually decreasing strength as the newer regiments gained the bulk of the incoming enlistments and conscripts. The Confederacy, on the other hand, sent most of its human resources into the older proven organizations, in pretense of keeping them up to reasonable combat status. Even as early as the Battle of Antietam, some Federal regiments present contained barely 150 men. On the Rebel side it was frequently little better. At Antietam, or Sharpsburg to the Confederates, the 12th Georgia had present only 100 men and was commanded by a captain. The 21st Virginia in the same battle numbered 87, with one company listing a single man on duty. There are numerous reasons for such small and depleted regiments, which should have counted approximately 1,000 men. Here is what a Connecticut captain said about that subject in August of 1862:

> There is a constant drain on troops in the field, much heavier than a civilian would suppose. Something like one fifth of the men who enlist are not tough enough nor brave enough to be soldiers. A regiment reaches its station a thousand strong, but in six months it can only muster six or seven hundred men for marching and fighting duty; the rest have vanished in various ways. Some have died of hardship, or disease, or nostalgia; as many more have been discharged for physical disability; others are absent sick, or have got furloughs by shamming sickness; others are on special duty as bakers, hospital nurses, wagoners, quartermaster's drudges, etc.; a few are working out sentences of court-martial....
>
> Meantime the government is raising new organizations, instead of filling up the old ones;...[21]

Coincidentally, this officer's unit, the 12th Connecticut, had not yet been in a battle which would have added additional casualties; these losses of deaths, wounded, deserters, and prisoners would have further reduced it to three or four hundred effectives or less.

It was not uncommon for an infantry regiment during its tenure to suffer as high as nineteen percent losses in dead and mortally wounded alone. The Union infantry regiment which took the highest percentage of dead and mortally wounded was the 5th New Hampshire, with 18 officers and 277 men killed outright, or who died of their wounds after battle. As to Confederate service, no figure exists to break unit losses by percent for the entire war, but a few other examples may be enlightening. The average number of men killed in Confederate regiments was about 150, but in a few units the losses were much higher. The 1st South Carolina mourned 21 officers and 260 enlisted men as killed and mortally wounded. And in separate, single engagements over 50 Southern regiments received in excess of 50% casualties. For example, the 1st Texas at Antietam had 82.3%; the 10th Tennessee at Chickamauga had 68%; and the 9th Georgia at Gettysburg had 55%.[22]

But these high and horrific figures do not tell the whole story. They do not contain the numbers of sound, vital men who were wounded and survived, only to return to their units, or, as Colonel William Fox stated, "...to drag their marred and crippled lives along a lower plane of existence." In the 2nd Wisconsin this was particularly true. Out of an enrollment of 1,203 during the war, that midwestern unit lost nearly 900 men either killed or wounded, leaving very few who were not permanently scarred by the war.[23]

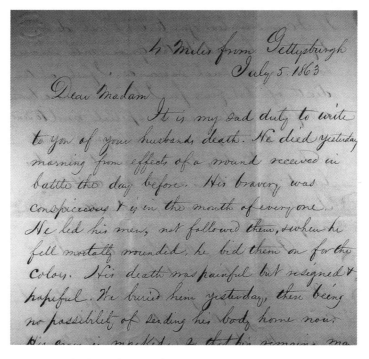

A portion of a letter bearing bad news to the soldier's family. (GAC)

BUILDING THE ARMIES

The noisy speakers of 1861, who fired the Northern heart and who fired the Southern heart, never did any other kind of firing.

General D.H. Hill, C.S.A.

Troops for the infantry and all other branches of service during the Civil War were obtained by recruitment and conscription. All of the first calls for enlistments came as volunteers because a draft was not instituted in the Confederacy until April 16, 1862, and not in the North until March 3, 1863. Of the approximately 3,500,000 men who entered Union or Confederate service between 1861 and 1865, about 170,000 were drafted by the United States and possibly 100,000 by the secessionist states. The Union army also accepted 178,000 enlistments of free blacks or former slaves. Both governments permitted the hiring of substitutes, and these proxies may have outnumbered the draftees. In the North nearly 120,000 were hired substitutes, and the Confederate army allowed in possibly between 50,000 and 100,000; unfortunately, these figures are not reliable.

In the first few months of the war, enticement and recruitment of volunteers was relatively easy as the "fever" of patriotic impulse blocked out more rational ideas or thoughts. Then, as the names of those who succumbed to disease or fell in battle began to crowd the columns of the local newspapers, it became harder to enlist even the most young and naive.

To the individual about to volunteer for infantry service, contemplation of the deed was often worse than the act itself. Warren L. Goss of Massachusetts recalled the day he enlisted:

> "Cold chills" ran up and down my back as I got out of bed after the sleepless night, and shaved.... I was twenty years of age, and when anything unusual was to be done, like fighting or courting, I shaved.
>
> With a nervous tremor convulsing my system, and my heart thumping like muffled drum-beats, I stood before the door of the recruiting office, and, before turning the knob to enter, read and re-read the advertisement for recruits posted thereon, until I knew all its peculiarities....
>
> I was in no hurry to open the door. Though determined to enlist, I was half inclined to put it off awhile. I had a fluctuation of desires. I was faint-hearted and brave; I wanted to enlist, and yet—. Here I turned the knob, and was relieved. I had been more prompt, with all my hesitation, than the officer in his duty; he wasn't in. Finally he came and said: "What do you want, my boy?" "I want to enlist," I responded, blushing deeply with upwelling patriotism and bashfulness. Then the surgeon came to strip and examine me. In justice to myself, it must be stated that I signed the rolls without a tremor.[24]

As the excitement of the first months of conflict waned it proved harder to obtain troops to fill the new regiments. More and more men were called up throughout the Northern and Southern states when it became obvious that the war would not end in less than a year. Recruiting stations sprang up in all large towns and cities, but often, recruiters attempting to enlist men (usually to obtain a commission) were forced to go farther afield to entice citizens into the armies.

As Josiah M. Favill noted in the summer of 1861: "Then, [in April, 1861] everybody wanted to go; now, apparently, most people wanted to stay at home." Like others recruiting nationwide, Favill had difficulties. On one occasion after signing up about 30 men, he saw them all desert and join another organization. This young man finally got his commission, but not without traveling from New York City to Oswego and even to Poughkeepsie, New York. He found himself going deeper into his state to search out the often reluctant village or farm boy who seemed less and less inclined to go to war for $13.00 a month, bounties aside.[25]

When an appropriate number of volunteers was secured (and held on to), the state governor placed the men on an official roll in the state militia. Then the recruiters, who

Civil War recruiting broadside.

were often local leaders in the community, and had undertaken the chore of raising the companies, would receive commissions from the state as lieutenants or captains, once they were elected by their respective units. Providing uniforms, arms, equipment, shelter, and provisions was often handled haphazardly, sometimes by the men who raised the companies, or even by the surrounding community, but usually by the states themselves.

Recruitment of volunteers continued unabated until the end of the war. Each day as the fighting went on unceasingly, notices like this one appeared in newspapers throughout the land:

Central City Blues

We had the pleasure yesterday of grasping by the hand, Capt. J.G. Rodgers,...He is in fine health, and he reports that although his command have endured much hardship and been in two battles; they are in excellent health and fine condition.

The "Blues" are in the 12th Ga. Regiment....Capt. Rodgers wishes to obtain thirty recruits for his company, to whom a bounty of $50 will be given, and uniforms furnished. We appeal to the men of Bibb county to join the "Blues" and fill up their ranks. It is a most excellent company—one that has seen service—commanded by a brave, high toned, noble and patriotic man. Come up then, and furnish Capt. Rodgers with your names. Let the thirty recruits be forthcoming immediately. "Delays are dangerous!"[26]

"Delays" were not the only danger. Just five months after that short article appeared in a Macon newspaper the entire 12th Georgia, not just Rodgers' company, needed over 900 men to fill its ranks. That organization which once numbered 1,000 effectives, then contained less than 100 men and Captain Rodgers no longer commanded his sorely depleted company; he was then acting regimental colonel.

As recruiting became more difficult, communities often resorted to shame or taunts to drive men toward service, and these unusual measures sometimes worked where cash bounties had failed. In Woburn, Massachusetts, this item was seen in the local paper during the summer of 1862: "Stay-at-home Guards are to have a new uniform the most striking feature of which will be a fringe of apron strings around the shirt and a baby's rattle suspended around the neck. They will be armed with wooden swords and quill pop guns." At another gathering a notice was posted which read: "TO-NIGHT! RALLY! BE ON HAND, EVERYBODY! Young ladies, can you not induce some gentleman of your acquaintance to enlist? TRY IT!"[27]

Soon, other measures became necessary to lure men onto the fields of death and anguish. First, bounties were established by the central government, states, and even later by cities, small towns, and counties to encourage men to enroll, in order that each community in every state could fill its assigned quota. Often when the local and state bounties were added up, a man proposing to enter the service might count on as much as $500 to $1,500 in cash, a significant sum in 1863. These large bounties drew in many unscrupulous persons who were avoiding the draft, and they used the system to enrich themselves. It was not uncommon for a "bounty man" to enlist, collect a healthy sum of money, then desert and repeat the process again and again. These "bounty-jumpers" were an embarrassment to both governments and were the object of hate, irritation, and derision by their fellow soldiers. Often when they were encountered at the front, volunteers would cry out, "Take good care of those men; they have cost the Government a great deal of money." Frank Wilkenson, who had enlisted in a New York unit described his experiences with bounty-jumpers while waiting to be sent to the field. For a month he was forced to live in prison with nearly 1,000 of these "ruffians:"

> A recruit's social standing...was determined by the acts of villainy he had performed, supplemented by the number of times he had jumped the bounty. The social standing of a hard-faced crafty pick-pocket, who had jumped the bounty in say half a dozen cities, was assured. He shamelessly boasted of his rascally agility. Less active bounty-jumpers looked up to him as a leader. He commanded their profound respect. When he talked, men gathered around him in crowds and listened attentively to words of wisdom concerning bounty-jumping that dropped from his tobacco-stained lips. His right to occupy the most desirable bunk, or to stand at the head of the column when we prepared to march to the kitchen for our rations, was undisputed.
>
> If there was a man in all that shameless crew who had enlisted from patriotic motives, I did not see him. There was not a man of them who was not eager to run away. Not a man who did not quake when he thought of the front. Almost to a man they were bullies and cowards and almost to a man they belonged to the criminal classes....[28]

Sergeant Austin C. Stearns, 13th Massachusetts, called these substitutes and bounty men, "the worst specimens of humanity," who were the scrapings from the slums of the cities. Many, related the sergeant, could not even remember the names they had enlisted under.[29]

Speaking of one substitute who came to the 17th Connecticut, Private Justus Silliman concluded: "...Mr. Hamilton is certainly a man of note [and] the citizens of Redding must prize his society very highly to pay $300.00 for the sake of keeping him within their borders[,] it is better that such valuable men should not sacrifice themselves for their country when they can be saved by the paltry sum of $300.00...." He also remembered that Rebel prisoners told him that their army conscripts were placed in the front ranks with ardent volunteers massed behind them with fixed bayonets.[30]

Sergeant Daniel Crotty, 3rd Michigan, was almost in anguish when he wrote, "Oh, why do not the young men of our land come down to help us crush this rebellion." He admitted that, "three hundred dollars is like a drop in the bucket to a rich man,...while the poor man must leave his home and those depending on him for support...." Crotty believed that draftees and bounty conscripts should be made to feel shame, and after the war "ought never to show himself in his native place..., but should fly to some corner of the earth, there to end his days in shame and disgrace,..." Lieutenant James G. Theaker, 50th Ohio, was more blunt on these characters, saying: "I could send a corporal & six men that would scare a township [full] of those draft-resisting, Canada-fleeing, weak-kneed Copperheads."[31]

In the long run, every regiment North and South was affected in some way by drafted men or substitutes. Wilbur Fisk's 2nd Vermont eventually had five distinct classes of recruits. "The first," he reported "joined the regiment in the Fall of 1861 at Camp Griffin, the second in the Spring of 1862 at Lee's Mill, the third in the Fall of '62 at Hagerstown, Md.; the fourth class was the drafted men and substitutes that came out here last Fall. [1863]. The last class are those that have come here under the last call of the President."[32]

As the bounty system quickly became corrupt, some citizens turned it into a profitable criminal business, operating organized rings of these "jumpers." Eventually the cost to the Union ran to nearly $600 million, not including the $300 base cost of equipping these soldiers, the same worthless recruits who soon became deserters and sold or threw away their weapons, uniforms and accouterments. Fortunately, the system worked well in some areas, although not well enough to eliminate the draft. But it did bring to the war effort in both countries, large numbers of men who helped to reinforce some of the seriously depleted combat regiments then at the front.

The conscription law was not absolute in either armed force during the war. There was always the opportunity for a drafted man to hire a substitute. As long as a man was mustered it did not matter how he was obtained. Consequently, in the U.S. a conscript could hire a substitute or pay the government a fee, (usually about $300) as commutation of service, a practice prohibited after February, 1864. Even if a citizen in a Northern or Southern state hired a substitute, (the Confederate system was much more limited and was abolished by 1864), he still could be called up for any succeeding draft, as he again became liable. For many, therefore, fraud became the only way out of an ever present and very uncomfortable situation.

Chaplain John Stuckenberg, 145th Pennsylvania, believed that substitutes sent to his regiment ruined the unit. He called them, "the worst of characters," and was often awakened by their "loud boisterous, vulgar and profane language," which he reported lowered the morale of the regiment. "It does not seem like the same regt; it being completely changed by the subs or conscripts (or convicts as some call them) for the worse. Our guard house use to be vacant—now it is full,..." Stuckenberg saw among them, "Germans, Irish, Englishmen, Frenchmen, a Russian, a Hungarian, Dutchmen, [a] Mexican and a number who were rebels once."[33]

Civil War draft notice sent to Amos C. Blodgett in the summer of 1863.
(DST)

TRAINING

The volunteers of the early sixties were hard to manage at best and when they were commanded by former playmates it was a trying ordeal for the officers. But we came down to it at last and plumbed the line like old regulars.

Pvt. Val C. Giles
4th Texas Infantry

Once enrolled, sworn in, and outfitted, the new soldier was ordinarily given some time to settle his personal affairs at home before having to report to a local rendezvous or mustering site or to a designated camp of instruction. Scores of these camps were located throughout Federal and Confederate territory, usually near the larger population centers.

Often the first taste of military service contained methods which to the fresh-faced volunteer seemed useless and ridiculous. Twenty-year-old Samuel D. Buck, 13th Virginia Infantry, explained in his memoirs:

> My first duty was on the Sunday following our organization. I was dressed in my best suit ready for church when orders came for me to meet my company at the armory [Harpers Ferry] for duty at once. I did not even have time to change my clothes. On arriving at the armory I was put on guard.... I was given an old greasy musket and for hours stood guard over a lot of old iron that nothing less than a mule team could have moved. In all my after experience as a soldier, I have never been able to see the sense or use of that day's duty. I was by no means pleased for I missed seeing my best girl to church. All loss and no gain to me, certainly no honor. Everything must have a beginning, so must the life of a soldier.[34]

Camp routine was both tedious and monotonous as recalled by the thousands of infantrymen who left behind descriptions in diaries, letters and recollections. William Tunnard of the 3rd Louisiana Infantry remembered:

> The men at this period were becoming initiated into the mysteries of camp life, and accustomed to its daily routine, which were by no means light. At early dawn the reville roused them from slumber. Roll being called, the companies were dismissed to put their quarters in order. Breakfast at 6 o'clock A.M. In the meantime ten men from each company were detailed to serve in the main guard, to enforce discipline and guard the camp. A police guard was also appointed, who cleaned up all dirt and filth about the tents, brought water for the company, wood for the cooks, and, in fact kept everything in order and cleanliness. During the afternoon, squad drills.... At sundown, company muster for roll call and supper. Tattoo at 9 o'clock P.M. when the men retired to their respective tents. Fifteen minutes later, three taps of the drum compelled every light to be extinguished and the camp was in darkness and quietude.[35]

Depending on the size or permanence of the camp, the soldiers took various steps to improve their overall living conditions. Wilbur Fisk of the 2nd Vermont Infantry described how he lived during his first winter in Virginia:

Early morning roll call in camp. (BL)

The tent I occupy is the smallest-sized army tent. To call these tents contemptible is using the mildest term that will apply to them. I don't know their exact dimensions in feet and inches, but a man any above the medium height, lying down, can touch the opposite sides of one of these tents with his head and feet at the same time, and the united breadth of five ordinary men will cover its entire length. Three others with myself make one of these our temporary home. When we are all in the tent, together with our bed blankets, overcoats, knapsacks, haversacks, canteens, guns and equipments, besides having a fire-place and generally as much as a half cord of wood on hand seasoning for use you may imagine there is but little room to spare.... We contrived to make so much of so little room by digging down and settling the floor (i.e. the ground) of our tent about two feet and then building up around this excavation with logs...about two feet more and over the whole placing our cloth tent. This basement protects us securely from the wind, is quite warm, and affords us a chance to stand erect.... We made a sort of platform for a bed on each end of the tent which gives us room, underneath for our wood, etc. On one side we excavated a fire-place with an opening to the surface of the ground outside the tent around which we built a chimney.[36]

From first to last, discipline and drill was a necessity. It was a major part of camp existence both early in the conflict and throughout the entire four years of war. An infantry regiment which was not drilled to perfection was a far less effective fighting machine. In combat situations the instant reaction to orders by squads, platoons, companies, regiments and brigades, had to replace normal "thinking" with "drilled in" immediate action. A well-drilled unit could make the difference between success and failure in battle, or between low casualties and total annihilation from enemy fire.

In some instances, superb discipline could backfire on a regiment when sent into action for the first time. Due to inexperience and overzealousness these units often did not realize the danger they were facing. A superbly drilled "green" regiment might

*A typical **infantry regiment in camp**.* (BL)

have "charged on" in battle to its possible demise, whereas veteran organizations may have pulled back to safety or called a retreat due to the unassailable rifle fire aimed against them. The 1st Maine Heavy Artillery fit this description closely on June 18, 1864 at Petersburg where out of 900 present it lost 632 men, killed and wounded. Only a month before on May 19, it had suffered 476 casualties in a previous action near Spotsylvania, Virginia.

Infantry drill was largely practiced in the "school of the soldier" as it was termed, and used the prevailing nineteenth century close-order drill system. The men marched in squads of eight, in a somewhat intricate set of movements. Squads went into "line of platoons and companies," in keeping with the linear tactics of the time. Each infantry-man, too, had to learn the motions of loading his rifle or musket. This set of nine separate motions were necessary in order to fire three aimed shots a minute, then considered a reasonable rate of firing.

An example of the "school of the soldier" which had to be learned by all recruits, but first by their instructors, comes from one of the instruction manuals available to officers and non-commissioned officers during the war. The command, in this case, would be "shoulder—ARMS."

> (First motion) Raise the piece vertically with the right hand to the height of the right breast and opposite the shoulder, the elbow close to the body; seize the piece with the left hand below the right, and drop quickly the right hand to grasp the piece at the swell of the stock, the thumb and fore-finger embracing the guard; press the piece against the shoulder with the left hand, the right arm nearly straight.
>
> (Second motion) Drop the left hand quickly by the side.

The soldier was required to learn and execute several dozen such commands, plus loading and firing a musket, squad drill, platoon drill, company drill, skirmish drill and battalion drill. Several of the official drill manuals or "infantry tactics" contained over 500 pages, along with scores of illustrations. Some of the typical maneuvers, and there were many, were entitled:

To change direction in column closed in mass.

To change direction in column at half distance.

To break to the rear, by the right or left, into column, and to advance or retire by the right or left of companies.

Formation of a company from two ranks into four, and reciprocally, at a halt, and in march.

To form the battalion on the right or left, by file, into line of battle.

The column arriving behind the line of battle, to prolong it on this line.

And so on.

A Massachusetts private expressed these sentiments looking back on his days of drill:

I was taught my facings, and at the time I thought the drill-master needlessly fussy about shouldering, ordering, and presenting arms. At this time men were often drilled in company and regimental evolutions long before they learned the manual of arms, because of the difficulty of obtaining muskets.... The musket, after an hour's drill, seemed heavier and less ornamental than it had looked to be. The first day I went out to drill, getting tired of doing the same things over and over, I said to the drill-sergeant: "Let's stop this fooling and go over to the grocery."

His only reply was addressed to the corporal: "Corporal, take this man out and drill him like hell...." It takes a raw recruit some time to learn that he is not to think or suggest, but obey. Some never do learn. I acquired it at last, in humility and mud, but it was tough.... Drilling looks easy to a spectator, but it isn't.[37]

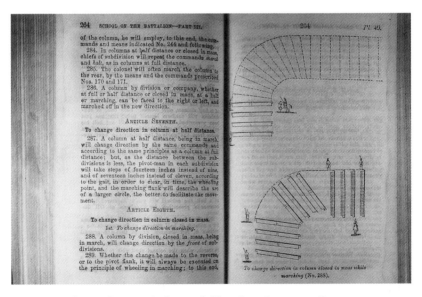

Pages from an infantry drill and tactics manual. (PBE)

Infantry regiments on parade. (BL)

In a letter home dated March 7, 1863, another private, Simon Hulbert, 100th New York, explained one drill session by saying, "A few mornings ago Capt. [Michael] Bailey started out to drill us. He commenced swearing. The men could not keep dressed [aligned] at all. He told Lieut. Cyrus Brown to Drill us. He started with us. We marched by the right & left flank, wheeled right & left without a word of complaint from our Officer. Kept dressed good."[38]

Austin Stearns remembered the light side of drill also (and the embarrassment) when his sergeant, who was a little tipsy, ordered a drill to show off for the people of Harpers Ferry. He recalled that, "His mind and tongue would not work together, for when his mind wanted to say a certain thing his tongue was sure to give the wrong order; after trying awhile and finding he could not make things work, he threatened terrible things and dismissed us. The citizens were all pleased with the Yankees performance."[39]

An infantry regiment did not always receive thorough training before it was placed in harm's way. It was not uncommon for a Civil War unit to be initiated into combat with but a few hours of drill under its belt, and with no actual practice in firing its weapons. A case in point is the 124th Pennsylvania Volunteer Infantry Regiment. Private Edward T. Harlan of Company E kept an account of his service with the 124th. After enlisting on August 13, 1862 he inscribed in his diary the following entries:

> August 18th. Lieutenant took us out to practice stacking arms; were drilled in afternoon.
> August 19th. Had our regimental drill by regular drill master; we were rather green.
> August 23rd. Had another regimental drill this afternoon by a little Dutch man.

Between August 28 and September 17, the 124th was kept active during the movements which led up to and included the Battle of Second Manassas, although the 124th took no part in that engagement. Near Antietam Creek, Harlan's diary was very much to the point:

> September 17th. We were awakened about 4 o'clock in the morning by picket firing, and were ordered to fall into line without breakfast. We were marched in line of battle to the field and put right in the fight....

Separated from the rest of its brigade, the 124th made several advances against the Confederates while marching alongside and through a portion of farmer David R. Miller's ripened cornfield. Fortunately, the regiment lost only 64 men, but astonishingly and by all accounts performed very well in the bloody engagement itself.[40]

Although the 124th acquitted itself respectably in its first battle, with few sessions of drill and no rifle practice, this was not the norm. David L. Thompson of the 9th New York was correct when he explained the importance of drill to any military unit: "Yet such a mass, [i.e., a regiment, brigade, etc.] without experience in battle, would go to pieces before a moderately effective fire. Catch up a handful of snow and throw it, it flies to fluff; pack it, it strikes like a stone. Here is the secret of organization—the aim and crown of drill, to make the units one, that when the crisis comes, the missile may be thoroughly compacted."

Thompson also saw the need for soldiers to be flexible on this idea: "Too much, however, has been claimed for theoretic discipline—not enough for intelligent individual action. No remark was oftener on the lips of officers during the war than this: 'Obey orders! I do your thinking for you.' But that soldier is best whose good sense tells him when to be merely a part of a machine and when not."[41]

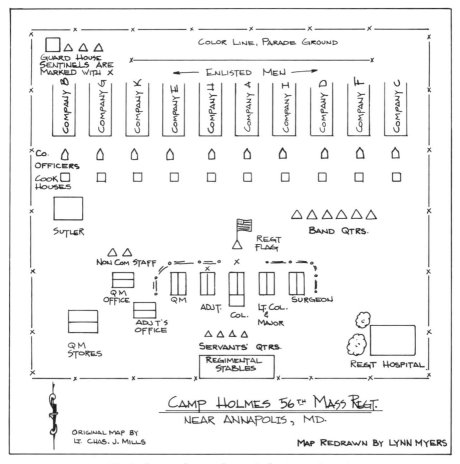

Typical camp layout for an infantry regiment.

PART
II

(WCM)

Food And
Equipment

RATIONS

I never was so tired of anything in my life as I am of Soldiers life.

Pvt. John L. Holt
56th Virginia Infantry

For infantrymen in all wars, food is of utmost importance. It can offset extreme fatigue, boost morale, and carry the soldier through great and demanding trials. Anyone who has not experienced army service can little understand the impact of good and abundant rations on the average soldier. This feeling was best exemplified by George Eggleston, a Confederate who occasionally suffered from a lack of food:

> But what is the use of writing about the pangs of hunger? The words are utterly meaningless to persons who have never known actual starvation, and cannot be made otherwise than meaningless. Hunger to starving men is wholly unrelated to the desire for food as that is commonly understood and felt. It is a great agony of the whole body and of the soul as well. It is unimaginable, all pervading pain inflicted when the strength to endure pain is utterly gone. It is a great despairing cry of a wasting body—a cry of flesh and blood, marrow, nerves, bones, and faculties for strength with which to exist and to endure existence. It is a horror which, once suffered, leaves an impression that is never erased from the memory,...[42]

For most Civil War soldiers hunger of the magnitude noted above was rare. For a period of almost five days, Eggleston had eaten only four hard biscuits and "one very meager slice of fat pork," all this while he did hard marching and rigid duty.

Generally, most soldiers remembered their time in the service as one when they almost always got enough to eat. Exceptions were expected, but not the rule,..."such as a man on an exposed picket post, or serving as rearguard to the army, or doing something which separated him temporarily from his company."[43]

A "ration" was defined as the amount of food authorized for one man (or animal) for one day. The Confederate government had adopted the Federal army rationing system at the start of the war, but by early 1862 they were forced to reduce it.

According to U.S. regulations in the 1860s, a Union soldier was entitled to receive daily 12 ounces of pork or bacon or one pound four ounces of fresh or salt beef; one pound six ounces of soft bread or flour; one pound of hard bread (hardtack, pilot bread, biscuits or crackers) or one pound four ounces of cornmeal. For every 100 rations (i.e., for the 100 men in a company) there was also issued one peck of beans or peas; 10 pounds of rice or hominy; 10 pounds of green coffee, eight pounds of roasted and ground coffee, or one pound eight ounces of tea; 15 pounds of sugar; one pound four ounces of candles; four pounds of soap; two quarts of salt; four quarts of vinegar; four ounces of pepper; one-half bushel of potatoes; and one quart of molasses. Additionally or as substitutes for other items, desiccated (dried) vegetables, dried fruits, pickles, or pickled cabbage might be issued.

Salt pork or beef was described by a Kentucky Rebel named Johnny Green. He called it "blue beef" and noted: "The cattle are slaughtered somewhere down south, cut up & put in barrels of very salt brine & shipped up here. I fear the cattle came near starving to death before being slaughtered, the meat is so poor & tough." He once called his meal ration, "the worst I ever saw; it was damp, musty & almost green with mould when issued to us.... My share gave me such a pain in my stomach that I could hardly walk."[44]

The dried or desiccated vegetables were often criticized. Corporal Joseph Van Nest, 101st Ohio, called them "compressed,... a combination of corn husks, tomato skins, carrots and other kinds of vegetables too numerous to mention." Van Nest said at first no one knew what to do with them. When boiled they swelled up and doubled in size. Lieutenant Abner Small remembered that the vegetables came in a handy portable form, "tons of it—in sheets like pressed hops." And when fully dissolved in a boiling kettle, the water, "would remind one of a dirty brook with all the dead leaves floating around promiscuously."

A Confederate writing near Atlanta in 1864 pointed out their use of "vegetables." He told his sister, "our men get a vegetable diet by cooking up polk, potato tops, May pop vines, kurlip weed, lambs quarter, thistle, and a hundred kinds of weed I always thought poison. I thought it trash...but the boys call it 'long Forage....'"[45]

Rations for marching and/or campaigning troops per day were one pound of hard bread, three-quarters pound of salt pork or one and one-quarter pound of fresh meat plus the above sugar, coffee, and salt. Infantrymen cooked these items either individually or "messed" by squads. In the Union army, cooking by companies was prescribed in March of 1863. But individual or squad "messes" (groups) did not completely disappear during the war.[46]

The campfire was as familiar to the common soldier as any other part of army life. Cooking was a major duty, necessity and even pleasure for all infantrymen. Sergeant Crotty of Michigan recalled how meat was cooked when he wrote, "We are not very particular how we cook our pork. Sometimes we fry it in a tin spider, which we make by cutting in two a canteen; other times we punch our ramrods through a slice and let it fry over the camp fire, and, in order not to lose any of the grease, we hold a hardtack under and let the gravy drop on it, which answers well for butter."

Frying hardtack. (HC)

Vermonter Wilbur Fisk, in a letter home in May of 1863, described how his comrade made a savory dish called "hash." First, hardtack was crushed into fine flour in a small bag using a stone or heavy stick. Meat was then cut into small pieces. Next, a spider was filled with broth saved when the cook boiled the fresh meat. Then the meat and extra water was added and reduced. Finally the cracker flour was put in along with mashed up potatoes if available. When done, he pronounced, "it was a dish good enough for anybody,—a super-excellent one for soldiers."[47]

Campfires, while a necessity for cooking and warmth, often "turned" on the soldiers. Dozens of accounts described the hazards and fickleness of a roaring fire. Sergeant Walter A. Clark, 1st Georgia Infantry, explained:

"We had built a fire of rails, a favorite army fuel in those days. I do not remember what species of timber they were made, but I do recall the fact that it was a popping variety when subjected to heat. All through the night our sleep was disturbed by the necessity of rising at frequent intervals to extinguish our burning blankets, and one man had his cap nearly burned from his head before it awoke him."

Yankee infantryman Fisk said that on one cold, blustery night in February 1864, "a fire was more of an annoyance than a benefit." After trying to sleep, he and a friend finally had to give up; they were chilled through to the bone. Finally they built, "an awful hot fire, so hot that I...had to cover my knees with newspapers, and my face with a handkerchief to keep them from burning. If I uncovered my face I couldn't endure the heat a moment. Before me there was intense heat, behind me it was exactly the reverse. The wind made itself felt as much in the rear, as the fire did in the front. If some malicious fiend had been sponging my back with ice cold water the sensations could not have been less desirable." Fisk and his comrades also suffered from the brutal wind in another way, as it whipped the smoke and ashes into their faces. He closed by noting that their clothes showed the effects in the morning—and that it was, "the meanest experience I have ever had on picket,..."[48]

On the whole, though, the daily cook fires were gathering places for the troops and a comfortable "common ground" where the men came together for companionship, conversation, comfort, and sustenance. It replaced the security of the fireside back home where all young men had so recently gathered with their families and friends. For as John Stevens remembered, "[W]hen not engaged in camp duty we set around our fires, talk and gossip, and discuss the various fights, and the prospects of an early ending of the war, reading the daily papers and writing letters home."

In the Southern armies food was not as much in shortage as is generally believed. The problem was transportation. For instance, in February 1865 the governor of North Carolina declared that, "hundreds of thousands of bushels of grain now rot at various depots...for want of transportation." A short distance northward and just before Lee's surrender in April of 1865, a commissary official in Richmond stated that 12,500,000 bread rations and 11,500,000 meat rations could be obtained for army use if the government only had the means to purchase and transport them.[49] By war's end, while the Confederacy struggled to simply move some food to its armies, Grant's forces were then being issued 123,000 fresh loaves of bread made on site daily during the 1864 Siege of Petersburg, Virginia.[50]

Officers were fed differently than enlisted men. Infantry regimental field and line officers in both the Union and Confederate armies were given a monthly allowance to purchase their food. For example, an infantry line captain and his two lieutenants

Going into camp. The rail fences quickly disappeared. (HC)

received four rations per month worth $36.00, plus an allotment to be used to hire one servant each. Field officers such as colonels, lieutenant colonels, and majors had an allowance for horses and their forage authorized by regulation.[51]

Line companies found interesting ways to distribute the daily rations in a fair manner. One popular method was to spread an oil cloth or poncho on the ground and on it pile little mounds of coffee, salt, sugar, or meat; one mound for each man in the unit. Sergeants tried to get each ration as perfectly even as possible. As the waiting

Issuing rations. (HC)

soldiers stood by, the orderly-sergeant would turn his back to the oilcloth. Someone would point to a pile, and say, "Who shall have this." The sergeant then, without turning, would call out a private from his company roll and the named person would appropriate the specific foodstuff. The process would continue until all rations were dispensed. Daniel Crotty likened the scene of the men "around him [the sergeant] like chickens around an old hen.... To us in the field it does not seem anyway strange to flock around and receive our coffee and sugar by the spoonful as fast as the names are called, but to an outsider the sight must be a strange one."[52]

All companies kept, and jealously guarded, a selection of cooking implements. As the war progressed, the number and quality of these items dwindled as regulations were passed that limited the amount of baggage an infantry regiment could carry as it traveled. Early in the war these "camp chests" were fully loaded, as aptly demonstrated by John H. Worsham of the 21st Virginia. His squad's mess chest was made of oak, three feet long and eighteen inches wide and deep, and was strapped securely with iron.

> We had in it a dozen knives and forks, two or three butcher knives, a dozen teacups and saucers, a dozen plates, several dishes and bowls, a sugar dish and cream pitcher, salt and pepper boxes, a tin box containing a dozen assorted boxes of spices, a dozen glasses, a sifter, rolling pin, coffee tin, etc. Besides these, we carried outside a frying pan, coffee pot, camp kettle, teapot, bread oven,...two water buckets, ax, etc.[53]

Soon, these large "kits" of extraneous items gave way to each man carrying a small tin cup or a "boiler" which was a larger cup with a wire or "bail" handle, plus a spoon and maybe a knife. Each mess, or sometimes a whole company if it was small enough, carried along on campaign a bread oven or "spider" as it was called, or a frying pan. The cast iron "spider" could be used in both applications; it simply had three legs and a cover. The men took turns toting the spider or the squad's frying pan, and it was used equally by all in the mess or by the assigned cook of the company.

The "spider." This one recently found in a Union camp in Virginia. (GAC)

As usual, there were exceptions. Private Edwin Smith, 54th Ohio, told a story in 1888 about how just days before the Battle of Ezra Church, Georgia, he had found a very large and heavy coffee-boiler. His company was determined to keep it, so they took turns carrying it. During the battle, Smith's turn came so he strapped it to his rubber blanket, and swung it around on the middle of his back. As his regiment maneuvered all over the "Southern Confederacy," he recalled, "We marched straight to the front, right-about to the rear, filed to the right, then to the left, left-oblique, right-oblique, left flanked, right flanked; in short, having exhausted Hardie's [sic] tactics...as well as our patience.... All this time the coffee-boiler clung tenaciously to my back, catching in the brush and briars...." During several running retreats Smith was tempted to pitch the boiler, along with his own accouterments, onto the ground. However, during that trying and eventful day he held tenaciously to the monstrous kettle, and "at length, [when] night closed the bloody drama,...I unslung the coffee-boiler and a few of us dirty-faced, powder-blackened coffee-cookers gratefully partook of the soldier's invigorating beverage."[54]

Infantrymen in all theatres of operation, both Yankees and Rebels, supplemented their rations by living off the land. Although armies were usually prohibited by their governments and commanders from appropriating civilian goods, these orders did little to stop foraging by common soldiers. Private Matthew B. Scofield, 21st Missouri Infantry, illustrated this general attitude while on a campaign in central Mississippi in February, 1864, written in a letter to his friend at home: "We lived on half rations part of the time, but the forageing parties made it full rations out of the rebels beef cattle & their hogs, & when we came to a Town we would find Stores of rebel Supplies Such as pork & meal & flower & Shugar. So you See that would make our rations all right."[55]

Infantrymen often resorted to desperate means to obtain the needed daily food allowance. General E.M. Law recalled how at the Battle of Spotsylvania, his men luxuriated in coffee and other rarities from the haversacks of the Federal dead:

It was astonishing into what close places a hungry Confederate would go to get something to eat. Men would sometimes go out under a severe fire, in the hope of finding a full haversack. It may seem a small matter to the readers of war history; but to the makers of it who were in the trenches; or on the march, or engaged in battle night and day for weeks without intermission, the supply of one article of coffee,...was not a small matter, but did as much as any other material agency to sustain the spirits and bodily energies of the men,...[56]

Edward H. Wade, 14th Connecticut, was even more descriptive. After the Battle of Gettysburg, he reported that he and his comrades had eaten very little since June 30, 1863. On the night of July 3 Wade said, "we crawled out on the battlefield and took the haversacks from those who had been killed in the fight that day; these haversacks were nearly all full of nice hoe-cakes. Some that we found were stained with blood where it had run into their haversacks from their wounds. But we were so hungry that we didn't stop for that."[57]

It is no wonder that the Confederates were loaded down with hoe-cakes, the Southern equivalent of hardtack. One Yankee officer who became a prisoner on July 2 said that he saw, behind the Confederate lines on Seminary Ridge, "...long lines of Negro cooks baking corn pone for rebel soldiers at the front."[58] Hoe-cakes were a thin bread made of cornmeal without milk or egg, originally baked on the blade of a hoe over an open fire. They went by several other names, such as pone, corn-cakes, corn-dodgers and ash-cakes. Corn-fritters and flap-jacks were popular as well. A 90th Pennsylvania man recalled the hoe-cakes he had seen as "plate-size."

Stealing food from civilians was an ordinary pastime, but edibles were just as often honestly purchased. In this way the average enlisted man and even his officers could procure milk, butter, chickens, eggs, molasses, cider, berries, peaches, apples, melons, pies, cakes and light breads. Sutlers also enlivened the soldiers' fare, but normally these private, army-wide storekeepers set up shop near safe regimental bivouacs only when the armies were in camp for long periods of time. Other dietary supplements included wild game where available, such as deer, rabbits, squirrels, turkeys, pheasants and doves. There is also much extant evidence that Civil War soldiers consumed fairly impressive amounts of horse and mule meat, dogs, rats and even an occasional domesticated cat.[59] Then too, many soldiers resorted to the generosity of family members to compliment their normal rations, or to the kindness of the U.S. Sanitary and Christian Commissions in the North and other similar patriotic institutions which grew up in various Southern cities and towns as well.

Hardtack, coffee, and salted meat (beef or pork) soon became the standard issue for the U.S. infantryman while in field service or on campaign. Confederates essentially existed on similar types of foods, except their "hardtack" may have been corn pone, hoe cakes, and corn bread, and their coffee ration quickly became a thing of the past, replaced with substitutes brewed from white or sweet potatoes, peas, parched peanuts, corn, rye, bran or wheat germ.

There were periods in both armies when rations were inferior, or substandard, and days when both Yankees and Rebels were well supplied and contented. Looking at the larger picture though, it is obvious that overall, Northerners were better fed than their Southern brethren. One Confederate observed the variances in July 1864 after being captured. While in the rear of the Union lines he saw a sutler dispensing lemonade, beer, ice cream and other luxuries, all especially enticing in the oppressive Georgia heat. That infantry officer, Colonel James C. Nisbet, 66th Georgia, recalled: "This seemed strange to me. I was forcibly reminded of the difference in the resources of our government and the United States. We were glad to get a sufficiency of cornbread, fat meat, sorghum and rye coffee."[60]

But some soldiers, no matter which side they fought on, were never content with their provisions. Sergeant Stearns commented on this phenomenon: "Some of the boys were always satisfied with what they received and went and ate it; others were so happy they danced for joy, while others were never satisfied, never received what they ought, what in their own eyes belonged to them; if they had received the whole then they would not have been any more satisfied."[61]

Hardtack, of which so much has been written, was nicknamed "sheet-iron crackers" or "cast-iron biscuits." They resembled a square or round biscuit made of flour, water and salt, only harder in consistency. John Billings described them as being approximately 3 1/8 by 2 7/8 inches in size, and half an inch thick. A daily ration was about 10 to 13 to each man. When relatively fresh, the crackers were nutritious and generally enjoyed by the troops. But mostly, these biscuits were issued in a very hard state and could not usually even be soaked soft. If not hard, they were moldy or wet, or had become infested with maggots or weevils. The weevils, according to Billings, were a small, slim, brown bug about 1/8 of an inch long, and were great borers. They could nibble a hardtack completely through and through.

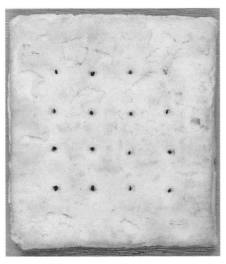

Army "hardtack." (DST)

A favorite way to prepare hardtack was by boiling, crumbled up in coffee or soup, or fried in grease. After boiling, it was not uncommon to see the surface of the coffee or soup swimming with weevils, which were then easily skimmed off. Maggots, it was said, were not easily budged in this way.

Private Perry Mayo, 2nd Michigan, in speaking of his 1862 Thanksgiving dinner in a letter to his parents, mentioned that he got one cup of coffee, two pieces of fried pork, and four crackers, "each cracker contained from ten to thirty worms varying in length from 1/8 to 1/2 an inch.... We broke [the hardtack] into our coffee to scald them and dipped them out with a spoon as they came squirming to the top."[62] An officer of the 65th Ohio declared that "it was no exaggeration to say some of [our hardtack] were so hard that the stoutest teeth in the brigade could make no impression on them. It was like trying to eat a stove-lid.... They would have made a prime article of half soles for army shoes."

A similar portrayal of hardtack came from Private George White, 19th Massachusetts, who "had a notion of saving some of the SOFTEST ones to make me a coat of mail previous to going into battle, but I'm afraid the rebels would smell the bread, surrender themselves and in their starving condition eat me up."[63] The 13th Massachusetts was issued the circular variety, and one man in that regiment recalled them as:

...round cakes about as large as a saucer and about half an inch thick; [and about 6" across] to break it was impossible; water made very little impression on it.... The boys said that [O.H.] Perry [in 1853] carried it with him to Japan for balls for his cannon; as he had no occasion to use them, they were issued by mistake to the infantry when they were intended as balls for the artillery. Those who saw the boxes said they were marked B.C. 2400; that would bring it back to Noah's time. I cannot vouch for this.[64]

In January 1862, the 55th Ohio drew its first issue of hardtack in Grafton, Virginia. Private W.A. Keesy reported that some men called it sea-biscuit, and it came in three sizes: "one size about three, one about five, and the other about seven, inches square, all being about three-eights or a half-inch in thickness, with perforations on one side and having a hardness and a durability quite remarkable. Some had the letters 'B.C.' embossed on them and the boys grotesquely asserted that the letters stood for 'Before Christ.'"[65]

The coffee ration was especially appreciated by the rank and file, but more so after hard marching in cold or rainy weather. It quickly became a universal drink in the Union forces, and the chosen method of preparation was black with ample sugar. On a halt, infantrymen would be seen moving in a mass and at a quick scramble heading for the nearest fence rails. Campfires were quickly ignited along the lines of march, as each soldier or group of messmates cooked their little boilers and cups of the strong brew.

Lieutenant Albert A. Pope, 35th Massachusetts, commenting on the importance of coffee, said: "I think there is nothing like coffee to stimulate a soldier, for they can dispense with almost everything but that."[66]

In essence then, Federal infantrymen lived on coffee and sugar, hardtack, boiled or roasted fresh beef, or the other variety, salt "horse," as it came to be known, punctuated at times by flour mixed with water and salt and cooked twisted on a ramrod or stick, and dried vegetables. The "Rebel" on the other hand, survived on the same types of beef, but with more pork in use as a rule, coffee substitutes, corn meal prepared in several ways, and field peas and molasses. All soldiers by design or by skill or cunning, supplemented their diets with various and sundry food items obtained from multiple lawful and not so legitimate sources.

Pvt. William C. Dry, 52nd North Carolina Infantry. (GNMP)

UNIFORM AND CLOTHING

I enjoy this life very much. I can go as dirty as I please, wear government shoes, haven't washed myself today and don't intend to.

Pvt. Francis E. Pierce
108th New York Infantry

The regulations of both governments during the Civil War prescribed certain official codes of dress and provided for their issuance. Since initially most uniforms originated from the states where the troops enrolled, many and varied styles and colors made their appearance. The most common and most standard uniform piece issued by either the Confederate or Federal government, or by any of the states involved in the conflict was the frock coat, used by both officers and enlisted men of both armies. An ex-Massachusetts soldier gave a fine portrayal of the coat and its major drawbacks and advantages:

> The coat was much too heavy, [especially when] the thermometer [was] in the eighties. It was made with long skirts, and when fitting the wearer was not a bad-appearing garment; but as very few of them did fit, our personal appearance was not improved. They were made large in front, to meet an abnormal expansion of chest. Until we grew to them, it was a handy place to stow some of the contents of our knapsack.[67]

In the Union army the government allowed $42 annually per man as a clothing issue. If the soldier did not overdraw this allowance, he received the balance in cash at the end of each year. Simon Hulbert, 100th New York, calculated some of his uniform items in 1864 as follows: white shirt $1.30, a pair of socks 22 cents, a pair of shoes $1.05, one pair of drawers 90 cents, one cap 58 cents, and one blouse [coat] $2.40. In January of the same year, Sergeant Nixon B. Stewart, 52th Ohio, recalled his monthly clothing allowance as $4.00, and the prices for items he purchased were: overcoat $7.50, pants $3.50, [fatigue] blouse $3.12, shoes $1.48, boots, $2.87, hat $1.68, cap 54 cents, drawers 95 cents, shirt $1.35, dress coat $6.25, and socks 32 cents. He added; "our clothing was good in quality, as good as we could ask for the price paid, but it was often poorly made."

Infantry line officers' uniforms customarily cost somewhat more than privates', and officers were required to purchase their own clothing rather than receive a government issue. Captain Thomas Stevens of the 28th Wisconsin recorded some general figures. He placed the prices of pants at between $15 and $18, "fancy, white, or buff" vests at $5 to $8, shoulder straps were $8, a dress coat for $35, and sword, belt, sash, and sword knot were $57.[68]

At the end of the year, some men were often "in the red." Perry Mayo wrote at the close of 1863 that his account amounted to $66.26 which put him about twenty-five dollars over. "Some of the boys," he confessed, "are $50 behind." In a letter home to Montpelier, Vermont on December 22, 1864, Private Wilbur Fisk reiterated all of the above information but added, "...it is a pretty difficult thing [after a year of hard campaigning] for a soldier to come out even with the Government. Sometimes it takes the whole of two months' pay to make it even, and quite frequently it takes more. It is apt to dim a fellow's bright anticipations of pay-day somewhat at the year's close...."[69]

Year's end overpayments were not always the fault of rough service or the government. Infantrymen, North and South, threw away literally hundreds of tons of perfectly good military clothing and equipment during forced marches, while in battle, when abandoning winter camps, and often even during sudden changes in the weather. Private Justus Silliman was only one of hundreds and surely thousands of soldiers who succumbed to this easy way of lightening his load. In early May 1863 while on a march near Fredericksburg, he admitted that, "[i]n the afternoon the heat became so intolerable that I tore off my dress coat and threw it away." Oddly enough, just about two weeks earlier he had written to his mother that the men in his regiment "...had our overcoats, dresscoats, and other clothing and things which we would probably not need during the hot season...sent to Hope Landing where they are to be stored for us." Silliman should have heeded the actions of his comrades, as he was then out $6.25 hard cash.[70] Considering that a private's pay was $13.00 per month, (raised to $16 in 1864) this type of carelessness soon added up. Lamentably, these calculations likely made little impression on the lowly infantryman as he struggled along under a burning sun on a dusty uphill road, carrying in excess of 50 pounds of equipment, and encased in a heavy, sweat-saturated woolen uniform.

Some soldiers were a bit more particular about what they wore and made attempts to add some comfort to their rough lives. Almost every soldier at one time or another wrote home for, or purchased himself, items of clothing not usually issued by his government. In an August 8, 1863 letter, Henry W. Prince of the 127th New York sent his mother money to buy flannel. He enclosed these confusing instructions, information, and requests:

> Government shirts is poor & coarse. Will do very well in cool weather. I would like a shirt made of soft light (not heavy) flannel. (I have changed my mind) I think a cotton shirt will be best for it will be cooler in day time, & at night if cool I can put a flannel over it. We have had 2 months of scorching weather & we soldiers have to wear wool enough without [a] woolen shirt. [We] wear woolen pants without lining & woolen coats. I want to try a cotton shirt. If I like flannel better I can wear it. I used to think I could not wear flannel in summer but I find a man can do most anything if obliged to & very soon get accustomed to it. Yet I fancy a cotton shirt would be more comfortable. I want to try it....I don't want a white shirt for white shows dirt too plain. Good stout calico is best & will not weigh so much as checked shirting. No collar or waist bands. Simply a binding around the neck.[71]

While normal infantry regiments were clothed in standard military garb, some units were more fortunate and were allotted a few "extras." For instance some men of the 100th New York received overalls to keep their uniforms clean during fatigue details, and were allowed to wear comfortable jackets called "round-about coats" at roll call. The soldier who reported these facts was upset that other regiments went to drill in shirt sleeves and even in their "drawers," a shirt, and a cap, while his comrades were ordered out with full uniform. Perry Mayo expressed on several occasions that he considered his 2nd Michigan one of the best uniformed regiments in the army. During the summer of 1861 they were even furnished with "good suits of linen clothing and straw hats." He added that the men had their "hair cut close to our heads on account of the intense heat and to save combing."[72]

In almost all cases time, expedience, money questions, common sense, and especially outdoor life reduced the United States infantryman's uniform to a couple of shirts, sky blue wool pants, a dark blue fatigue blouse or coat, a good pair of heavy army shoes, several pairs of socks, and a slouch hat, forage cap or kepi. Eventually most of the fancy, oddball, and strange foreign-inspired uniforms became a thing of the past, memories of early war excesses. Regiments like the 62nd Pennsylvania sent their "new French [Zouave] uniforms to Washington," in February 1862, and the 3rd Michigan threw off its "dirty, shoddy suit of gray, furnished us by a shoddy contractor at Grand Rapids, who made a fortune out of the speculation."[73]

The image of all Confederate infantry wearing cheap, ragged, multi-colored uniforms or non-uniforms throughout the war is a myth that has been hard to dispel. In reality, large numbers of Rebel soldiers were outfitted either by their army, or with help from home, in good, serviceable clothing acceptable to the difficult tasks at hand. Differing from the North, the new Confederacy early on paid its soldiers a reimbursement for clothing and other necessities brought or obtained from home. This practice stopped when the C.S. government, like its adversary, began to issue uniforms and equipment directly to its troops.

It was not unusual though, especially in the early months of the war, to see Southern soldiers in civilian clothes. Several accounts from the Seven Days' Battles of 1862

Many Confederates adopted the waist-length jacket called a "round-about." (GAC)

report Confederates fighting entirely in non-military attire. Perry Mayo verified this fact in a May 1862 letter to his father: "A great many deserters come into our lines every day. They are a hard looking set. They are not dressed in any particular uniform, and most of them are dressed in citizen's clothes." New York Private Simon Hulbert said practically the same thing on May 11, recalling "we could tell a rebel when we came across them for they have no uniforms, only citizens clothing."[74]

In letters home to his wife Amanda White, Sergeant Marion H. Fitzpatrick, 45th Georgia, kept one of the best records available of the types and changes, requisitions and issues of both civilian and government clothing he received between 1862 and 1865. According to his inventory it is clear that he was well supplied during most of his military service. Only occasionally did he want for necessary items; usually it was shoes. On November 7, 1862 he sent news to Amanda that: "...our wages are raised to $15.00 a month and we are to be clothed by the government and not draw any more computation money.... If that is the case, I will get no credit for anything you send me and it will be best to draw altogether from the government except socks.... We can draw clothing here much cheaper than they can be bought in Ga. Some of the boys have already drawn good clothing at reasonable prices...."

The sergeant, from necessity, became quite handy with needle and thread. On December 15, 1862 Fitzpatrick told his spouse that he wore both pairs of his britches, and had done so for two months. The outside pair became rather "holy," but he managed to mend them nicely. His only problem was that "...we have nothing to patch with.... One of our company burned a hole in one of his shirts and throwed it away or rather gave it to any of us...to patch with. It was a pretty good checked shirt—I took the back off and hemed it with long stitches—washed it and made a first rate hankerchief. I have saved enough to patch my coat pocket and the hole that was burned in my coat..., which task I expect to perform now pretty soon."[75]

A Florida sergeant named Washington Ives who was stationed in Chattanooga, Tennessee in late 1862, described his newest wardrobe to a sister, along with prices: "Our boys are drawing shoes and drawers the feeblest are drawing blue woolen under-shirts at $2.11 a piece...." He also wrote, "...I have just drawn a pair of kersey pants for $2.62, [and] 1 coat of the same material as Mr. Burtchaetts' suit for $5.25...." Sergeant Ives would have been surprised to learn that less than three years later in late April, 1865, a set of underwear cost, according to Colonel Alfred Belo, 55th North Carolina, "...twelve hundred dollars in Confederate money," which normally would have been "some two dollars and fifty cents a suit."

Speaking of "drawers" or underwear, a Yankee from the 100th Indiana, Theodore F. Upson commented: "Evry [sic] one was givin [sic] a suit, hat, coat, pants and shoes - also shirts and drawers. If they fit, all right; if not, we had to trade around till we could get a fit....The drawers are made of canton flannel. Most of the boys had never worn drawers and some did not know what they were for and some of the old soldiers...told them they were for an extra uniform to be worn on parade...."[76]

Regarding uniform prices, which varied widely in Confederate service, Lieutenant Charles Denoon, 41st Virginia, voiced that government shoes sold for eight to ten dollars and the short waisted jackets, called "round-abouts" or conversions, ran 12 or 14 dollars. According to the young officer it took a soldier four months' wages to buy a suit of clothes. Another Virginian, John L. Holt calculated in August 1861 that his uniform would cost $33.00, and he expected to receive "roundabout coats" as they took less cloth in construction than frock coats. He requested from home an overcoat and a pair of "oversocks," and wanted the wool for his coat to be mixed, "about 3/4 black to 1/4 white [which] will make it about the proper color...." He asked his wife Ellen to make for him "some yarn drawers just single wove yarn cloth [which] will be nearly equal to flannel." Holt then informed Ellen that he could get calico for 25 cents per yard, and that the company had just drawn new uniforms at $7.50 apiece, which were "good ones made of heavy woolen goods."[77]

Even early in the war homemade military items were common in the South where no one really enforced the standing regulations. A 1st Georgia non-commissioned officer, Sergeant Walter Clark, remarked on an unusual style of cloth not often utilized in Confederate clothing. On December 8, 1861 in Winchester, Virginia a supply of blankets had arrived for his company from the citizens of Augusta:

"One of the contributors had no blankets, and in lieu of them donated a handsome crumb-cloth, which like Joseph's coat, was of many colors, red and green being the prevailing tints. In the distribution this fell to Elmore Dunbar, the wag of the company. Not needing it as a blanket he took it to a tailor in Winchester, had it transformed into a full suit, cap, coat and pants, and donning it had an inumerable company of gamins, white and black, following in his wake all over town."

In 1861 there were many infantry companies completely undecided as to what colors should be used in their uniforms. A 5th Texas soldier, John Stevens, recalled in his memoirs that after someone in his unit suggested that soldiers should have uniforms, no one could decide on a shade. Even the captain remained silent as each man gave his opinion. Finally it was proposed and agreed upon, "that each man get just what suited his fancy and have it made up in any style he chose—jes' so it was uniform."[78]

Of course, infantry uniforms soon became austere and fairly standardized, but still came in an assortment of colors ranging from dark cadet gray to almost a white gray, to browns and tans, and yellow and white, and even dark blue closely resembling Union clothing. Valerius C. Giles, 4th Texas, verified that "...[i]t was sometime after the war began that the Confederacy adopted any particular style of uniform. The color was universally gray, but the cut of the cloth varied materially." He recorded, "We were a motley-looking set, but as a rule comfortably dressed. In my company we had about four different shades of gray, but the trimmings were all of black braid."

Giles and his comrades even attempted to waterproof their outfits, using hot goose grease. He concluded that, "it penetrated the felt and leather like benzine...[but] stayed with us like a brother. Our hair, faces and hands were covered with it, and it wouldn't wash off. So we went through that campaign as slick as goose grease could make us." Giles believed that "dressy" uniforms helped to make good soldiers, as pride, he said, was one of the best qualifications a soldier could have: "If he takes pride in his personal appearance, it's two to one he has sufficient pride of honor not to run." Ironically, Private Giles would have been sorely pressed to locate a "dandy" in a bright new uniform in his regiment by late 1862. As of December of that year many of his comrades were looking pretty ragged; he described one man in particular, Private John Griffith: "John was reduced to a flannel shirt of a very thin texture, a pair of cotton pants with one leg off at the knee, an old slouched wool hat, and one cheesecloth blanket." Griffith had no shoes but eventually made a pair of moccasins out of fresh cut beef hide and rawhide strips.[79]

Although many Rebels were so poorly clad, many issues of new and sturdy clothing were received by Southern troops throughout the war. In December of 1864 for example, John Green told how the 9th Kentucky quartermaster, had brought out of Savannah suits of "cotton under clothes & grey Jeanes Jacket & trousers...for his men."[80] Even a Yank could vouch for the good condition of some Confederates late in the war. Lieutenant Galwey of Ohio documented this appearance of veteran Southern soldiers near Spotsylvania Court House, Virginia, in May of 1864: "...[T]hey were all clad in neat gray jackets and pantaloons with entire seats. In contrast we were in rags, scarcely one of us having a complete garment of any sort."[81]

Further to the southwest and over in northern Georgia later in September, an eye-witness encountered General James Longstreet's command and remarked that most of his troops had just drawn new uniforms consisting of dark blue shell jackets and light blue trousers. These men, who had come from Lee's army, impressed the Army of Tennessee veterans by the uniformity of their outfits, and the "...superior style of their equipment, in haversacks, canteens and knapsacks. The contrast between them and General Bragg's motley, ragged troops was striking in the extreme...." Oddly, a Federal, William Miller, 75th Indiana, described the dress of Longstreet's men as "uniformed in White Jackets and Blue Collars and cuffs and blue pants," while Chesley A. Mosman, 59th Illinois, said it was "bluish-gray" with sky blue pants.[82]

"Butternut" was one of the colors generally associated with Southern infantrymen during the Civil War. Butternut dye was made from the crushed hulls of walnuts (often mixed with copperas) and the pigmentation varied from a dull-brownish tan to musky yellow. A 9th New York soldier, David Thompson, documented this tint of color from his experiences in the Antietam Campaign. He had observed many dead on the field of Sharpsburg who were, "...undersized men mostly, from...North Carolina, with sallow, hatchet faces, and clad in 'butternut'—a color fluctuating all the way from a deep, coffee brown up to the whitish brown of ordinary dust."[83] A Confederate officer, Robert Stiles, called it a "sickly, jaundiced, butter-nut hue, like the clothes some back-woods, cracker regiments wore when they first came to Virginia." Corporal James Hosmer of the 52nd Massachusetts peered intently at the Rebel dress he spotted after the surrender of Port Hudson, Louisiana:

> Here they were, the real truculent and unmitigated reb, in butternut of every shade, from the dingy green which clothes the unripe nut, to the tawny brown and faded tan which it wears at other stages,—butternut mixed with a dull characterless gray. There was no attempt at uniform, yet something common, in the dress of the whole company,—a faded look, as if the fabric, whatever its original hue, had felt the sun until all life and brightness had wilted in the web and been killed out of the dye. Still the clothing was whole; and, upon closer inspection, looked strong and serviceable, though very coarse.

One man, Lieutenant William Berryhill of Mississippi, dyed some of his clothes on August 25, 1864, using chestnut bark and copperas to tint his military jacket, one pair of drawers, and two shirts. He decided not to dye three other shirts, one linen, one new Irish linen, and a hickory stripe. He ended his letter by telling his wife, Mary, not to laugh at the idea "of my sweating over the dye pot for there is no telling what a man can do untill he trys."[84]

Often the butternut color was mistaken for "yellow," as recognized by Private Smith, 54th Ohio, who in the Georgia summer of 1864, recalled "a mingled line of yellow and gray in all the pomp, splendor and circumstance of glorious war." Smith was viewing an infantry battle line 300 yards distant and ready to advance. Another Yankee, Lieutenant Thomas Galwey pronounced some benefits associated with the butternut color. In the summer fields surrounding Gettysburg, his men "found that the enemy [skirmishers] kept close to the ground so as to afford an uncertain target, owing to his dun clothes, we began, as the boys called, to be scientific in our fire."[85]

There are countless accounts available which chronicle the dilapidated conditions of a fair share of Southern infantrymen. Perry Mayo, even as early as 1861, saw through his field glasses four Rebels near a fort, "...poorly clothed, ...all of them having holes in the seat of their pants and in a ragged condition generally." And Sergeant John Worsham, 21st Virginia, was very descriptive of his fellow Confederates in July, 1863. He wrote:

> At this time our army was in a sad plight as to clothing. Hundreds had no shoes. Thousands were as ragged as they could be—some with the bottoms of their pants in long frazzles; others with their knees out, others out at the elbows, and their hair sticking through holes in their hats. Some of the men patched their clothing, and it was usually done with any material they could get. One man had the seat of his pants patched with bright red, and his knees patched with black. Another had used a piece of gray or brown blanket. There were, however, so few patches and so many holes that, when a Pennsylvania girl on the side of the road saw us pass and asked her mother how the officers were distinguished from the privates the mother replied that it was easy enough: the officers' pants were patched, and the privates' pants were not.[86]

Scores of Confederates, even whole regiments, eventually resorted to confiscating and wearing captured Union clothing and equipment. For instance, after the Battle of Shiloh in April 1862 it was normal to see Rebels in large numbers uniformed and equipped through the courtesy of the U.S. government. Lieutenant James Williams who commanded Company A, 21st Alabama in that engagement, wrote his wife Lizzie on several occasions. In these letters he spoke of his "immense pair of Yankee army shoes," together with a captured blanket, haversack and canteen, which he had covered over with "reddish gray cloth." Just prior to the battle, Williams requested that she make him a blue coat to complete his regular uniform. But after seeing the Federal troops at close quarters he explained to her:

> Since the battle I have regretted that I ever ordered a blue uniform—it is just like that of the enemy and it is feared that in the confusion of battle some of our officers were killed by men of our own side—I will never go into battle with my blue coat on that account but will wear my old gray jacket.... [I will] observe what you say about appearing upon the field in the fatal blue uniform; I have no desire to be killed by my own friends in mistake though many of our officers wear the blue coats all the time.

Lieutenant Williams soon ordered a new coat. It was to be neat, light and suitable for summer, very cheap, he said, and should cost about $16. He still liked his blue coat, as it was fancy and he could use it for evening dress parade. Later on May 3, he received a new sword, socks and a hat. Turned up on one side, and fastened with a gold star and a black silken loop and tassle, the hat was greatly admired by everyone. Lizzie had been petitioned to find a full black feather for it, but was asked not to use a gold band on the hat or any other gold if possible.[87]

Many other Confederates were forced to use Union apparel and accouterments. Sergeant Worsham remembered that by the close of the war, "...nearly all equipment in the Army of Northern Virginia were articles captured from the Yankees.... Most of the blankets were those marked 'US,' and also the rubber blankets or clothes. The very clothing that the men wore was mostly captured, for we were allowed to wear their pants, underclothing, and overcoats. As for myself, I purchased only one hat, one pair of shoes, and one jacket after 1861."

Still another Virginian, John Casler, 33rd Virginia, in July 1862 wore a Federal issue coat. He once became a little careless, as he later remembered: "One morning, as it was a little rainy, I put on a blue blouse, and that evening was on the skirmish line. As we were going through a piece of woods I thought I had better pull off my blue blouse, as I might be taken for the enemy by some 'Johnnie Reb' and popped over. So I took it off and hung it on a bush,..." John Green captured a fine overcoat in Tennessee in 1862 which belonged to Colonel A.B. Moore of the 104th Illinois. And in November 1863 near Mine Run, Virginia, Lieutenant Galwey, 8th Ohio, saw one of his men, "...during our advance [run] amongst a lot of Confederates, thinking them, from their blue overcoats, his own men. He learned his mistake...[and] broke away and joined us."[88]

Occasionally, due to the appropriation of the enemy's clothing, a Rebel would be killed or injured by his own men. In a 1903 memoir, Robert Stiles tells of such an event, which occurred during the final fighting near Petersburg, Virginia in 1865:

> I had cautioned my men against wearing "Yankee overcoats" especially in battle, but had not been able to enforce the order perfectly—and almost at my side I saw a young fellow of one of my companies jam the muzzle of his musket against the back of the head of his most intimate friend, clad in a Yankee overcoat, and blow his brains out.... I tried to strike the musket barrel up, but alas, my sword had been broken in the clash and I could not reach it. I well remember the yell of demoniac triumph with which that simple country lad of yesterday clubbed his musket and whirled savagely upon another victim.[89]

Life as an infantryman in army service was rife with opportunities for boredom, adventure and even some short periods of excitement. But what was unquestionably guaranteed was the chance to live in filth and squalor. The armies of the 1860s paid very little attention to cleanliness in general, leaving that aspect to the individual soldier and his officers to uphold. The commanders on the other hand sometimes left this task to each man who then set his own particular sanitary code. There were many exceptions to this code. In the 100th New York, for instance, the captain of one company ordered his squad sergeants to be responsible for the cleanliness and health of their men. "Every man," he said, "is to have his hair cut short, whiskers short & feet washed twice a week."

More often it was infantrymen like Rice C. Bull, 123rd New York and his companions who took it upon themselves to keep themselves reasonably clean while campaigning. Bull explained: "It took time to wash and dry [our clothes] so we had to know we would halt for at least a day before we could undertake the job.... We [then] borrowed a kettle from the regimental commissary for the 'boiling' and by ten in the morning were at work." Bull usually waited for a warm sunny day so his uniforms and underclothes would dry quickly. Later a body bath was indulged in and afterward, "wearing our clean clothes, we felt like new men."

Within the army there was an element of the population who never washed and were so shiftless and ignorant that they had to be forced to maintain even a semblance of neatness. Simon Hulbert became attached by circumstances to one such character named Gilbert J. Potter. Potter, according to Hulbert, "got so dirty & filthy that I could scarcely bear to have him in the bunk [in prison] he stunk so.... [H]e was so dirty looking that no one would have him in a tent...[and for] four weeks...he never washed his shirt nor bathed his body...& we used to take off our pants & shirt once or twice a day to kill the lice, & he did not have his off...in four weeks. He looks kind of scurfy [sic] now. [Oct. 15, 1862]. This morning the Lieut. G. Lynch ordered the orderly to send a Corporal with four men [to] take the gentleman Potter to the river & gave him a good scrubbing." Another 100th New Yorker caught the critical eye of Private Hulbert. He was named Disbrow and chewed tobacco. "He has hair all over his face. You can hardly see his mouth. His whiskers are all wet with tobacco juice, & when he eats, (My O), he has a meal of victuals in his mustache, or enough to last 24 hours."

In the campaign which terminated at the Battle of Antietam, the Confederate army under Robert E. Lee was in an unusual and distinctively poor condition. A Texas volunteer confessed that the men, many of whom were barefooted, had worn the same clothes for five weeks. Pants, jacket and shirt, he said, were present "through the dust and mud marching, fighting and sleeping on the ground." It became so bad that on or about the 7th of September 1862, General Hood ordered his entire command to wade into the Monocacy River near where they were camped, fully clothed and wash the dirt out of themselves and their uniforms. "In we went," commented John Stevens, "and I guess we got a portion of the dust out of our clothes. We then came out and stood in the sun and dried off."

Even an army's leader was not spared from the scourge of filth that accompanied infantry life. Fourth Texas Private Val Giles testified to that fact on the retreat from Gettysburg when he spied General Lee mounted on his horse at Falling Waters, Maryland, watching his men cross on a "rickety old pontoon bridge." He "sat calmly in the saddle near the river...with a few staff officers and couriers near him. He had always appeared to me before that morning as a model of elegance. On that gloomy occasion he looked pale, haggard, and old, but sat old Traveler as knightly as a Chevalier Bayard. He was bespattered with mud from the spurs on his boots to the gold cord on his black Kasruth hat. Old Traveler, whose original color was light iron gray, on that memorable morning was a veritable claybank. General Lee was calm but wore an anxious look...."

During the Nashville Campaign, according to Sergeant Clark, 1st Georgia, the men he soldiered with "did not wash their faces nor comb their hair at less than weekly intervals," and the washing when it came was merely a patting of water from the canteen to the face. Once just following this period of service, Clark found a woman in Mississippi who agreed to wash the underclothing of his mess. When they took the items to the woman all apologized for the condition, as they had been worn for over a month without a change. "No apology is necesseray," [sic] she assured them. "I have washed some for Forrest's cavalry that was so stiffened with dirt that they were able to stand alone." And once when a member of his regiment was searching for a pot to begin the midday meal, Clark said he sang out, "Where is the oven?" A messmate some distance away shouted back, "Can't you wait til I finish washing my feet in it?"

Following the Seven Days' Battles during the summer of 1862, Sergeant Fitzpatrick, 45th Georgia, described in a letter to his wife that he was finally having his clothes washed after five weeks of hard campaigning. During that period he had "dabbled [them] out in cold water and no soap once." He mentioned that he had adopted a common solution for not only carrying his extra clothes but keeping himself presentable. Fitzpatrick wore both his shirts at once, and also put on "both pairs of my britches and have been wearing them for two months. The outside pair got nearly impossible [with dirt, holes, etc.] but I worked on them late the other day and they do finely now." A prevalent and habitual remedy used within the infantry, it was not an oddity to find soldiers even during the summer clothed in two pairs of underclothes, shirts and trousers. When dirty, they were simply switched until all could be properly washed.

No better description exists of the foul atmosphere of an army camp when not suitably policed or when the site chosen for the bivouac was not intelligently considered, than that which was left by William Keesy as he portrayed a Union encampment near Washington in 1862. Unfortunately, within this camp boundary there was a beef slaughtering area which supplied the troops with meat:

> The hides and offal of the beeves for miles upon miles around, under a sweltering sun and sultry showers, would gender such swarms of flies, armies of worms, blasts of stench and oceans of filth as to make life miserable. Like the plagues of Egypt the pestilence would fill the air, come up into our tents and pollute the very water of the pure springs.... Taking into account the dead horses that were slain in battle, dying of wounds and daily perishing from the inconceivable wear and tear on horse flesh in moving, maintaining and equipping such an army [of 100,000 men]; and add to this the refuse, the sinks [latrines], the garbage, the waste, hides and entrails of the slaughtered beeves in droves and you will readily see that even the sanitary interests of the army is no small matter.

The stench and filth of camp life was also compounded by the living things of nature which often mingled with human beings on campaign, when both attempted to occupy the same space. In their writings, infantrymen complained of the constant tortures of worms, woodticks, bed bugs, chiggers, scorpions, lizards, centipedes, snakes, fleas, mosquitoes, ants and flies. But the real curse of the army, conceded Private Keesy, was not so much the dirt and stink, but a small pest he called the "immortal, illustrious, ever-memorable, ever-present, lion-backed 'Gray-back.'" They lived with the army and lived off the army he documented, and "[w]hoever had been gored under the fifth rib, or been tickled under the armpit, or been probed in the muscle of his weary body and has had his night slumbers disturbed by the rasping scrape of the dull tusk," will remember him, "I assure you."

There was not an infantryman anywhere that would have disputed Keesy's claim, although many would have denied their presence on his own body. Once when Keesy's friend Jake Wilt swore he was not pestered by the insect, Keesy bet him five dollars he could find one on Jake's person: "He soon divested himself of the underwear and as I rolled back the seam of the part worn under the arm-pit there rolled out some very fine specimens of the old lion-backed, glossy-shelled gray-backs, while there were nits enough adhering to the fabric to start a colony for the army."[90]

Unlike "Uncle Jake," the majority of infantrymen simply admitted that they harbored the nasty critters and accepted it as part of the unpleasantness of soldiering for their country. Before Antietam, Thomas Galwey deemed he was "very dirty and very lousy.... We all scratch alike, generals and privates. The lice have grown to be a perfect torture to us. While I was on picket one night, one of my men, a hard case but a jolly fellow, Jack Sheppard, amused himself by stringing vermin on needle and thread for a necklace, gathering his jewels from the inside of the ankles of the men's pantaloons. I can't imagine that anyone can become accustomed to lice."

For soldiers who came from clean households in civilian life, the first introduction to lice infestation in the army was an eye-

The "immortal...everpresent...'Grayback.'" (HC)

42

opening experience. Theodore Upson of Indiana related how in his first days of service he and his comrades refused to sleep in previously occupied barracks because they thought lice were present. It took their commander to convince them none of the bugs lived in the building: "Boys, I have been in the Army for a long time and I know what gray backs look like. Have seen thousands of them. And felt 'em too! That [pointing to an insect held by one of his men] is not a gray back, not even a louse—only a harmless little whitewood tic. You go back to camp. I give you my word of honor it is clean, and I will give five dollars apiece for all the gray backs you can find there."

To Texas Private William A. Fletcher, who was recovering from an illness in the regimental hospital, the thought of having body lice was repugnant. When accused by a friend of harboring these creatures he was insulted and angry. But reality soon overcame his wishful thinking when, upon scratching an itch, Fletcher had to give in:

I drew out my hand...and held it to the light, and there, sure enough, was something alive, for I could see its legs working. I was on my feet instantly...with a full-grown louse crawling before my eyes—such a feeling of disgrace one rarely has. I made an examination of clothing and bedding and saw that I was well supplied with them of all sizes and nits by the hundreds. There was a good fire in the grate and scuttle of coal nearby, so I kept a fire while I held my clothing and bed covering to the heat and cooked the life out of the most of them. My clothing and bedding was well scorched when I got through, but the nits in the seams seemed to be but little changed.

Fire might have been the only threat the louse understood. Walter Clark who labeled them "pediculus corporis," described the infantry custom of "before retiring at night, to take our flannel or hickory shirts, close the neck and wrist, suspend them over a blazing fire and hold them there until the air was filled with the odor of frying meat." In early 1862 Samuel McIlvaine's 10th Indiana had their first encounter with these little parasites, which they nicknamed "Southern body guards." As soon as their presence was detected, "[s]hirts were jerked off, hurriedly examined, and many of them committed to the flames."

Another method found successful in de-lousing one's clothing was to let bug battle bug. John Casler, 33rd Virginia, discovered this novel approach while a prisoner of war and detailed it in a memoir 30 years later: "There was an ant bed in the lower end of the yard, and every day there would be from five to ten prisoners around that bed, picking off lice and having them and the ants fighting. They would have a regular pitched battle, and would get up bets on them. Sometimes the aunts [sic] would drag the louse off, but often times a big louse would stand them off. It was great sport for the prisoners."

To illustrate the insidious nature of the body louse and how it became the curse of every man, officer or enlisted, is the following from John W. Stevens, 5th Texas, who recalled a story involving "the blight" and his brigade commander, General J.B. Robertson:

In size...he is about as large as a small grain of wheat. May be, hardly so large—37 or 38 years since I saw him last. It is said he has legs—how many I do not know, as I never tried to find out. I know he has a mouth and he understands how to use it.... His usual haunts are about the seams of the clothing, especially around the shoulders and outside seams of the pants legs; he's there in force and the force is continually aug- menting. He is never idle;...no soldier on duty can hope to escape him; he will eat the skin off and gnaw into the flesh.... They seem to be indiginous [sic] to army life.

While we were camped...near Winchester...our [general] undertook to lecture our regiment one evening while on dress parade, on the matter of clensing [sic] ourselves of these "bugs".... The old general meant well, his lecture was given in kindness. But we noticed all the time he was so earnestly addressing us he was busy with first one hand and then the other scratching himself on the shoulder, on the arm, then around the waistband, his pants, and then his hips, then quickly the other hand went to the shoulder and under his arm; the boys observing it began to titter, then the whole regiment began to laugh, and some one called out, "Say general, what makes you scratch so," the old man saw the "pint" and breaking out into a laugh, dismissed the parade. Fact is, he was about as "bug-y" as any of us—we could not avoid the bug, he was everywhere, he was no respecter of person. He could wear the gray or the blue, he was at home in both armies, was loyal to both flags....

When speaking of this critter, many infantrymen like Stevens used humor to get their point across. Eli W. House, 52nd Indiana, even sent his cousin at home a poem about the louse: "Well, Cal, I will have to tell you a little prayer that we had when out on the raid in Missouri...its, every time I lay down to sleep, the greybacks all around me creep, and if they bite before I wake, I hope by God their jaws they break."

The lice who resided in Company K, 13th Massachusetts Regiment, were called "Army Crums" according to Sergeant Stearns. He remembered a humorous story about them which took place during the Gettysburg Campaign:

One day while in Pa. one of the boys had his shirt off skirmishing [with the bugs] when an old citizen came along and stopped to look at him, the soldier taking no notice. "Are they Fleas?" said the old citizen. "Fleas!" said the soldier in a voice of thunder and expressing great indignation. "What do you take me to be, a d____d dog? No, I'm a soldier, and they are lice."

To be constantly dirty and crawling with biting insects was not very enjoyable, especially for years on end. Lieutenant A.B. Isham of Michigan has left an account which proves how trying these creatures could be to the human mental state. Isham was lying wounded in a field hospital and was speaking poetically of a man in a bed adjacent to him who had just died:

The full daylight sometimes made disclosures not engaging to look upon. It revealed that a soul had "slipped its moorings" in the night, and the deserted "tenement of clay" not seldom presented an aspect too hideous to be viewed with calm complacency. If, as sometimes was the case, the subject had been the host of a horde of crawling vermin, these disgusting things swarmed out the hair and off the body, to make their way down the sides of the cot. It made the flesh creep, it filled the soul with horror, to lie helpless, within hands reach of such a spectacle, without the ability to move a muscle or make an effort to prevent it, and feel that this dreadful mass might in a little time be transferred over to riot on one's tissues. Such sights were not so uncommon in a field hospital. The loathing, the dread, the nameless terror, the despondency, they induced in those of gentle breeding who were making a brave struggle for life, in not a few instances turned the scale against them.[91]

Like all military clothing, the category of footwear and headgear could appropriately be part of a separate chapter. But a few comments should suffice to reinforce what has already been said on the subject.

Northern infantrymen were issued forage caps, French "kepi" style caps, and large dress hats complete with brass insignia, a large feather, and blue colored hat cords. As time passed and the troops learned to cope with the discomforts of field service, many soldiers turned to more comfortable wide brimmed civilian-style hats. Hermon Clarke, 117th New York, for one, wrote home on June 13, 1864, asking to be sent a, "...black soft hat, not very heavy, size 7 or 7-1/8, and a pound [of] smoking tobacco."

Lieutenant Abner Small of the 16th Maine called the average soldier's headpiece, "a cap as shapeless as a feedbag." But to J. Smith Graham, 140th Pennsylvania, a hat was quite precious, as he explained in a letter to his brother in September 1864 demonstrating the hardships they were enduring: "To make things worse it was raining. Several of the boys lost their hats...and this was my fix too, and as a soildier [sic] only has one hat, we had to go three days before we could get another. You may think this is hard but a soildier thinks nothing of it."

Private Theodore Upson was not favorably impressed with the regulation dress hats of the U.S. infantry. He called them "rediculous things" that made him "think of the pictures of the Pilgrim Fathers. They are high with a cone shaped top and a wide stiff brim. They have a brass oval [bugle] in front and a brass eagle to loop up one side." The 13th Massachusetts did not care much for these hats either, and they did something about it, just as surely as Upson's 100th Indiana must have done:

> The hats were neither useful nor ornamental. They were made of black felt, high-crowned, with a wide rim turned up on one side, and fastened to the crown by a brass shield representing an eagle with extended wings, apparently screaming with holy horror at so base an employment. On the front of the crown was a brass bugle containing the figure 13. Now it so happened that the person who selected the sizes was under the impression that every man from Massachusetts had a head like Daniel Webster—a mistake that caused most of us much trouble, inasmuch as newspapers were in great demand to lessen the diameter of the crown....later on [the hats] mysteriously disappeared.

Confederate Private John Green may have been happy to possess a hat as "classy" as just described, because he had lost his cap when it "was shot away during the fight at Missionary Ridge...." His solution to the problem though, was unique. Green explained: "...Capt Mort Perry got a new coat [and] I told him if he would give me the tails from his old coat I would make him a new cap & make one for my self also. My proposal was accepted & my success was such that I was beset by several in the regiment to make them caps. The scarcity of the material however prevented my being worked to death in the cap industry."

Prior to leaving Texas for the "seat of war," Val Giles was escorted by his father, who did not like Giles' new military cap, to "Sampson and Hendrick's big store on [Congress] Avenue [in Austin]. He told Ben Hendricks he wanted the best hat in the house....After making me try on a dozen or more, they finally agreed on [a] monster... but it didn't suit me. I took it off and crushed in the sides, then set it on my head a little slanting. 'Don't do that,' Father said. 'It makes you look like a rowdy....' Hendricks agreed with him, so I had to submit and wear the thing straight." Later while having a photograph taken of his new uniform, Giles said he was talked into placing a star device on the brim of his hat and pinning it up. The photographer had convinced the new private that it would make him look much more fierce. And John O. Casler of the "Stonewall Brigade" reported that just before the Battle of First Manassas, he and his comrades, "...tore all the feathers out of our hats, because we heard the Yanks had feathers in theirs, and we might be fired on by mistake, as our company was the only one that had black plumes in their hats."[92]

In the letters, memoirs and diaries left by Civil War infantrymen, the subject of feet and footwear often arises, usually in connection with "forced marches." Theodore Upson's introduction to army shoes and socks was typical for a Civil War soldier. In August 1862 this seventeen-year-old private described his new uniform down to the last detail: "The shirts are rather coarse and scratchy and the sox—well, I think I shall wear the ones I brought from home and have Mother knit me some more when they are worn out. As to the shoes, they are wide and big enough, goodness knows! No danger of cramped feet with them! They may be very good but surely they are not very stylish."

A pair of well-worn army shoes. (THS)

At least two Confederates would have definitely switched places with Upson later in the war. In November 1862, shoes were so scarce that the chaplain of the 4th Texas wrote a letter to the Richmond *Whig*, asking the locals to furnish 100 pairs for his men. Val Giles of that regiment testified that General Longstreet had, "...suggested that the barefooted men go to the slaughter pens, procure the hides that came off the beeves killed for the army, then make moccasins for their feet by taking the green hide, cutting out a piece large enough to cover the foot, then turning the hairy side in. The order said to 'whang the moccasins on with rawhide throngs....'" The chaplain himself verified it, as did other soldiers, including Douglas Cater, 19th Louisiana, who in early November, 1864 explained: "My shoes had worn out and for two days I had been wearing a pair of moccasins made of cowskin freshly taken off a poor beef.... A soldier brought me a pair of shoes number four size.... A number six was as small a shoe as I could wear, but by cutting away enough of the vamp to free my toes, I could wear them. They were quite an improvement over my moccasins."[93]

The numbers of men on both sides who went barefoot at one time or another during their service is phenomenal. As a token measure of this problem, in October 1863 the 9th Virginia had nearly 200 men without shoes, and this regiment was by no means even close to its full compliment, i.e. 1,000 men. Orderly-sergeant John Lewis of the regiment reported 17 out of 57 in his company in that condition; this was during November when the Shenandoah River was iced over to one-half inch thick. In this same month Longstreet's Corps reported 6,466 barefooted men, while eight months later, fully one-quarter of Lee's entire army was shoeless.

Lewis also spoke of "hide" shoes, saying they were made from, "green hides of the cattle killed for food, sewed up with thongs of strips...the hair side being inside, next to the foot." When they dried, Lewis emphasized, they were impossible to get off without cutting them. Their length was 16 inches when "fresh." He added: "It was lucky that there were no dogs in camp or they would have given us trouble." But Sergeant Lewis admitted that not every soldier who went shoeless did so from having worn them out. On one occasion he saw a private who, upon hearing gunshots up ahead as his unit prepared for battle, threw his shoes in a nearby canal as if to say: "...you came very near getting me in trouble this time." The cowardly man then retired to the rear, giving "no shoes" as an excuse.[94]

It was more rare to see a Union soldier without something covering his feet, although the idea that Northerners never went barefooted is also untrue. But in one case it was cause for something akin to the circus coming to town. Charles Barber, 104th New York, recalled that near Waterloo, Virginia on or about July 27, 1862 he went foraging for a meal: "I went to a farm house to buy some potatoes and I over heard a young lady say oh ma do come see this bare footed Yankee and the whole house hold looked out of the doors and windows and even 20 negroes of all kinds come in to the yard to see the barefooted Yankee."

Going barefoot as a civilian on a warm summer day or even as a soldier out looking for food was a far cry from being in such a state as part of your military duty. To a man loaded down with 50 or 60 pounds of clothes, equipment, weapons and ammunition, this was nothing less than pure torture. Lieutenant Galwey gave a hint of this condition in July 1863:

> I am barefooted.... A good part of our marching is on mountain roads, made of sharp-cornered broken stone, or through the open wastes on the side of the mountains, where the briars and blackberry bushes cut my feet at every step. But I have plenty of company. Almost half of us are barefooted now.

A couple of months later in northern Georgia, a Florida soldier, Washington Ives, recited that the "whole army is in good spirits but it is bad to see barefoot men marching on such roads.... I tell you it is enough to make you shed tears to see what some of the boys are enduring...." Georgian Marion H. Fitzpatrick verified that the roads were the cause for the loss of shoes, as well as the pain from not having them. He told his wife in a letter dated December 4, 1862 that his, "shoes are nearly worn out. I would wear out anything the way we had to march and the kind of roads we had to go over. A great many are entirely barefooted." A lieutenant in the 41st Virginia verified this last statement by Fitzpatrick. Just four days later Charles Denoon wrote his father: "Everything is in frozen condition here [near Fredericksburg, VA]. Many poor soldiers are totally barefooted, and badly clad, but they stand it without much murmering [sic]."

Texan John Stevens endured the shoeless condition for 21 days, days of long marches and rough duty during the Seven Days' Campaign near Richmond in 1862. Stevens lost his shoes in a deep, boggy marsh and failed to replace them even from the dead due to his shoe size being "high up in the teens." At times he was able to pull socks off the corpses, but these did not last long. Therefore, Private Stevens explained, "[I] was forced to move through this exciting campaign with [my] little pink toes(?) all exposed to the wicked gaze of the daisies and violets that lined our pathway...." And in March of 1863 Stevens found himself barefooted again. This time there were no daisies blooming and the hardship did not just pass away:

> Now its snowing very heavy—it snows all day. The snow is nearly knee deep, and I am once more bare-footed. Now I guess you think I suffered. Not a bit of it; I did not suffer then, but I have suffered the results ever since—I suffer now as I walk the streets of Hillsboro [Texas, 1902]. Every day of my life I am reminded of that day's march, and as I grow older it gets worse—both of my feet are diseased from the effects of that day, and at times I can't keep my shoes on.[95]

Principally early in the war, but even at other times, soldiers believed that boots were preferable to shoes. Shoes were less than adequate in mud, deep dust, heavy rain and snow. But there were also problems with boots. W.A. Keesy described a classic case of overreliance on this product when he purchased a "very fine pair of oil tanned, double soled, iron nailed high-kneed, horse-hide $8 boots,... [which] everybody envied...."

In camp, Keesy's much envied boots were delightful, but on the first march things changed. Said Keesy: "...[my] boots were the envy of all, and more than once was I offered their price in gold. But after a few hours' marching I confess I did not think so much of them. By night I was not proud of them at all. They hung on my poor crippled feet like iron bands." The next day before he had gone six miles he was in "an inexpressible state of torture." By nightfall Keesy was five miles behind the rest of the army. The next day he sold them to his friend Jake Wilt, for $2.00 plus Jake's "tumbledown" old shoes. Years later when remembering the incident and the adventures Jake's shoes eventually went through, Private Keesy declared: "If I had those old army shoes now, I don't think I would take a $100 bill for them."

Correspondingly, Confederate M.H. Fitzpatrick was also put out of commission by a pair of boots he was forced to borrow from his captain in March, 1864: "I wore the boots till we got here [Orange, VA] which was three days and they broke me down and nearly ruined my feet. This morning I have not put them on at all, nor do I expect to any more if I can help it. I put on an old pair of socks over one of my new pair and am taking it shoeless. I am so stiff that I can hardly walk at all...."

Sometimes as infantrymen learned severe lessons they adapted well. Charles Barber opted for lambskin boots which would have been far more comfortable than Keesy's horsehides mentioned earlier. Barber asked his wife to send a "pair of boots, size 8, wide toes[,] my instep is size 20 and heel 28 put a pair of taps on the outside soles make the upper out of heavy kid skin without lining." Generally though, the majority of infantrymen made do with the issues of their governments, sometimes improvising or

Charles Barber, 104th New York, who asked his wife to send him boots from home.
(RGB)

improving what the army provided, as in the example of John Holt, 56th Virginia. Instead of purchasing boots, he wrote his "beloved wife" Ellen Lawson that "a good pair of shoes made" would do nicely and would she "make me another pair of gaiters & have them Smartly larger especially at the top.... If they are too large I can move the buttons so as to make them fit." These gaiters or leggings imitated the useful qualities of boots, without the weight and discomfort.

All infantrymen sooner or later suffered from blistered feet whether wearing boots or shoes until their feet toughened up. Wilbur Fisk, after a difficult march following the Battle of Gettysburg, "saw some feet...[of men who had fallen out of ranks] that if they had been on me, I should consider had done their duty faithfully...." He described the sensation: "Blistered and raw, every nerve was a magazine of pain, and every step exploded them."

EQUIPMENT

I tell you the less a soldier is burdened with the better he can get along.

Sgt. M. Hill Fitzpatrick
45th Georgia Infantry

All Civil War enlisted infantrymen carried a weapon and various accouterments and equipments either prescribed by regulation, or personally chosen for comfort, usefulness or necessity. Accouterments may be described as a canteen and cup, haversack, knapsack, blanket(s), poncho, and/or shelter tent. Accouterments also included the cartridge box, percussion cap box, bayonet and scabbard, and waist belt and belt plate (buckle). The knapsack was the largest piece of equipment the soldier carried; its use is also the most controversial. In many circles there is a strong belief that only Federal infantrymen carried the knapsack. This is a blatantly false notion, because too much easily obtainable evidence contradicts that idea. As a rule, Confederate foot soldiers probably used knapsacks nearly as frequently as their Yankee foes.

Sergeant Fitzpatrick best summed up the feeling of most Northern and Southern infantrymen who used the knapsack as a tool of the trade: "I have no use for a knapsack on a march but they are very useful in Camps." The sergeant explained to his wife in November 1863, why on his last march he had "throwed away my knapsack..., but I drawed another since we came here."

Knapsacks, although heavy, were still very much in service in both armies even into the last days of the war. The sergeant-major of the 4th Florida, Washington Ives, boasted in a letter to his father during the Atlanta Campaign, written on September 23, 1864 about a march of 20 miles "over a bad road and the men carrying knapsacks ect. [sic]."

In place of the knapsack, thousands of soldiers wearing either the blue or gray turned to a lighter weight and less cumbersome substitute. Lieutenant Denoon offered his brother, who was about to enlist, this advice learned from months of soldiering: "...all he needs is one pair pants, one coat, two shirts, two pair drawers and two pair socks..., haversack, canteen, tin cup, one blanket (small), oil cloth or piece of Yankee tent.... You may put your shirt and drawers in your blanket and roll them up in a round roll, tying the two ends together and place it on your shoulder as you would a game bag or horn with strings around it to keep it from unrolling...."

In stark contrast to the plain blanket roll, the rigid or soft painted cotton cloth knapsack of the Federal army, John Worsham's 21st Virginia used a more fancy variety. Said he: "Our knapsacks were a specialty. They were imported from Paris, made of hairy calfskin wrapped around a frame box, and red and white in color. Inside they were divided into partitions.... There were straps on the outside for blanket, overcoat, oilcloth, and shoes." Early in the war Worsham carried these items in his gaudy knapsack: "...a fatigue jacket, several pairs of white gloves, several pairs of drawers, several white shirts, undershirts, linen collars, neckties, white vest, socks, etc.—filling our knapsack to overflowing. Strapped on the outside were one or two blankets, an oil-

Cpl. Austin C. Wellington, 38th Massachusetts, carrying his knapsack topped by a poncho and blanket. (WCM)

cloth, and extra shoes. Most...weighed between thirty and forty pounds, but some...weighed fifty pounds!"

It seems plausable that only early war troops loaded themselves down to such extreme out of ignorance or lack of experience. This unusual account by a Confederate written in the summer of 1863 concerns one of his close companions in the 1st Tennessee Infantry:

> ...Tennessee Thompson, always carried bigger burdens than any other five men in the army. For example, he carried two quilts, three blankets, one gum oil cloth, one overcoat, one axe, one hatchet, one camp-kettle, one oven and lid, one coffee pot, besides his knapsack, haversack, canteen, gun, cartridge-box, and three days' rations. He was a rare bird.... Tennessee usually had his hair cut short on one side and left long on the other, so that he could give his head a bow and a toss and throw the long hairs on the other side, and it would naturally part itself without a comb.

Wilbur Fisk of Vermont provided his readers at home with information on the constant aggravation a soldier must endure when in preparation for an upcoming march. "Often a knapsack would have to be unpacked and its contents sorted over and over again, and other articles selected out and doomed to stay behind, to the no small regret of the wistful owner." As Fisk exclaimed in this mournful lament: "How can we get along without them?" or "How can we carry them?"

Private Fisk described other uses of the much maligned knapsack. "It furnished us a seat in the daytime when we stopped, and was our pillow at night when we slept. It was our bed, band-box, and storehouse." But for some it was still a nuisance. Fisk found that, "[v]ery few had no knapsack at all, and some had allowed their affections to become so alienated from the troublesome articles in the late campaigning, [June-July 1863] that it was difficult to persuade them to adopt another." Like Private Fisk, Michigander Daniel Crotty, took pride in his knapsack. He admonished that "the knapsack of a tidy soldier is worth looking at. The overcoat is folded in a nice roll and strapped on top; the blankets, shirts, drawers and socks, with a soldier's album, which almost every soldier carries with the pictures of dear and loving friends at home. All have their proper places in the knapsack."

Knapsacks were often disliked, but when loaded and wet they were particularly detested. Charles Barber evoked this complaint after a tedious march in January 1863. "[I]t rained all night we slept but little; we packed up again at daylight without fire or breakfast.... it still rained the roads was horrible...; our blankets and all our luggage was soaked through which doubled the heft of our knapsack...." But the very best composite of the infantryman's "weighty companion" was penned by Maine officer Abner Small, who wrote:

> The knapsack...is an unwieldy burden with its rough, coarse contents of flannel and sole leather and sometimes twenty rounds of ammunition extra mixed in with these regulation essentials, like beatitudes, are photographs, cards, huswife [housewife], Testament, pens, ink, paper, and oftentimes stolen truck enough to load a mule. All this is crowned with a double wool blanket and half a shelter tent rolled in a rubber blanket.

One duty associated with the history of the knapsack was more than uncomfortable; it was sad and melancholy as well. Captain Porter Farley of the 140th New York, who was familiar with the many unhappy tasks following a battle, explained:

Abner Small, 16th Maine, who best described the contents of a knapsack. (HAS)

> Of the knapsacks which had been piled together [before the fight in the Wilderness, VA] only half had been reclaimed by their owners. When all hope of seeing any more men come in was lost, the unclaimed knapsacks were opened, and the friends of the missing men tried to save such trifling mementoes of their lost comrades as would be most precious to their families.... but most of the clothing of the missing men had to be abandoned.[96]

Unquestionably, the soldier's blanket and poncho were more essential to life in the field than was the knapsack. Blankets issued by the Federal army were generally pure or mixed wool, colored gray or brown with the letters "U.S." stitched in black outline, measuring 7 x 5.5 feet in size. Confederate blankets were very diverse in color, material, and size. Many were homemade; quilts were common and even an issue item of the C.S. government. The Southern infantryman more than likely carried a blanket furnished from home, or pilfered from a dead, wounded or captured Yankee. Sergeant Fitzpatrick of the 45th Georgia claimed that he could draw an "excellent" blanket from his government at a cost of $4, while Union Sergeant Stewart, 52nd Ohio was charged $3.25 for his woolen blanket.

Ponchos, or gum-blankets, referred to as rubber-blankets, became a favorite item of the infantryman due to its multiple purpose, i.e., as a ground cloth, raincoat, and shelter tent. First issued in November 1861, it was approximately 45" x 79" and fitted with brass grommets. Some even came with a buttoned slit in the center for use over the head and shoulders against inclement weather. The army also supplied "painted blankets" due to the shortage of rubber blankets. These too could be worn as rain cloaks. Rebels by the thousands coveted these articles which along with the U.S. regulation canteen, became two of the favorite items to be scavenged from their Northern enemies. Often the use of knapsacks gave way to the blanket alone as a means of securing and carrying one's effects. Corporal Lee Stillwell, 61st Illinois, gave his views on that subject early in the war, on June 16, 1862:

The army issue poncho. (NA)

*Capt. James Young, 60th New York,
adopted the "blanket-roll."* (GNMP)

> It was about this time that the most of the boys adopted the "blanket-roll" system. Our knapsacks were awkward...[s]o we would fold in our blankets an extra shirt, with a few other light articles, roll the blanket tight, double it over and tie the two ends together, then throw the blanket over one shoulder, with the tied ends under the opposite arm— and the arrangement was complete.

Multitudes of soldiers grew fond of their blankets, even when they failed to provide the basic necessary comfort, as Wilbur Fisk said in November 1862: "[A]t this time of the year, it is difficult for a fellow to keep himself warm. I know my time honored woollen blanket, the very one that I picked up on the battle-field of Gettysburg, I have found to be provokingly insufficient to keep me warm a great many times these cold, stormy nights, and my wrath has gone up to the swearing point on several occasions on account of it."

Fisk needn't have worried however, because soon afterwards on "one cold morning" his worn out old blanket was stolen by a member of the 4th Vermont. Later, Private Fisk immortalized the army poncho or rubber blanket. On a rainy, dreary day in 1863 he and his companions had built a comfortable fire which they kept blazing from nearby fence rails. The army was in the mountains and the men were both cold and wet. Fisk poetically described the "[s]tragglers [who] kept streaming in and huddling around the fire, their rubber blankets, dripping wet, thrown over their heads, and looking for all the world like a flock of sick turkeys in a stormy day."

In contrast to the scenes above, warm weather often produced just the opposite feeling toward blankets, as related in this account by Justus Silliman, 17th Connecticut. He experienced an uncomfortable march in May 1863: "Overcoats blankets and tents which had been thrown away by those in advance lined the road and covered the ground at their halting places. I do not think a hundred thousand dollars would more than have covered the loss in manner. Sambos & Phillises collected in squads,...[and] would gather up an armful of clothing and march off in great delight,...."

Every infantryman sooner or later shared the experience of Private Silliman. Confederate Johnny Green recalled that on July 20, 1864 his Kentucky regiment moved from position to position all day preparing for battle. By the morning of the 21st they were "still three miles from the point of attack; it has been a terribly tedious march. The sun comes up & makes the heat so oppressive that many of the boys throw away their blankets rather than carry them over their shoulders." Those who abandoned good blankets later regretted their actions, even on scorching days. The weather always changed, night invariably came, and a blanket could make all the difference to a damp or cold infantryman. Theodore Birmingham, 23rd Michigan appreciated a real bed so much that he took pains to prepare one whenever possible. He described how to a woman friend back home:

> First we leveled off the ground as smooth as possible. Then we lay down two poles about four feet apart (each pole was a little longer than I am) and one across the foot. Then we cut some fine [pine?] bows and threw them in and since got some straw and put in.... Then for the under sheet we use an overcoat. For oversheet we use a blanket and for coverlids we use another blanket. For [a] pillow we use our knapsack and coat unless it is cold weather. Then we throw the coat over us and use our shoes to assist for [a] pillow.

The popular "gum-blanket," first supplied to the troops in late 1861, was expertly eulogized by T.F. Upson in a letter mailed from Memphis, Tennessee: "We have drawn rubber blankets (or "ponchos" they are called); they are about 6 1/2 feet long and 3 1/2 feet wide with eylet [sic] holes in the sides and ends. We can lace two of them together at the sides and then with a forked stick at each end and a straight peice [sic] for a ridge pole can make a little tent that two can sleep under. So we have an extra one to close up one end and one to put on the ground it makes it better, so Taylor and I have drawn two each, which we are allowed to do." Sergeant Austin Stearns of the 13th Massachusetts also characterized the use of the rubber blanket for a shelter-half or tent. In March 1862 he "...first saw what was soon to be our tents for the remaining time of our service, Ponchos. [General Louis] Blenkers Division of German troops were camped here having those tents for their shelter."

One of the most novel uses ever invented for that humble piece of soldier's equipment was explained by Lieutenant Thomas Galwey. Describing how gambling is carried on in the army, he said of the game called Chuck-Luck:

> Six numbers are painted on a cloth, and the speculators put their money on what number they like. If the chosen number is thrown by the Banker's dice, the Better wins; if not of course he loses. Naturally there are no fancifully ornamented tables for this enticing game; but go where you will, if you pick up any gum-blanket, you will find the numbers "1, 2, 3, 4, 5, 6" marked on the white side of the blanket, in various degrees of artistic excellence.[97]

Although as the war progressed many infantrymen discarded the heavier canvas two-man tents for a poncho or rubber blanket, the portable "shelter-half" tent saw heavy use. The Southern army did not officially issue many of these field tents. The average soldier of the Confederacy made use of captured specimens. The Union army supplied an 1862 version of the shelter tent, which measured 5' 2" x 4' 8" and was fastened together by bone buttons. In 1864 a second, somewhat larger version came out; this one was 5' 6" x 5' 5", complete with metal buttons. These two-man shelters had various nicknames, such as "A" tents, "fly tents," "dog kennels," "wedge tents," "picket tents," "dog-houses," "dog tents," "pup tents," "shanties," or "shebangs." Sergeant Stearns described them as: "...simply a piece of cloth about six feet square with a row of buttons and button holes on three sides; two men pitched together by buttoning their pieces together and getting two sticks with a crotch at one end and one to go across at the top and then placing their cloth over it and pinning it down tight;... On the whole, after we got used to them, we liked them quite well."

New Yorker David Thompson proposed that when a third man entered the process it was usually in rainy weather: "...[a] piece of rope about four feet long is...tied to the top of one of the stakes and stretched out...and pinned there. The third man then buttons his piece of muslin to one slope of the roof, carries the other edge of the piece out around the tightened rope and brings it back to the edge of the other slope, to which it is buttoned." Thompson pointed out that this third piece could be moved to either opening of the "pup" tent depending on the direction of wind or rain. It was advisable during wet weather not to touch the inside of the cloth, for the water would then come in "drop by drop." His advice included the construction of a small trench, about three inches deep, to be dug around the tent, "close up so that the rain shed from the roof will fall into it." He concluded that for three quarters of the year, "it is all the shelter needed...."

Fortunate to have his own tent, Sergeant Fitzpatrick commented that: "These Yankee tents are very light, and button together so that one man can carry one piece and another man the other piece. Three men can sleep under one of them very well. The one I got is right new and I would not take a pretty for it,..." A Yank, Theodore Upson, 100th Indiana, also left a record of his "cotton" house. "We are supplied with what the boys call pup tents. We each have a piece of canvass nearly 7 feet long, 3 1/2 feet wide, with eylets along sides and ends. Two men go together, lace up the sides of the canvass, get end sticks and ridge pole and have a good little tent to sleep in." Instead of being used by merely one to three men, W.A. Keesy, 55th Ohio, recounted how with the side and end buttons, "[j]ust as many men as saw fit could unite their tents and thereby tent together." Keesy added that in the beginning using them was like being outside, but "after getting used to, and learning how to use it, it answered every purpose. Besides the convenience of always having your tent with you,...it relieved an army of wagons which now could bring up the needed crackers."

The shelter tent. (HC)

In more permanent camps during the summer these small tents could be made larger and cooler by some minor adjustments and a little ingenuity. Lieutenant Galwey explained:

> The tents [with a view to warm weather] are placed facing the company streets in the usual manner. A framework like a bedstead is made by driving four stakes into the ground and laying slats made of springy saplings across these, about three feet from the ground. Then we set up at each end of the bedstead a tall stake forked at the top, across which a pole is laid. The tent is then stretched over the pole. Thus the air is allowed to circulate freely everywhere and the tents can be kept free of dirt and vermin.

Wilbur Fisk, on March 20, 1862 called his tent "nothing more than pieces of flaxcloth about a yard and a half square" which when held up by two poles or two inverted bayonetted rifles, resembled a "hencoop" with the ends open. Again on August 10, 1863 he described the tent as "nothing more nor less than two pieces of cotton or linen cloth, about five feet square," which when dry were light, but when wet, became very heavy, "and to carry these in our knapsacks with all the rest of the clothing..., was going to make a pretty heavy draft upon the strength of a fellow's back bone."

In late 1862 Confederate John Worsham commented:

> [T]he 21st Virginia had by this time learned to live without tents, [and] it was easy for the men to move. The only shelter the men had were oil or rubber cloths and cotton flies. The latter were of cotton about four by six feet in size and hemmed around the borders. Button holes were worked around these borders and buttons sewed on at certain places....
>
> In moving, all that was needed was to roll up our fly or oilcloth to take with us, put our small lot of cooking utensils in the wagons, put on our accouterments, and take arms. Then we were ready for a march to another camp, or to meet the enemy.

19th Louisiana infantryman Douglas Cater used his piece of tenting, or duck cloth as he called it, to top a unique "house" made of cornstalks. The "walls were three feet high and long enough and wide enough to spread a blanket over a bed of straw on the inside." A little ditch on the outside around the structure, "conveyed the falling water [from the roof] away from my bed."

One of the best and easiest ways to construct a quick shelter to protect men from intermittent showers or a hot sun while on a halt during long marches, was described by Lieutenant William Wood of Company A, 19th Virginia. His men often "stretched a blanket by 'putting on' the bayonet and sticking [the muskets] in the ground, and then catching each corner of the blanket in the lock of the musket, a shade was [thus] secured...."[98]

The haversack also was carried by Civil War infantrymen. Unlike the knapsack, which often held the blanket, extra clothes, personal items, and even the shelter tents, the haversack could be found dangling from the torsos of nearly all soldiers who saw field service. Contrary to the "come and go" attitude toward the knapsack, the haversack was in constant use, and along with the musket and canteen, was a real necessity to the foot soldier.

Described by John D. Billings, the average regulation haversack was a bag constructed of Russia sheeting or painted cotton cloth, "about a foot square, with a broad strap for the shoulder [1-2 inches] into which soldiers soon learned to bundle all their food and table furniture." There were dozens of varieties and sizes of these articles, some of cotton drill painted black, others unpainted, all at a cost to the soldier of about 50 cents each. Often an extra bag was included which could be buttoned to the inside back of the haversack to keep the various food items separated. Smaller string-tied or drawstring bags were added to hold rice, coffee, sugar, salt and pepper, etc. However, Daniel Crotty, 3rd Michigan, dispels the notion that such implied neatness meant very much:

> It is a curious sight to see the men gather around and get their variety of provisions - salt pork, hard tack, sugar, coffee, salt, and just enough pepper to make one sneeze, all of which is stowed away in the best possible manner in the haversacks. Sometimes when we go on a double-quick, everything is mixed together in solid mass, and it takes us no little time to get our provisions in shape again. But we have to take a mixture of pepper and salt, coffee and sugar, once in a while, as we find it impossible to part our provisions.

Daniel Crotty, 3rd Michigan, wrote about keeping provisions in a haversack. (BGP)

Lieutenant Abner Small described the infantrymen in his 16th Maine as having on "[o]ne shoulder...[his] 'commissary department'—an odorous haversack, which often stinks with its mixture of bacon, pork, salt junk [meat], sugar, coffee, tea, desiccated vegetables, rice, bits of yesterday's dinner, and old scraps husbanded with miserly care against a day of want sure to come."

Vermonter Wilbur Fisk questioned if anyone reading his letter could survive living on what he and his comrades were allotted for six days: "From an inventory of the contents of my haversack when we started from Warrenton [VA—Nov. 1863], I noticed that I had just forty-eight hard tack, and about one pound and a half of salt pork, besides sugar and coffee of which I had plenty." Fisk declared, "we soldiers often have but little else to think of, except what we shall eat and what we shall drink and where-withal we shall get our rations; and sometimes this subject becomes to us one of painful importance."

In a letter composed to his mother in Connecticut, a few weeks after the Battle of Chancellorsville in May, 1863, Justus Silliman declared that the "secesh carry no knapsacks, haversacks or tents, [and] carry their food in their pockets replenished every day, have neither coffee or sugar." Hundreds of eyewitness accounts in letters, diaries, and memoirs contradict this statement. Even late Civil War photographs of captured Southern infantrymen prove that the haversack stayed in favor with the majority of Confederates to the end. In July 1864, for instance, Lieutenant Edwin Weller, 107th New York, wrote to his friend from near Marietta, Georgia with strong proof that this item was in use and even in production: "...[N]ear here, we captured some four hundred women, who were at work in a factory making knapsacks and haversacks for the Rebel army. They are said to be a hard looking set of females by those who have seen them."[99]

Along with the haversack, and carried on the same side of the body, (usually the left) hung the infantryman's canteen, which was often accompanied by a tin cup. Whereas numerous soldiers buckled their coffee "boilers," "dippers" or "bailers" to the haversack's outside flap-cover, when carrying a smaller cup it was often left to dangle from the canteen strap or stopper chain.

Canteens were made from several materials throughout the Civil War period, but tin and wood were by far the most prevalent. The canteen had to be light, strong, and sized to hold between 2.5 and 3 pints, the amount of water an average infantryman needed on a daily march. U.S. regulation canteens were oblate-spheroid in shape and made of "two convex circular pieces of pressed tin soldered together around the rim." The mouthpiece was pewter, accompanied by a cork and metal stopper topped with an iron ring and chain. The cover was of blue or gray fabric with

Haversack, regulation U.S. canteen, and tin cup.
(THS)

a brownish cast, usually wool or cotton, which muffled noise and helped to keep the contents cool; a cotton strap completed the whole. If lost, it cost the soldier about 44 cents.

Southern-made tin canteens were produced in a drum or cylindrical style, rather than the Federal oblate-spherical shape, due to the lack of stamping dies required for the construction process. The Confederacy also issued thousands of wooden canteens, usually constructed of cedar or cherry, which had a tendency to leak after extended use. Because the rebels' wooden canteens were so unique as military equipment and had such a "homespun" look, Yankee soldiers went out of their way to acquire them as war relics. These canteens were sometimes personally identified as to the owner and/or captor.

This cedar canteen was acquired after the siege of Port Hudson by Corp. S. Mendall, 4th Massachusetts, and brought home as a war relic. The other side has the original owner's name carved into it, Pvt. John Echols, 15th Arkansas. (GAC)

Sergeant Fitzpatrick was one Confederate who "switched allegiance" during the Battle of Second Manassas. During the action his unit was driven back off an embankment, but not before he had shot into the Federal attackers who were "fifteen ranks deep." Afterward he told his wife: "I went to where I fired last and three of the devils were lying there. I got me a good Yankee zinc canteen which fortunately was nearly filled with water."

Properly made to hold water, extra canteens were often taken apart and turned into frying pans or portable bake-ovens, and even corn-graters which allowed the squad cook to make corn cakes and hasty puddings. In battle, full canteens could also cool and clean heated and fouled musket barrels, or even fill the sponge buckets of a nearby artillery field piece. The former use was described by Private Ed Smith, 54th Ohio during the Battle of Ezra Church, Georgia, on July 28, 1864: "Charge after charge was made by the massed rebel forces.... Our guns would get so hot that we could not hold them. Three times when the rebels were driven back we let them cool, and twice poured water in them to clean them out."

Finding water on a long march or during or after a summer battle like Ezra Church was, by many accounts, a trying ordeal. An excellent recollection of this grueling trial was left by Wilbur Fisk in August 1864:

"One of the greatest evils we have to contend with is a scarcity of water...Day before yesterday on the march, I took a handful of canteens, and started off by the side of the road to find water,.... I traveled five or six miles;... and I examined every place where the lay of the land seemed to indicate the possibility of a spring or a creek, and I tried at several houses where there were inhabitants, but could find no water." Eventually, Fisk located a source and filled the canteens, but on his return to the regiment he was besieged by thirsty soldiers all along his route, some "half dead with thirst;...offering as high as a dollar, and some a drink of whisky in exchange for a drink of water."

Finding water was one thing, but getting it into the canteen could be another problem altogether. The following event took place in the Shenandoah Valley in June 1862, while 55th Ohio infantryman William Allen Keesy was on a lengthy march under a broiling sun:

We had just crossed a stone culvert under which is running a nice stream of clear spring water. I broke for the tempting liquid, for to keep up this terrible strain and great perspiration we must have water. A comrade called to me and said, "Al, let me take your gun and you fetch me a canteen of water." By the time he had taken my gun and given me his canteen, a half dozen other comrades had unstrung and were giving me their canteens. I thought it an easy task, relieved of my gun to bring the water. But as I went down the bank to reach the stream, a great many more men from the passing column were on the same errand and had completely obstructed my way. Determined to get what I went after, I struggled until I reached the stream. It is a tedious experience, as the soldier knows, to fill a half dozen canteens. You might as well try to hurry a balky mule, or frozen molasses on a cold day, as to hurry this business. Try to immerse them as much as you will they will persist in bobbing up and getting their necks out of water. I succeeded, however, after a time, in getting them filled and started out...to overtake my company.

It took Keesy several hours to push through the crowded turnpike back to his regiment. By then he was overtaxed and close to sunstroke. He ultimately had to pour the water out of all the canteens just to have the strength to return, remarking that "the process of emptying those pestilential canteens was just as tedious and just as taxing on my valuable time as the performance of filling them was." That experience left him "physically so injured that I never recovered my former vigor."

Keesy was fortunate in one respect. The water he procured was sweet, clean, and cold. Often there were unseen hazards lurking in water. Near battlefields there was always the chance that a water supply such as a well, pool, or brook would be contaminated by human or animal excrement or blood, and mud churned up from the bottoms by constantly moving troops, artillery carriages and supply wagons. Bacteria was of no concern, and insects, scum and other plant matter would be simply brushed aside. An example of the filthy consistency of water often encountered is told by a New England sergeant while near Chancellorsville soon after that battle:

> The weather was excessively hot,..; water was scarce, good water could not be found, the creeks were low, and near all the fording places were filled with dead horses or mules[.] I remember of comming [sic] to a creek and, being very thirsty, thought to fill my canteen before leaving, so I started up creek to find clear water. After going quite a distance I looked and thought I was above all impurities,... and [so] took a long draught and was filling my canteen when a comrade asked me "how I liked the water." "First rate" I replied. "I thought so," he said, "when I saw that dead mule there," pointing at the same time to a bunch of bushes just above me in which lay the swollen carcass. The water being down and canteen filled, I thought it is good as any I could find so, saying nothing more, I went on my way.[100]

Winter had the opposite effect. It often became so cold that, according to Texan Charles Leuschner, "I have poured water out of a cup and before it would touch the groun [sic] it was ice." And in December 1863 near Brandy Station, Virginia, Wilbur Fisk related that, "[s]ome idea of the weather may be understood from the fact that several of the canteens that I helped fill late in the evening, were frozen solid in the morning, and some had burst open and were spoiled."

Through heat or cold, camp, march, or battle, the canteen was a constant companion of the fighting soldier of both armies. As Captain James Smith remembered, its sound was their calling card, and "...the rhythmic click of the canteens of marching infantry" was never far away.[101]

Old battered tin cups or "dippers" and boilers were found to be as useful as a canteen. These army cups came in all sizes and styles, some issued from the governments, others purchased from private sources, and many made by the soldiers themselves. Leander Stillwell reconfigured an "oyster can of a quart's capacity, with a wire bale attachment" for a coffee-boiler. Another soldier used an old tomato can for the same purpose. Used for more than boiling coffee, a 3rd Michigan private pointed out that "our burnt tin cups...serve to cook our meat, beans, soup, coffee, tea, and everything else we get to cook."

An infantrymen could become very attached to a personal army cup or "dish." Sergeant Stearns made that clear during the fighting around Spotsylvania Court House, Virginia in May 1864: "The zyps, zyps of the bullets were coming thick and the prospect of warm work ahead caused me to unhook my knapsack and let it drop. When it struck the ground I heard the old dish rattle and the thought of coffee, soup and the other dishes that had been made in it, and besides it was the same old dish that I had started with, caused me to stop, turn around, and unstrap the dish from my knapsack and, taking off my canteen, run the strap through the bail and, slipping it over my head, go on."

While this Massachusetts sergeant may have had great affection for his old "bailer," he was not adverse, like many men, to appropriating a new one if the opportunity arose. Earlier in his military career, Stearns revealed these circumstances: "[Near] Cedar Mountain, there arrived an instalment [sic] of recruits for the regiment.... The Chaplain,...seeing the recruits had nice clean dippers, warned them that if they wanted to keep them, they must keep their eyes open all the time, for if there was one thing that a 13th man envied, or wished to get possession of, it was a nice clean dipper." These simple infantryman's "kitchen implements," i.e., a plate, cup and canteen, could be as adequate to the soldier's needs as a civilian's house full of pots, pans and dishes. Private Fisk made it all sound easy and even enjoyable: "I had an excellent breakfast [this] morning; if you doubt it, allow me to tell you what I had. I had a slice of fat pork, good enough for anybody to eat, plenty of hardtack and coffee. I had a tin plate and tin cup; on my plate I fried my pork, and in my cup I made my coffee. My hard tack I converted into fried cakes, superior to ordinary doughnuts,...I doubt if ever the Prince of Wales enjoyed a meal better."[102]

Knapsacks, haversacks, blanket rolls and uniform pockets contained a whole assortment of personal items. Not all soldiers carried each and every piece here listed; a few kept none on hand, and some only a few items. The selections were almost unending: a diary or journal, pencil, writing pen and steel tips, ink bottle, razor and strop, coin purse, photograph album, sheath knife, bible or testament, candleholder, pipe, tobacco bag, matches and case, comb, brush and mirror, toothbrush, wallet, playing cards, cap cover, portable chess or checkers set, handkerchief, assorted clothing, stencil, writing paper and envelopes, stamps, identification disc, rifle tools, corps badge, and other insignia. Some of these products came in "kits" made especially for the soldier by merchants or his own family, such as writing kits, toilet kits, knife-spoon-fork combinations, or sewing kits sometimes called "housewifes" or needlecases. This last object was a favorite of countless infantrymen.

T.F. Upson was nicknamed "Little Mother," "all because when we first came out I had a needle book with thread and needls [sic] all very convenient. And when the boys lost a button or tore thier [sic] trous[or]s, what more natural than to go and get 'Mother' to fix it." Perry Mayo, 2nd Michigan, liked his "needle book" or as, "we call them a Housewife. Like the original it is a nice thing in a family, but it doesn't sew on the buttons." And John Worsham called the "needle case" the "best article carried by the soldiers...containing needles of various sizes, thread, buttons, etc. It soon became the most valuable of our possessions. When we went into camp we would see the men occupied in sewing or patching their clothing, and towards the last of the war it was in almost constant use."[103]

Both sides of a Civil War "ID" tag. These were private purchase items. (GNMP)

WEAPONS AND ACCOUTERMENTS

These rifles cost $42, and it would not be prudent to...lose one, as I could not pick up another on the road, as they sometimes do in the Common Infantry, as we say.

Lt. Charles Mattocks
1st U.S. Sharpshooters

Fully armed infantrymen in both the Federal and Confederate service usually carried a rifle musket, musket, or in rare cases even a breech-loading or repeating rifle. But by far, the majority of soldiers both North and South used the slower-firing, easy to maintain and reliable muzzleloading weapons. The infantryman was also outfitted with a cartridge-box for ammunition, a cap pouch for percussion caps, a waist belt and belt plate and a bayonet and bayonet scabbard. Since American soldiers by experience were not fond of carrying accouterments of any kind, including canteens and knapsacks, etc., commanders, if motivated to abide by regulations, had to be alert to the fact that any and all parts of a soldier's equipment could disappear at any time.

The cartridge-box was one of the most important pieces of a fighting man's load. It had to be strong enough to withstand rough handling and to protect the paper cartridges from abuse. The box must be waterproof and constructed so that in the excitement of battle an infantryman could get to his cartridges quickly and instinctively. The standard cartridge-boxes of the 1860s were made with black bridle leather, had double flaps and contained generally two tin inserts. Suspended from the shoulder by a leather belt, it could also be worn on the waist belt without the shoulder strap if desired. Both systems had advantages and disadvantages. To prevent injury in case of an explosion of the cartridges the stitching in better constructed boxes was sewn so as to blow the box outward away from the body.

Cartridges were issued to Civil War infantrymen from supply wagons in pine crates containing 1,000 rounds; when full these crates weighed less than 90 pounds. The ammunition or "ball-cartridges" were paper wrapped, containing a "round," that is, a musket ball or Minie ball, and a powder charge of approximately sixty grains. Single cartridges were packed or wrapped ten in a bundle and came stacked in the crates as follows: The bundles were arranged in two tiers of five each, alternating front to back. In each bundle a package of twelve percussion caps was placed. When the soldier was issued his cartridges, normally between 40 and 60 rounds, he placed them inside the tin inserts of his cartridge box. The tin inserts were removable. Twenty individual paper cartridges stood upright in the upper sections of the inserts and could be withdrawn for firing as needed. In the lower sections of the inserts were two more packages containing twenty reserve cartridges; these could be opened and transferred to the upper sections when necessary. Any extra packages of cartridges were carried in the soldier's knapsack, pocket or blanket roll.

Cartridge-boxes came in various sizes depending on the ammunition size itself, i.e. .58 cal., .69 cal., etc. A standard U.S. .58 caliber box size was 6.8 x 1.4 x 5.2 inches. A

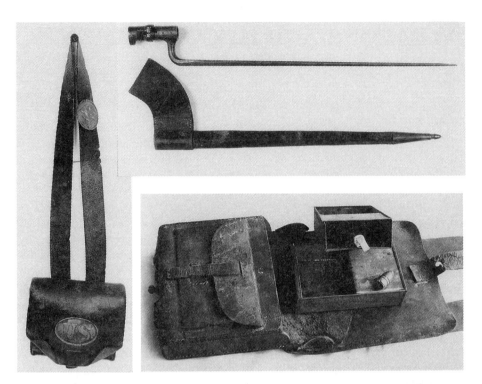

(Above) Complete cartridge box with sling, close-up of open box showing tins that held cartridges, and bayonet with scabbard. (DST & GAC)

(Right, top to bottom) Confederate belt buckle, Union belt buckle, Confederate "frame" buckle.
(HS & DST)

(Above) Union and Confederate infantry buttons
(DST)

stamped brass, lead filled oval "U.S." plate was affixed to the outside flap, and on the inside was sewn a small rifle tool/implement pocket. The shoulder strap was buckled to the bottom of the box, and it too was adorned with a plate, this one circular with an "eagle" device stamped into the brass. Confederate boxes came in more varieties of leather and styles, with or without shoulder straps. Many Southern-made boxes were not fixed with a brass flap plate or even an inside implement pouch. The tin inserts have been found to be more crude and in general, of a lower quality than U.S. manufactured tins. Straps and even the boxes themselves have survived which were constructed of painted cotton canvas, solely due to the scarcity of leather in the South.

The percussion cap pouch of bridle leather was carried on the front of the waist belt, which also supported the bayonet and its scabbard. Normally about 2.6" x 1.0" x 2.0", it had double flaps, a lambskin lining to keep the caps safely in place and one or two vertical belt loops sewn on the reverse.

The infantryman's waist belt was usually constructed of buff or bridle leather and measured about 1.5 inches wide. Federal regulations prescribed a "U.S." belt plate of stamped brass, with lead filled reverse and hooks, to be worn with the belt. Confederate belts came in several types of leather and styles; the plates were either cast solid brass, stamped, or stamped and lead filled. The shapes and sizes and devices varied greatly, such as oval, rectangle, two-piece interlocking, and square, with the letters "C.S." or "C.S.A." used on some. The most common buckles in use however, were unadorned, sturdy open-frame styles; countless civilian models and captured Union plates filled out the balance of the need.

The Confederate War Department produced few cartridge-box plates, no shoulder belt plates, and little or no hat insignia, such as the "bugle" or French hunting horn device which was stamped out in great quantities and adorned the hats and caps of Federal infantrymen throughout the war. Rebel soldiers were happy to procure U.S. made equipment or weapons in order to outfit themselves with the best and most serviceable items possible. In contrast, Yankees often captured, took from the dead, or gathered from battlegrounds or camps, discarded Southern military accouterments to send home as war relics. Confederate officers' swords, canteens, "Bowie" knives, and even belts and belt plates were popular as souvenirs.

Warren L. Goss of Massachusetts, exasperated about his equipment early in the war, griped: "My canteen banged against my bayonet, both tin cup and bayonet badly interfered with the butt of my musket, while my cartridge-box and haversack were constantly flopping up and down—the whole jangling like loose harness and chains on a runaway horse." William Keesy also recalled the movement of equipments whether in battle or on a forced march. In May 1862 while campaigning against General Thomas J. Jackson's army in Virginia, Keesy talked about one fast-paced trek:

> We are puffing and panting, sweating and pulling into it for dear life.... Hurry up men! Hurry up! For God's sake hurry up! Look ahead boy, look ahead. They are double quicking! My Lord, will they kill us? Some are throwing away their blankets. Flap! flap! flap! You can now plainly hear the flapping of the cartrage [sic] boxes upon the men's hips as they double quick, trying to keep up with those ahead.

Other soldiers like Henry Prince, 127th New York wrote about discarding accouterments while on the march or in action. Prince simply said: "[M]uch is cast away in battle," and he meant everything from muskets to extra socks.

If mentioned at all, the cartridge-box is often described as being moved into a fighting position just before entering combat. Confederate John Casler in the First Battle of Bull Run was hit by a bullet, "tearing a piece from my side, just under my cartridge box, which I had pulled well around on the right and front of my waist." Eighth Ohio officer Thomas Galwey described the same preparation for battle with his company near the Ny River, Virginia in 1864: "Before dawn on May 18 we were in position and lay down for an hours sleep. Scarcely more than that, for by daylight I woke and we were all getting up in our position, slinging knapsacks, swinging cartridge boxes around to the front of the body, and examining our arms."

Quite late in the war, the Federal government issued to some regiments a new style of box invented in 1863 by Colonel W.D. Mann, which hung on the front of a soldier's body. Lewis Bissell noted the switch in his regiment on January 17, 1865: "They have been changing our old Enfield rifles for Springfields—our cartridge boxes for the patented ones. These are carried on the front of the body. They are made to carry sixty rounds. Our old ones carried only forty. There is a knapsack to go with the new cartridge box."

Cleaning and caring for accouterments were part of a soldier's duties. Like many infantry enlisted men, Simon Hulbert took this in stride. However, in a September 10, 1863 letter home to New York, Hulbert explained: "You know I am generally busy. Well, The first thing this morning my gun I thought could look a little cleaner. So I went at it, took it all apart, cleaned it nice. Then Blackened my Belts, Brightened my brasses, Black [sic] shoes, & then I washed my shirt."

Not all soldiers looked upon their accouterments as just another piece of army equipment. Some men saw these mundane items as physical testaments of their military service, and thousands took or sent home miscellaneous pieces that appealed to them. So it was with Charles Barber, of the 104th New York when he wrote to his wife and children on September 7, 1863:

> I have the same gun and bayonet[,] cartridge box and belts that I first drew when I entered the Army. I want to bring them all home but it is doubtful whether I can[.] I would keep my gun and equipments as long as I live then give them to Charlie [his son]. I am the only man in our company but what has [not] lost their gun.
>
> I have carried my gun safe through 8 or 9 battles and mean to get it home if I can.

In still another letter to his spouse on February 18, 1864, Barber emphasized: I sent some things [home]...a brass plate and some eagle buttons to Charley to wear across his breast.... I have had the plate on my belt all the time and wore it in every battle[.] let Willie scour the plate and buttons with sand paper and they will look bright and make Charlie shine.

Private Hulbert also mentioned an interest in purchasing his "good rifle." "I think I shall buy it when I am discharged & bring it home & let you all see it." As much as Charlie Barber desired to take his weapon home at the end of his enlistment, he never did, for it was lost in a subsequent engagement. Ironically, had Private Barber been discharged in 1865 he would have had the opportunity. In May 1865 U.S. General Order #101 gave honorably discharged volunteers the authorization upon muster out, "to retain their arms and accouterments, on paying therefor their value to the Ordnance Department."

Muskets, all kinds, "with or without" accouterments at war's end cost $6.00 each. Many soon to be discharged infantrymen availed themselves of this order, which allowed them to take home the old companions of their army days. It also gave the government some much needed revenue, and saved it from storing and caring for a surplus of arms no longer needed by the rapidly dwindling army. Even today there are families in this country that retain the weapons and cartridge-boxes, etc., brought back by the Union victors of the War of the Rebellion in 1865.[104]

Between 1861 and 1865 Union and Confederate infantry forces were armed with between 40 and 50 types and models of muskets, rifle muskets and other infantry weapons. As E.P. Alexander explained: "The old idea was still widely entertained that, because the percentage of hits [in battle] is always small, the fire of infantry should not be rapid, lest the men waste too much ammunition." These weapons were mainly muzzle loaders, capable of firing between two and three aimed shots per minute. In a series of loading steps, the soldier tore open the cartridge, poured powder down the barrel, rammed the ball down into the bottom of the barrel and onto the powder with a steel ramrod, then placed a percussion cap on the nipple at the breach, all before the act of firing. Smooth-bore muskets were smooth-barreled guns, and shots from these arms were not precise much beyond 50 to 75 yards. Rifle muskets were a world apart, true and deadly at longer distances. This system used the bands and grooves of the bores' rifling, in conjunction with the new Minie balls (bullets) which were invented by French captain Claude Minie, and perfected by American James H. Burton. Made of soft lead, it was elongated, with a hollow, cone-shaped base. Slightly smaller than the rifled bore, it slid easily past the rifling unless the barrel became fouled. When fired, the hollow base was forcibly expanded into the rifled grooves of the bore, causing a tight fit and spin to the bullet, elevating accuracy. Hundreds of Civil War soldier accounts and modern tests report that the rifle musket, caliber .58, shooting a 500 grain bullet (the weight of eleven copper pennies or about 1.31 ounces) had a minimum accuracy of ten shots in a four inch bullseye at 100 yards, or an 11 inch bullseye at 333 yards. At 500 yards the bullet still penetrated almost six inches of pine boards. The rifle could be used in excess of 500 yards, but the majority of Civil War combat took place at ranges under 200 yards.

In tests conducted in 1971, for example, targets 72" x 72" in size were set up at 400 yards. When 15 shots were fired by several Civil War muskets, the results varied:
> Enfield M1853 rifle-musket—13 hits out of 15 at 400 yards
> Springfield M1863 rifle-musket—7 hits out of 15 at 400 yards
> M1842 Smoothbore—0 hits out of 15 at 400 yards
> Austrian rifle-musket—3 hits out of 15 at 400 yards
> Whitworth rifle-musket—15 hits out of 15 at 400 yards

Similarly, in a test completed in 1968, "a marksman could break a saucer ten times out of ten at 50 to 75 yards with a Richmond Confederate Rifle or a Springfield. But

British pattern 1853 rifle musket (Enfield). The labels read: "Rebel rifle used against the Union troops at Port Hudson on June 14, 1863. Captured and brought home by Jesse L. Delano." [52nd Massachusetts] (GAC)

three men in a row, firing a smoothbore musket, failed to hit even the backstop, which measured four by six feet.... With the rifles in use by both armies in the Civil War, a soldier could be killed easily at a range of 200 to 300 yards, often farther."

Using British Whitworths and other target or sporting rifles, the distances employed by sharpshooters to kill a man were even longer, sometimes 800 to 1,000 yards. Lieutenant Mosman, 59th Illinois, pronounced that men opting for these accurate guns could at times even hit moving targets at 1,000 yards. The bullet, he concluded, was "a poured ball about an inch and a half long." After an eyewitness interview with a company of New York sharpshooters Private Roland Bowen underscored the power of these deadly weapons: "Each rifle has a telescope running the whole length of the barrel. The average weight is about 35 lbs., the lightest weighing 17 lbs. and the heaviest 50 lbs. I talked with one of the men a few minits [sic], he told me that he could hit a man every time at half a mile and every other time at the distance of a mile."[105]

Not all sharpshooters needed these specially made weapons. One fellow in the 15th Arkansas nicknamed "Old Thousand Yards" was a famous backwoodsman and hunter, who, according to James Hosmer, armed with an infantry rifle "was really sure of a bear or buffalo at the distance of a thousand yards." Hosmer called him a good natured man with a fine frame and noble countenance whose vigor and masculine beauty was apparent. At the siege of Port Hudson he had used his skill on many a poor Yankee.

In the initial stages of the war there were any number of models and calibers of arms in the hands of Northern and Southern infantrymen, many seriously outdated. The old smooth-bore musket, caliber .69, made up the bulk of the Confederate armament at the beginning, but even as late as 1863 some units still contained flint locks and shotguns. The garrison at Port Hudson, Louisiana is a case in point. In January 1863 several infantry regiments still relied on flint lock arms: the 42nd Tennessee, 11th, 12th and 17th Arkansas, 1st Mississippi and the 1st Alabama. The entire complement of troops there, about 6,000, needed 2,000 guns and 4,000 bayonets just to be fully armed.

The diary of William Chambers, 46th Mississippi, is an object lesson on this point. On April 15, 1862 he records that the government had just appraised the regiment's weapons for purchase—and they were still at that late day armed with "double-barreled shot guns." The arrival of June 1st, 1862 had brought no relief. Chambers wrote: "[O]ur company was unarmed...." By December, "[t]here were not enough guns by fully one-third to arm the effectiveness in the regiment and less than 30 rounds of ammunition for what guns there were." On November 11, 1863 he was informed that the regiment would be armed with Austrian rifles. And after another year of campaigning, he wrote on March 8, 1865 that they were again issued Austrians, but, "there has not been a cartridge box in the brigade since I joined at Verona [in January]. It seems hardly credible, yet it is true, that all the picketing we have done here, [near Mobile], though in sight of the enemy, has been done with 'empty guns.'"

A different problem which confronted the Confederate government, and even some Union regiments, was the use of multiple weapons and calibers in a single unit. Colonel William Allan, an ordnance officer with the Army of Northern Virginia, confirmed the distribution of smooth-bore muskets, caliber .69; rifle muskets, caliber .54; Springfield muskets, caliber .58; and some Belgian rifles, caliber .70, all found in one brigade during the winter of 1862-1863; "and the same wagon often carried the three kinds of ammunition required."

Pvt. Albert W. Dyer, 13th Massachusetts, poses with his accouterments and regulation dress hat complete with all insignia. The photo is also nicely framed with a patriotic mat. (GAC)

The goal of the ordnance department was to correct this deficiency, which was essentially accomplished after the Battle of Chancellorsville. According to Colonel Allan, gleaning the battlefields was one of the important duties of the field ordnance officers. After Chancellorsville all undamaged arms and equipment were methodically gathered up, in addition to 20,000 damaged arms which were sent to Richmond for repair and reissue. The first day's field of battle at Gettysburg and other battlegrounds were likewise scoured.

John Worsham supported the words of Colonel Allan. In his own 21st Virginia, "one company of infantry had springfield muskets, one had Enfields, one had Mississippi rifles, and the remainder had the old smooth-bore flintlock musket that had been altered to a percussion gun." Another Confederate gave a bleaker picture. In April 1862, just before the Battle of Shiloh his 9th Kentucky regiment was encamped at Monterey where, "a blacksmith shop [was kept] busy turning out old fashioned pikes to arm some of our troops who had no guns."

The North met with similar difficulties in the early days of the war. The Comte de Paris stressed that to keep up with the demands of the thousands of U.S. regiments, "the refuse of all Europe passed into the hands of the American Volunteers." Eventually though, manufacturers like that at Springfield, Massachusetts, were able to provide the Federal forces with sufficient weapons of superior quality, going from 10-12,000 muskets produced yearly in 1861 to 250,000 weapons delivered in 1863. The Springfield or its counterparts became the "ideal" weapon of choice in both armies, a rifle the Comte described as having the "advantage of not requiring heavy charges, of giving a great precision of aim at a distance of from six to seven hundred metres, and of being easily loaded and managed. It was therefore introduced throughout the army as fast as the ordnance department was able to meet the demands...."

Every soldier had his preference for a particular weapon. James L. Graham, 62nd Pennsylvania, expressed satisfaction with his weapon in a letter dated January 9, 1862: "We have just received our new guns today. They are the Springfield rifle of '61. They are a splendid gun, just new and bright as a new pin." In September 1862, the

17th Connecticut Volunteers were given the most popular European weapon, and Private Silliman reported: "Saturday afternoon we were furnished with our arms. They are Enfield rifles of English manufacture; taken from a vessel which tried to run the blockade; they are excellent pieces but have the old fashioned bayonet."

A New Yorker, Simon B. Hulbert, had the opportunity to employ several different weapons during his enlistment. In March, 1863 he wrote to his friends at home: "Well, we went over to Hilton Head [S.C.] & got new guns for the whole Reg't. The Austin [Austrian] rifle. This makes four guns that I have had in the service 1st the Enfield, then the Springfield, & Enfield again, & now the Austin. I like the Enfield better than all of them." Four months later his 100th New York was handed a fifth weapon, this time the Springfield, which Hulbert contradictorily testified, were guns "that we can trust now." He also took time in one of his letters to describe to his folks the drill involved in firing a rifle:

> I suppose that you would like to know how I get along learning to be a marksman. I have never fired my gun yet, but I have loaded it several times.... it is contrary to the rules of the camp to fire a gun any where near the Camp....
>
> But now I open my cartridge Box, take one [cartridge] out & tear it, put in the powder & then shove out the ball, take it, put it in the muzzle, draw the rammer, turn it & ram the ball home very able. But I do not cap the piece till the order really comes,...

While the Springfield and Enfield usually received high marks from the average infantryman, the Austrian and Belgian rifles did not. T.D. Upson drew arms in August 1862 but "[w]e don't like them much" he complained, "they are Belgian muskets with a great cheek peice [sic] on the side of the stock and are about the poorest excuse of a gun I ever saw. I don't believe one could hit the broadside of a barn with them." The soldiers' cost [if lost] for this weapon was $22. Georgia Sergeant Walter Clark made a comparison in his circa 1900 memoirs. During the Atlanta Campaign he once fired three well-aimed shots at a Yankee stationed behind a tree, all three missed, and Clark was forced to explain why:

> And now in at least partial extenuation of what seemed very poor markmanship it may not be amiss to say that the weapon used was an Austrian rifle and was considered a very inferior gun. With an Enfield or Springfield rifle I think I could have made a better record, provided always that my nerves had not been rendered unsteady by the necessity of dodging minies for six or eight hours.

John Green, of Kentucky's famed "Orphan Brigade" quickly took advantage of the Union defeat at Shiloh on April 6. After overrunning the position of General B.M. Prentiss, he and his companions, "...swapped our very indifferent guns for their splendid Endfield [sic] rifles." Washington Ives, 4th Florida, eventually received the same rifle as Green but under different circumstances. In August 1862 near Chattanooga, Ives told his sister Katie that, "[our] arms heat so by firing that Gen. Ridgely is going to issue Enfields to our company and Mississippi Rifles to the balance of our reg't."

The Enfield was usually appreciated by any Southern troops who acquired them after using other weapons of lesser quality. In the spring of 1863, Sergeant Fitzpatrick, 45th Georgia, made reference to this in a letter to his wife, Amanda. After commenting on the weather, he returned to drill and guard duty, and said: "I have got another good Enfield rifle and excellent equipments, which I am very proud of."[106]

During infantry service, men could become attached to their muskets. Some even personalized the gun itself; this was done more frequently in the Confederate army, due to the strict accountability that Federal regiments required for the care of their arms. In most cases, the soldier merely carved something into the stock of the weapon for quick identification, or to keep it from being stolen and switched by another in his unit who carried a dirty or inferior arm. Often, however, these personalizations went farther, due to the affection felt for their "closest companion." Marking a rifle was a sensible idea for practical reasons, because what happened to Vermont infantryman Wilbur Fisk was not uncommon. Fisk left camp once seeking a decent breakfast. Returning, he noticed his "gun had changed its appearance most remarkably. The decently clean and polished musket that I left there had become transformed into a carelessly kept and miserable rusty affair that any other soldier would have been ashamed to carry. Evidently somebody had swapped with me."

During the Battle of Second Manassas, Val Giles, 4th Texas spent some idle time, "in front of the line of battle cutting the initials of my name on the breech of my musket...." And after the Battle of Gettysburg, civilian Leander Warren found an Enfield near the body of a dead Confederate. "He had the finest gun I ever saw. It was made in England. On the stock was eng[r]aved his name, "T.J. Knight, Co. G, 12th Georgia Vigilantes." William A. Hughes, 1st Tennessee, owned a gun he called "Florence Fleming." Private Sam Watkins, a comrade in that regiment, recalled that Hughes had put the name on the weapon in silver letters. Mortally wounded while saving Watkins' life, Hughes gave the gun and his blanket and clothing to Watkins before he was carried off the field.

Pvt. McLaughlin personalized this Enfield rifle at Vicksburg in 1863. (GAC)

The sad parting of a soldier from his cherished weapon was depicted by William Keesy in June 1865 during his muster-out. Keesy had his gun stolen in camp in December 1864. So he took another rifle and was "determined that if that gun was stolen from me, it would speak for itself. I therefore cut my name in large, deep capital letters, on the broad side of the butt. After this was done I became greatly alarmed for fear that the first time inspection should come around, I would be arrested for mutilation of goverment property." Upon discharge, "the regiment was called to turn over our guns. Instead of stacking them," said Keesy, "we threw them on a pile like cord wood.... In the pile of guns, as I stood and gazed at them, I could see my name so plainly that I could hardly find it in my heart to part with my faithful friend. Thirty-two years are now passed, and I would give $50 for that gun."

As early as June, 1861, the 2nd Michigan Infantry had been given the "Harpers Ferry Rifles and muskets," which Perry Mayo called "Southern arms with Northern principles." In September, pleased to have the opportunity to see how the ammunition for some arms was made, he called it "novel and interesting." At the Washington Navy Yard, Mayo observed and reported to his father:

> [the]...manner of making musket and rifle balls.... They are no longer in moulds, after the old method, but the whole thing is done by machinery. The lead comes in rods the right size [i.e., calibre]. They are fed in a machine like wheat, and the balls come out like hail.
>
> The cartri[d]ges too are all filled by machinery. The famous Minnie, [sic] which most of the troops here use, are just like the long balls belonging to your [civilian] rifle with the exception of the large end which is hollowed in the same shape as the point. When the gun explodes, this thin shell spreads and fills the bore, thereby gaining all the strength of the charge.

By March 1862, Mayo's regiment had received a "new rubber patent tent" and, "...new Minnie rifles...[which] can hit a barrel head 120 rods [about 65 yards] twice out of three times. They are a beautiful gun."[107]

With regard to actually shooting these weapons, it was rare in many Civil War regiments to get much time in for target practice before being sent to "the front." But in other units, some practice was allowed and even encouraged. "It is drill, Dress Parade & target shooting all the time," Simon Hulbert remarked on December 5, 1862, but so far he had, "not got to be a great marksman yet, But am improving every time that we go out to shoot. Two days in the week we go out & fire five rounds a piece,..." This may not seem like a lot of practice, but in a majority of 1860s infantrymen's experiences, it would have been almost excessive.

The 17th Connecticut, as late as April 1863, was still trying to improve its aim. Once during that month they "went out target shooting, each company having previously constructed a target in shape of a man and of usual size." Perry Mayo's Michigan regiment however, did not use targets. He reported that "[w]e go out every day to practice shooting and have shot down ten acres of grass...." Captain Tom Stevens, 28th Wisconsin, indicated that officers also needed target practice. On November 27, 1862 he "shot a match...with revolvers" with several fellow line and field officers. Stevens declared that we "[s]hot by count, and [I] made the best 6 shots, & the best 10 in 12 at 30 paces. I also did pretty well with a rifle at 40 rods, beating nearly all the company at it."

Target shooting with special long range rifles was mentioned in several accounts. Sam Watkins, 1st Tennessee, described a match to decide who in his army would receive a small number of British Whitworth guns, which he called "the finest...in the world." He explained, "The mark was put up about five hundred yards on a hill, and each of us had three shots. Every shot that was fired hit the board, but there was one man who came a little closer..., and the Whitworth was awarded him."

For long distance hits, Theodore Upson claimed that his Henry repeating rifle was as good as any. He boasted to several officers that at 500 yards he could "put half the shots in the magazine [it held 15] of my rifle into [a man] size target at that distance. Well to make a long story short we went out to a Shooting Range as they call it, and I took of[f] my coat and put 12 shots, one after another, into thier [sic] target and did not half try. Those fellows opened thier eyes; said they had no idea such shooting could be done. It realy [sic] was no shooting; lots of men could beat me all hollow." Sergeant Fitzpatrick reminisced about a time in 1864 when the company of Georgia sharpshooters he belonged to was called out for practice each day. They shot "two rounds apiece at the distance of 600 yards. Out of 98 shots, only five hit the board. I was one of the five and I missed the cross [i.e. "X" or "bullseye"] some distance." The sergeant claimed that they improved each day. Coincidentally, these Georgians were using common Enfield infantry rifle muskets, not special target weapons such as the Whitworth or Kerr.

Washington Ives commented on a special breed of these killer marksmen. In July 1864 during the Atlanta Campaign he attested that: "[b]oth armies have sharpshooters who often kill men and horses at 1 1/2 miles." In May 1864, Johnny Green described a "sharp shooting corps" that had been organized in the Confederate Army of Tennessee, and were doing effective work: "They were armed with Kerr rifles, english guns, I believe, brought in through the blockage. They were of long range and in the hands of good marksmen did dreadful havoc in the enemy's ranks. There were but eleven in the brigade, three of them from our regiment [9th Kentucky], chosen for their expert markmanship. They became a great terror..., for they could kill at much greater range than the infantrymen." An interesting phenomenon concerning the mystique of marksmanship, was discovered by Lieutenant Ralsa Rice, 125th Ohio. He realized that,

> ...[a]n erroneous idea prevailed [within our forces] that the enemy had superior rifles, superior ammunition and, with the hands of expert riflemen, were doing the shooting. The fact was [that] their arms, as a general rule, were but the ordinary smoothbore muskets. I took special pains to determine an answer to this question, searching the field after the battle, examining captured arms and only in one instance saw anything different.... The enemy had a similar idea concerning us, that we had marksmen armed with rifles having telescopic sights. Our Eastern army had a few such weapons, but I only saw one man so armed in our Western army.

This notion of the enemy being better armed, when placed into the context of daily combat, could easily be construed by both sides as the losses mounted in battle.[108] During the course of a fight, an infantryman might notice several types of shooters. One variety of soldier fired wildly or hurriedly without aiming or picking out a target. Another group of riflemen shot very coolly and deliberately, while a small percentage refused to fire at all, or purposefully wasted their bullets on anything except human beings. A fourth type should be listed: the rare individual who purposefully killed or wounded his own officers or comrades.

William Keesy recalled a man in the 64th Ohio named Reiff who during the Battle of Nashville, "was nervously firing away, but while he seemed to take aim toward the enemy's lines he fired every bullet into a log not more than two feet from his gun. I called to him, with my mouth at his ear,...'You will likely burst your gun.'

"'Oh, I'se gibben it to 'em, I bets you I'se gibben it to 'em!' and on he went, pegging his balls into the log."

Sergeant Clark of Georgia remembered a man named John Carroll, who, "ten feet to my left, kept firing when I could see no game, and I said to him, 'John, what are you shooting at?' 'Well,' he said, 'they are down that way.'"

It is possible that Carroll and Reiff were taught to shoot that wildly. Simon Hulbert mentioned in a May 1862 letter to his family that, "[s]oldiers do not take aim after the first shot because the smoke is so thick, but they only bring the gun to the Shoulder & then pull. But I think I should take good aim the first shot." Again in March 1863 Hulbert was sounding the same advice: "We never have a chance to take deliberate aim here [in practice]. We have to do it quick. It is shoulder arms, Ready, aim, fire, like 1, 2, 3. Load, ready, aim, fire again, fast as you can."

Other riflemen were more careful and made each shot count. Charles Barber, 104th New York, revealed his actions at Gettysburg: "I loaded and fired my gun as coolly as if I was shooting at woodchucks." During one of the 1862 Seven Days' Battles, Louisianian Henry Handerson wrote of peering, "vainly through the dense undergrowth to find some target worthy of my aim.... At last,...I knelt down in order to look beneath the bushes...."

John Green described coolness under fire on September 1, 1864, when he helped to press back a Federal assault aimed at a breastwork that his Kentucky regiment was defending: "I rose from a stooping posture in the trenches to shoot but...a Yankee with the muzzle of his gun not six inches from my face shot me in the [face] and neck but fortunately it was only a flesh wound.... But my gun was loaded and the other fellow had had his shot. I rose & put my gun against his side & shot a hole through him big enough to have run my fist through."

At Murfreesboro, Tennessee, Washington Ives did his best to maintain his equilibrium in battle. Several bullets cut through his clothing and two men nearby were shot, but Ives found that he "did not feel any different under fire than I did doing any other kind of work and I took 20 deliberate shots picking my man every time[,] one time I saw the man fall but the others I could not see on account of my smoke."

A few men put into the position to kill refused to do so. At Chickamauga, Val Giles saw a Texan who fit this portrait:

[I]...saw a fellow shooting straight up in the air and praying as lustily as ever.... This fellow was blazing away at the sky, and when Lieutenant Killingsworth remonstrated with him, he paid no attention to him whatever. Captain Joe Billingsley threatened to cut him down with his sword if he didn't shoot at the enemy.... He retorted...: "You can kill me if you want to, but I am not going to appear before my God with the blood of my fellow man on my soul."

Even though it was against the nature of most Civil War soldiers to voice knowledge of the purposeful killing of their own officers, an occasional reference can be found in a letter, diary entry or memoir. James W. Groat, 1st Minnesota, speaks of an incident in his company concerning Captain Wilson B. Farrell who he called "brave to a fault but [who] did not understand human nature.... I regret to say that his promotion to the Captainery of Co. C proved fatal to him in the end, for as he was leading his men into the very Jaws of death at Gettysburg some member of his company, it is supposed shot him in the back and he fell dead."[109]

In battle, a soldier carried 40 rounds in his cartridge box and 20 or more rounds elsewhere. And when needed, the men on the firing line were supplied with pine boxes containing 1,000 rounds. These crates, when full, weighed 85-90 pounds each. Pack mules sometimes substituted for wagons or human carriers and maneuvered the wooden boxes to the front line. According to J.W. McFarland, 140th Pennsylvania, "[o]ne man would lead four mules, each carrying from two to four hundred pounds of ammunition,.... They proved to be much more serviceable than wagons; especially in bad roads."

Extra cartridges placed in pockets, knapsacks, or the like could be dangerous. Sergeant Nick Wilson, 138th Pennsylvania, at the Battle of Locust Grove, Virginia, related, "my knapsack [was] blown entirely off my back by the explosion of forty rounds of cartridges which I had in it[,] being ignited by a Rebel bullet going through the knapsack."

The number of rounds fired during a battle varied. For example, at the Battle of Spotsylvania, G. Norton Galloway, 95th Pennsylvania, shot off four hundred cartridges while many others near him dispatched as many or even more. Galloway verified that pack mules were brought up, each carrying 3,000 rounds. "The boxes were dropped close behind the troops engaged, where they were quickly opened by the officers or file-closers, who served the ammunition to the men." By the end of the day Galloway and his comrades found their "lips were incrusted with powder from 'biting cartridge.' [Our] shoulders and hands were also coated with mud that had adhered to the butts of our rifles." He remembered that the guns became "choked with burnt powder, and would receive the cartridge but half way...;" although that did not deter the discharge.

In one case not setting the bullet down onto the powder fully interfered with the firing of a musket. During a clash near Harpers Ferry in late 1862 Sergeant Marion Fitzpatrick found, "[t]o my greatest mortification [that] my gun failed to fire, but I soon recollected that it was charged with a Yankee cartridge which had to be rammed hard. I drew my stick, gave it a hard ram, tried it again and [it] went clear as a whistle."

Bullets and cartridges from the Civil War. (DST)

The Georgia sergeant was fortunate. In such cases, often the bullet would have to be "pulled" from the gun muzzle, using a "worm," a threaded device much like a small pointed screw that fit onto the rear end of the ramrod. When twisted, it locked into the lead bullet enabling it to be extracted from the bore. A member of the 88th New York humorously described a soldier in Company E who got a ball stuck half way down a hot musket barrel. This man was a "stutterer" and during a battle called out loudly to a friend nearby: "Have you iver a Wur-r-r-m?"

The 400 rounds fired off by Private Galloway at Spotsylvania was by no means a usual occurrence. An infantryman might fire off as few as 10 or 20 cartridges, or up to 200 or 300 rounds. Going into a fight there was no sure way to determine how many cartridges an individual man would use. One June day during the Atlanta Campaign, Sergeant Walter Clark consumed far less ammunition than his companions, who carelessly shot away 80 or 90 rounds. Clark said he did not feel "authorized to waste my ammunition [so] I fired only when there was a blue target in sight."

Lieutenant Thomas F. Galwey reported that his much reduced 8th Ohio fired 56,000 rounds between May 5 and early June, 1864. Lieutenant Chesley A. Mosman, 59th Illinois, computed that "150,000 rounds of rifle cartridges are fired every 24 hours [near Kennesaw Mountain, Georgia] in ordinary skirmish work by our Corps, and we nearly double that when ordered to fire constantly."

Added together, the hundreds of similar units in both armies must have gone through uncounted millions of bullets in the various campaigns. In another example, it is believed that in the three-day Battle of Gettysburg the 165,000 plus men present could have shot away between 7 and 9 million rounds during approximately 26 total hours of combat. During that same engagement the 104th New York was on and off the skirmish line for three days. Charles Barber claimed that his friends George Thomas and George Stryker only "fired sixty rounds each." Others, especially in the Culp's Hill region, expended 300 or more bullets against the Confederates.

But at Spotsylvania, Barber declared that he "loaded and fired my gun till it was so hot I could not hold it only by the stock and strap[,] it was so foul I could hardly ram a ball down so we stopped firing to cool and clean our guns and get more cartridges[.]" The problem of bore fouling was common. At Murfreesboro, Tennessee on January 2, 1863, for instance, Washington Ives said he fired, "exactly 20 rounds and could have fired 30 if my gun had not got so dirty that I had to tear cartridges and wet every load of buck and ball...."

Heated weapons were a serious and recurring problem for infantrymen who did most of the heavy firing in any engagement. Sam Watkins verified the above statement while on the Kennesaw Mountain line near Marietta, Georgia on June 27, 1864. On that day he alone "shot one hundred and twenty times. My gun became so hot that frequently the powder would flash before I could ram home the ball, and I had frequently to exchange my gun for that of a dead comrade." In the Battle of Nashville, William Keesy said he "worked" his gun, "until it got so hot that it actually burned my hand clear across the palm into a great blister. I at first wondered why the balls would spring up and shove the ramrod two-thirds of the way out of the barrel when putting down a load. I soon learned that it was so hot that gas was generated, and I feared that a premature discharge might be ruinous to my hands." Perry Mayo, while engaged at the First Battle of Bull Run in July 1861, had already fired off four rounds successfully when the "fifth charge exploded just as I was turning [the powder] in, blowing the cartridge off close to the ball. Some of the powder is in my right hand yet."

To prevent fouling of the bore when consuming large numbers of cartridges in combat, a group of 37th Mississippians found a clever solution. Private Washington B. Crumpton explained how they began using Yankee cartridges that were "two calibers" smaller than their own weapons: "[W]e abandoned the slow method of drawing the rammer to load. We tore [open] the cartridge, placed it in the muzzle, stamped the breech butt on the ground; the weight of the bullet carried the cartridge home, so we only had to cap and fire. It was almost like a repeating rifle."

This raises the question why there were not more breech loading and repeating rifles used during the Civil War. At the commencement of the hostilities the rapid fire versus single shot concept often came up as the two sides prepared for war and began the development of quality firearms for their armies. The argument persisted, and gained converts to both viewpoints during the course of the four-year conflict. Confederate Colonel E.P. Alexander shed some light on the problem and solution when he wrote:

> The old idea was still widely entertained that, because the percentage of hits is always small, the fire of infantry should not be rapid, lest the men waste too much ammunition. After a year or two some of the best breech-loaders got admission among cavalry regiments, and common sense and experience gradually forced a recognition of the value of a heavy fire. By 1864, the Spencer breech-loading carbine had been adopted as the regulation arm for the Federal cavalry, and by the fall of that year brigades of infantry began to appear with it....
>
> There is reason to believe that had the Federal infantry been armed from the first with even the breech-loaders available in 1861 the war would have been terminated within a year.

After using both a Belgian and an Enfield rifle during his service with the 100th Indiana, Theodore Upson eventually purchased a Henry "repeater" for $35, $10 cheaper than its original cost. It held 15 cartridges, with an extra in the breech, and he said of it: "They are good shooters and I like to think I have so many shots in reserve." Upson asserted too, that he thought "the Johnnys [were] afraid of our repeating rifles.... This I know, I feel a good deal more confidence in myself with a 16 shooter in my hands than I used [sic] to with a single shot rifle."

One other advantage of the breech-loaders and repeaters was that some models used a metallic cartridge which was waterproof. On one occasion soldiers of the U.S. Sixteenth Corps were crossing a river in Georgia when they were fired upon by Southern riflemen. While crossing, and submerged to the waist, the men discovered that they could still, "throw the cartridge from the magazine (of the Spencer) into the chamber of the piece, by working the lever, as well under water as in the air; hence, all along the line you could see the men bring their guns up, let the water run from the muzzle a moment, then taking a quick aim, fire his piece and pop down again, with only his head exposed.... We could hear [the Rebels] calling to each other, 'Look at them Yankee sons of bitches, loading their guns under water!'"[110]

PART
III

(ACHS)

Campaigning and Fighting

THE VETERAN INFANTRYMAN

Soldiering is a rough coarse life, calculated to corrupt good morals & harden a man's heart.

Pvt. Henry W. Prince
127th New York Infantry

An overall composite of the average soldier's experiences, does not give a total picture of the foot soldier as he appeared to himself and others after months and years in the field, undergoing the "seasoning" that was inevitable in camp, on the march and in battle. Just before the Battle of Gettysburg in late June 1863, a sharp-eyed Union newspaperman penned these stark distinctions between Northern and Southern infantry as he saw them in the two main eastern armies. Just how deeply these diversities may have pervaded all armies of the two nations is questionable.

> Physically, the [Rebels] looked about equal to the generality of our own troops, and there were fewer boys among them. There dress was a wretched mixture of all cuts and colors. There was not the slightest attempt at uniformity in this respect. Every man seemed to have put on whatever he could get hold of, without regard to shape or color. I noticed a pretty large sprinkling of blue pants among them,.... Their shoes, as a general thing were poor; some of the men were entirely barefooted. Their equipments were light as compared with those of our men. They consisted of a thin woollen blanket, coiled up and slung from the shoulder in the form of a sash, a haversack slung from the opposite shoulder, and a cartridge-box. The whole cannot weigh more than twelve or fourteen pounds.... The marching of the men was irregular and careless; their arms were rusty and ill-kept. Their whole appearance was greatly inferior to that of our soldiers....
>
> In speaking of our soldiers [in May 1863],...[e]ach man had eight days' rations to carry, besides sixty rounds of ammunition, musket, woolen blanket, rubber blanket, overcoat, extra shirt, drawers, socks, and shelter-tent, amounting in all to about sixty pounds. Think of men, (and boys too) staggering along under such a load, at the rate of fifteen to twenty miles a day.

By the summer of 1864 Major Robert Stiles drew a much neater picture of the veteran Southern infantryman in what he called, "campaign trim:"

> This meant that each man had one blanket, one small haversack, one change of under-clothes, a canteen, cup and plate of tin, a knife and fork and the clothes in which he stood. When ready to march, the blanket, rolled lengthwise, the ends brought together and strapped, hung from left shoulder across under the right arm; the haversack—furnished with towel, soap, comb, knife and fork in various pockets, a change of underclothes in the main division, [of the sack] and whatever rations we happened to have in the other—hung on the left hip; the canteen, cup and plate, tied together, hung on the right; toothbrush at will, stuck in two button holes of jacket or in haversack; tobacco bag hung to a breast button, pipe in pocket. In this rig,...the Confederate soldier considered himself all right and all ready for anything; ...and this "all" weighed about seven or eight pounds.

Abner Small observed that soldiers changed over time as their personalities blended, the men became less individualistic, and they grew toward a group identity. Stiles saw the loss of exclusiveness as the most notable conversion of their personality:

...[H]e no longer claims his enrolled name; he becomes simply an indistinguishable unit. In the first year of the war, the distinctive marks of environment were observed at a glance. The Wolverine, the Hoosier, and the Down-East Yankee were clearly defined. But long association and a oneness of purpose gradually merged individual character- istics, and men became composite—almost developed a new type. Marks of birth were always apparent, but there was no aristocracy among the privates; they were thoroughly democratic. A graduate of Harvard and an illiterate from the wilds of Maine were often seen affectionately picking lice together. Rich men and poor, Christians from pious back-country homes and heathen bounty-jumpers from the slums of New York, would cheat one another at seven-up. All would bathe in and drink from the same stream, whether prior or subsequent to the watering of the brigade mules.

In the early fall of 1863, Private Fisk cautioned that the Army of the Potomac was no longer made of the "fancy soldiers" that people were accustomed to at home:

Our clothes were begrimed with dirt,...and they had acquired a dirty look that all the soap and water in the world would not relieve them from. Our faces, too, from long exposure to the open air had been relieved of that delicate paleness which the dandy admires, but which the fighter for his country never wears. There was nothing of the ornamental sort about us, nothing superfluous or fanciful; we only had what stern necessity required. It was not our fault we looked seedy; to look otherwise they must keep us out of the field.

Many months later, Fisk had an opportunity to see some of Lee's infantrymen at close range. It was April 9, 1865, and the war had become a thing of the past:

Large squads of the prisoners were taken by here,...I thought they looked remarkably well, considering what had been said of their condition. Their faces looked grim and dusty of course, but I couldn't see any sign at all of their having suffered from starva- tion. And their clothes and general appearance were as good as ours generally are, after we have been marching and fighting for some length of time. Great, long legged, hearty fellows—they looked as if they might fight with a vengeance, if they were where they could, and thought it would be of any use.

An English visitor to North America in 1862 named Edward Dicey thought that American volunteers appeared more business-like as soldiers than his own country- men. "[T]here was no playing at soldiering," he declared. Dicey was impressed by the drill and distinctive dress and accouterments of the Federals and the fact that the men were not fighting for money, as often was the case in his native land. But he found fault, too, with the many "inaccuracies of military attire," the "slouching gait" of the men, the "indifference to rule" and the lack of "precision in the march." Dicey concluded with, "I have seen the armies of most European countries; and I have no hesitation in saying that, as far as the average raw material of the rank and file is concerned, the American army is the finest."

A second Englishman near Richmond in 1862 communicated to his readers that the Confederate soldier, at first sight, "presented a somewhat uncouth and even sorry appearance: about his person any kind of coat, or more commonly nothing beyond shirt and pantaloons; on his head, as the case might be, a cap, a straw hat, a slouch hat, or no

hat at all. A closer scrutiny, however, showed that essentials were well provided. Besides his musket and cartridge-box, every man had a canteen, most men a blanket and a haversack. A more suitable equipment for summer service in Virginia could hardly have been devised."

One captain in the 2nd Tennessee, C.S.A., noted that during the bitter combat of June 1864 in Georgia, his adversaries were a "hard looking sett of men." This feeling was not surprising, for as each army closely eyed its enemy, it clearly saw itself. Lieutenant Henry Dwight, 20th Ohio, knew this. Rough service and tough campaigning turned the handsome recruit into a vagabond. He wrote:

In the trenches before Atlanta...the pomp and show of war has become a matter of poetry rather than of fact.... Practical utility is what we look at in matters of dress and equipment.... The most elegant dress uniform will become torn and spotted, and the brightly polished boots will become soiled with mud when one is reduced to marching in line of battle through swamps, thickets and briar patches, and then sleeping night after night on the bare ground with only heaven's clouds for an overcoat.... Dusty, ragged and unshaven, [a soldier's] appearance is far more in accordance with his surroundings...than as the pictures [you have seen] represent him to be.

Campaigning not only wrecked an infantryman's attire, it was physically debilitating as well. Private Charles Barber had enlisted "under a higher and purer motive than the love of money;" and he would do it again, "if I am needed,..." but, said Barber, "it is doubtful whether I shall be fit for military service again[,] the rheumatism troubles me and grows worse[.] I am growing gray and older in constitution than I am in years[,] the hard knock of soldiering is making me grow old verry fast...." Many men could identify with Barber. Others, instead of being broken down by the trials of field service, actually thrived. This was true for Warren Goss who, "with hardened muscles, rendered athletic by long marches and invigorated by hardships, became stronger as time flew by."

The infantryman who spent months and years enduring the brutality of military life was eventually advanced to veteran status. The 100th Indiana chronicler, T.F. Upson, attested in November 1864 that "[s]uch an Army as we have I doubt if ever was got together before; all are in the finest condition. We have weeded out all the sick, feeble ones and all the faint hearted ones...." Private Hermon Clarke, in the late summer of 1863 proudly told his folks that: "I laugh sometimes when I think how I used to be troubled with rheumatism when I had a good bed and always dry clothes. Now I sleep in the open air in the mud and rain and sometimes don't have a dry thing on in 3 days, and [I live] on short rations of strong meat and wormy hardtack. [Yet] my health is good [and I] never felt so well in my life." And one year later he asked his family to:

> ...think of me once in a destitute condition, or nearly so. I have a cap, blouse, shirt, pants, and boots—all nearly worn out; had my knapsack and all my good clothes stolen: overcoat, rubber blanket, poncho, and everything; haven't had anything to eat in a month but pork (half the time raw), hardtack, and coffee; have marched, picketed, and fought in all kinds of weather but cool. A little more than half my face has skin on it; the rest covered with scabs where it is torn with brush skirmishing. Still I am well.

The transition from eager, naive recruit to seasoned infantryman came slowly but surely to those who survived fear, boredom, homesickness, disease, and wounds. Captain Harry T. Owen, 18th Virginia, saw the change in June, 1863: "The veterans' faces were tanned by summer's sun and winter's storms and covered by unkempt beards. Boys who had enlisted in their teens appeared with long tangled locks, changed and weather-beaten now, apparently, into men of middle life." William A. Keesy had the "face" of a vet as well. When he arrived home in June 1865, everyone he met asked, "Why Al, what makes you so black?" Keesy knew why. "The Southern sun and camp smoke had very materially changed my complexion."

Looking over his captors in November 1862, Union prisoner of war Simon Hulbert could closely determine their mettle. He expressed a prevailing sentiment, claiming that the Southerners,

> ...do not go in for making a great show [of] Blacking Boots, belts, scouring brass [and] burnishing guns to make them look Bright. But if the gun is only clean inside so that it will go off, it does not make any difference how rusty it is outside....
>
> The men are generally tall, slim & wiery [sic] fellows, quick as cats, real American people....They are mum as dead men as far as talking is concerned in the ranks. Every one knows what he has to do.

Private Lewis Bissell of Connecticut had a chance to look over 1,700 Confederate prisoners captured in the Shenandoah Valley. He called them the "flower of their army," and "smart healthy looking men," who "are very quick, walk like horses. Our men do not pretend to keep up with them." He described their uniforms as "light grey. The coat comes to the waist. They wear slouch hats. Caps are seldom worn. What few are seen are U.S." Bissell further declared them to be cheerful, talkative men who laughed and joked all the time. But a large number wanted to take the oath of allegiance to the Union, and, "all[,] from officers down to privates said they were tired of the war and that peace was worth more than the C.S.A."

Both Union and Confederate infantrymen had their moments of feast and famine throughout the war. As early as May 1862, Lieutenant Galwey called the look of his command, like that of "a pack of thieving vagabonds—no crowns in our hats, no soles to our shoes, no seats to our pantaloons." But as the war continued, the Rebels felt the pinch of shortages to a greater degree: not only of manpower, but in weapons, clothing and supplies.

By January 1865, William Chambers of the 46th Mississippi perceived that the end was near long before actually giving up. Expounded Chambers:

I find my regiment, the whole army in fact, in a deplorable condition. Twenty besides myself of Company B are here, but there is not a gun in the company. The regiment numbers about one hundred and fifty men, about half of whom are barefoot. All are ragged, dirty and covered with vermin, some not having sufficient clothing to hide their bodies. There are perhaps twenty guns, but not a single cartridge box in the regiment. The men are jovial enough...[but] fully convinced that the Confederacy is gone.

Two months earlier Major Stiles had observed the same dire circumstances in a brigade of troops that was stationed near Petersburg, Virginia: "We were shocked at the condition, the complexion, the expression of the men, and of the officers, too, even the field officers; indeed we could scarcely realize that the unwashed, uncombed, unfed and almost unclad creatures we saw were officers of rank and reputation in the army."

Even toward the close of the war, the veterans, especially in the Confederacy, had a grandeur about them, noticeable to all who cared to pause and look and reflect. Washington Ives, 4th Florida, remembered a scene from those days:

It makes one sad to see an old warrior reg't pass on the march bearing a flag with probably fifty holes through it and the names of from three to twenty hard fought fields [upon it]. [S]ometimes you will not see more than 50 rank and file in a regiment...look at their flag and you generally see...the numbers of 3 or 4 regiments consolidated. There are some regiments whose flags have inscriptions of honor on them, so numerous that it would almost be an impossibility to crowd another name.[111]

ON THE MARCH

In fact a soldier on the march resembles a pack mule.

Pvt. Washington Ives
4th Florida Infantry

An army on the march was a memorable thing. If seen from a distance it thrilled the imagination. Viewed from the ranks as an infantryman it can have many appealing and terrible faces. David Thompson's description of the Union army moving toward Antietam still stands as one of the best accounts of its kind ever written in wartime literature:

The gathering of such a multitude is a swarm, its march a vast migration. It fills up every road leading in the same direction over a breadth of many miles, with long ammunition and supply trains disposed for safety along the inner roads, infantry and

Union infantryman dressed and equipped for the march. (NA)

artillery next in order outwardly, feelers of cavalry all along its front and far out on its flank; while behind, trailing along every road for miles..., are the rabble of stragglers—laggards through sickness or exhaustion, squads of recruits, convalescents from the hospitals, special duty men going up to join their regiments.... Stand, now, by the roadside while a corps is filing past. They march "route step," as it is called,—that is, not keeping time,—and four abreast, as a country road seldom permits a greater breadth, allowing for the aides and orderlies that gallop in either direction continually along the column. If the march has just begun, you hear the sound of voices everywhere, with roars of laughter in spots, marking the place of the company wag—generally some Irishman, the action of whose tongue bears out his calling. Later on, when the weight of knapsack and musket begins to tell, these sounds die out; a sense of weariness and labor rises from the toiling masses streaming by, voiced only by the shuffle of a multitude of feet, the rubbing and straining of innumerable straps, and the flop of full canteens. So uniformly does the mass move on that it suggests a great machine, requiring only its directing mind....

"Route step."
(BL)

[In the distance] moved the baggage wagons, the line stretching from the bottom of the valley back to the top of the ridge, and beyond, only the canvas covers of the wagons revealing their character. We knew that each dot was a heavily loaded army wagon, drawn by six mules and occupying forty feet of road at least. Now they look like white beads on a string. So far away were they that no motion was perceptible.... [In the infantry line] motion...could be inferred from the casual glint of sunlight on a musket barrel miles away... each column a monstrous, crawling, blue-black snake, miles long, quilted with the silver slant of muskets at a "shoulder," its sluggish tail writhing slowly up over the distant ridge,....

Route step was the comfortable, relaxed change of gait appreciated by the infantry who so often walked long distances. John Worsham, a member of Stonewall Jackson's "foot cavalry," explained it: "At the commencement of the war, we were usually given the route step soon after starting the march. On passing a village town we were called to attention and marched through with military precision. Yet toward the close of the war we generally kept the route step throughout the march, for all had learned that the men got along so much better and could march much farther by being allowed to take their natural step and to carry their guns as they chose."

The view of thousands of soldiers in "route step" gave rise to this unusual comparison written by a newspaper reporter after the Battle of Gettysburg:

We see the mass of armed men filling the road, and wonder that...so many Union muskets could be carried so closely. One thing may be remarked of all illustrations of troops upon the march—they never give an adequate idea of the invariable irregularity of the position of the guns. They stick out like "quills upon the fretful porcupine;" they bristle like the hair of a sot who wakes up from a night in the gutter. Arms at will means a separate and distinct attitude for each individual rifle in the column, and, seemingly, no two are ever carried alike.

The route of march was planned for each day by the division commanders; it filtered down to the regiments and then company commanders who decided by different means who would lead the march that day. This was an important "draw" for the men at company level up through the brigade, because the closer to the front of the column one happened to be determined the amount of dust choked down by day's end.

Lieutenant Albert Pope, 35th Massachusetts, noted on May 5, 1863 that the day's march started at, "half past seven. We changed our [company] positions in line according to the rank of the captains. My company is seventh in line, fifth in rank." The time it took to prepare for any given march depended on the situation of the army, which could change at a moment's notice. It could be determined by the miles to be traveled that day, the weather, road condition, whether or not battle was imminent or the enemy was near or far. In the army, "hurry up and wait" has always been the norm, but sometimes speed of preparation was essential, and some individuals or units took the task seriously.

Simon Hulbert, for one, was proud of his ability to "break camp" in a short time. Said he: "[I have] a house that you can take to pieces in five minutes & pack it up in five minutes more. I can strike my tent, Roll my coat, fold my blanket & tent, pack them in my knapsack, & fasten the coat on the top, put on my harness, & be in readiness to move at any time in 10 minutes time, which I think is doing well."

The distance an army could cover in a day also varied. James Graham, 62nd Pennsylvania tried to explain these affairs to his Aunt Ellen Lee on May 20, 1862:

> Since I wrote...you will perceive we have been on the march again. We came...to this place yesterday, six miles the way we came but only making us four miles nearer Richmond.... The reason we do not march farther in a day is because of our supply trains not being able to move farther than that in a day. It is truly said that large bodies move slowly. Some people think we might be able to march 20 or 25 miles a day instead of what we do. If the whole country was one gravel road, it might be accomplished but without something of this kind it is impossible.

Graham was correct. When infantry moved on a parallel road away from army wagon trains, in good weather, and on improved roads, they could cover 15—30 miles a day. Average marches, however, seem to have been between 8 and 13 miles daily. In contrast, Roman legions 1800 years earlier, were expected to march on good roads about 25 miles a day, every day, carrying approximately 50 pounds of weapons and equipment.

The "halt and go" march was frustrating, tiring, and accomplished little to the military objective. Private Fisk demonstrated this in his letters home concerning soldier life in the 2nd Vermont. The march from Winchester, Virginia to Gettysburg through the mountains was one such march:

"Breaking camp." (BL)

It took all night to march about seven miles, the roads so clogged with teams and other things to hinder. Marching by rods is like dying by inches, and it gets an impatient man into a hell of a misery. Scolding and swearing is dispensed at an awful rate when a regiment is compelled to halt and wait every few rods, if the road is good and the journey long.... [T]he road was continually blocked up by some obstructions ahead, so that we had to halt three minutes where we could travel one. It was vexing beyond all control to stand there and hold our aching knapsacks, with [a] gigantic, never-ending hill looming up in front of us, and the long hard journey in prospect.

We rarely halted long enough to sit down, but if we did the column would invariably start just as we were fairly seated. Men fell out, whole companies at a time. Some companies took a vote to stop, and all fell out, officers and men. Our Colonel said he rode on till his men all left him, and he found himself without a command, when he concluded he would stop too.

Dropping out of a marching column and going it on your own hook was a great temptation for many an exhausted private. This was the only way some men could keep up with the universal flow. Otherwise they would have failed if obliged to keep their places in the ranks.

Thomas Galwey believed that being assigned to "wagon-guard" was an infantryman's worst nightmare. He said that a well-drilled body of soldiers could march for hours without either losing or gaining enough distance to make the march irregular, but mules could not be trained to do the same. Halting, checking the pace, trotting to catch up, slowing for rough ground or a creek, etc. was impossible to match walking alongside of wagons. "And so it goes," attested

A straggler going to the rear. (BL)

Galwey. "Slow walk, then run.... Imagine, then, the feelings of the infantry who have been detailed to guard the wagon train. Two men go with each wagon. Of course, they walk, creep, run or halt, just as the wagon which they accompany walks, creeps, runs, or halts, and in twelve or fifteen hours this becomes not only monotonous but maddening."

Not every march was recalled in detail by the rank and file soldier; there were just too many to remember. Some few stood out from the rest, others were simply too long, dreary and painful. In a routine way W.A. Keesy concluded: "Why, I have marched for whole days scarcely noticing even the general lay of the country, because I was too tired. Everything seemed a task. My gun was cutting into my shoulder. My accouterments felt like great iron bands. My knapsack was a load. The 60 or 120 rounds of cartridges were a dead weight, and my canteen and haversack very encumbersome, as, footsore and weary, sometimes hungry and thirsty, we dragged along."

Allen Redwood, 55th Virginia, wrote of a similar march: "There was no mood for speech, nor breath to spare if there had been—only the shuffling tramp of the marching feet, the steady rumbling of the wheels, the creek and rattle and clank of harness and accouterment, with an occasional order, uttered under the breath and always the same; 'close up! close up, men!'" Private Fisk remembered with a clear hatred the forced marches like the ones above. He said that the last miles were "doled out in suffering by inches." And, he added:

If a man wants to know what it is to have every bone in his body ache with fatigue, every muscle sore and exhausted, and his whole body ready to sink to the ground, let him...shoulder his knapsack, haversack, gun and equipments, and make one of our forced marches, and I will warrent him to be satisfied that the duties of war are stern and severe.... [especially] when every spark of energy seems about to be extinguished, and the last remnant of strength gone [and he is], tired, hungry, sick and sore,....

In many marches depicted by infantrymen of the Civil War, one factor which stood out in making these outings so distasteful was the heat and accompanying dust. On June 16, 1864 Austin Stearns confided in his diary that the dust "...was fearful; it covered every thing, away up through the country we could see the dust rising like a cloud from the army that was toiling along; the grass, trees, fences, and even ourselves were covered. Our faces were as completely covered as though we wore a mask and the sweat flowed furrows down our cheeks; the dust was in our eyes, and the sweat caused them to smart intensely."

In early June 1863 Wilbur Fisk wrote that "...every man was so covered with the gray dust that he looked for all the world as if he had just been immersed in an ash-heap." And W.A. Keesy believed that July 8, 1862 in the Shenandoah Valley was one of the most trying ordeals he ever lived through:

The heat was so intense that the dust burned us. Many of the men were falling out by the way-side, overcome by heat. The officers put leaves, dipped in water when it could be had, into their hats as a precaution against sun-stroke. The very atmosphere was aglare with the blazing sun and it was sad to see so many men collapsing under the blasting heat; many strong men with the look of despair upon their faces, with "death by sun-stroke," soon to be written after their names upon the roll.... The scene on this terrible, hot march was as appalling as battle itself.

Others commented in memoirs, diaries and letters about similar difficulties they encountered on Southern soil. Near Vicksburg, Mississippi in July 1863 John Green's regiment traveled only 14 miles, but he called it "about the most trying march we ever made" due to the heavy loads they were forced to carry and because "the sand was shoe mouth deep & so hot it actually blistered our feet. More than half the regiment fell by the wayside that day...." And on June 10, 1862 near Iuka, Captain Alfred Hough, 19th United States Infantry, also experienced the sacred dirt of Mississippi. He informed his wife Mary:

...the dust was fully from 3 to 4 inches deep, and you can imagine what an atmosphere we travelled in, 30,000 men stirring it up.... The dust rose in clouds, so that for a great part of the time I could not see 10 feet in front of me.... We passed hundreds of stragglers lying under trees and under fences waiting for evening to come up. Some were very sick, and here I saw something of the terrible realities of a hard march.... I saw a poor fellow lying under a tree just dead! The doctor had not reached him in time. As I passed I heard the doctor reading from a piece of paper taken from his pocket, "My name is N.O. Hack, I am from _____ Co., Ohio; If I am killed write to my mother."

Sunday, September 7, 1862 near Tenallytown, Maryland was a day to remember for Sergeant Thomas Evans, 12th United States Infantry. The road was composed of a fine white sand and the heat was severe, causing perspiration to gush out of every pore.

I cannot adequately describe it; sweat did not stand like beads on the surface, but it ran off us in streams. We wrung our blouses as we would have done after a shower, and moisture trickled from every finger end. The clouds of dust clung to the wet clothes and made us look like millers. Water was rushed for the moment it was seen, and drunk in enormous quantities. It was useless trying to hinder this; remonstrance was useless against the overpowering thirst. After that men could not keep in the ranks, they had either to fall out or fall down.

Straggling cannot be always prevented except by absolute brutality. Good men never straggle without cause. If exhausted by the length of march, intense heat, insufficient halts, and other causes, a man is kept in the ranks until he falls, he cannot be left there for the whole column to pass over him. It will take at least two men to get him to some place of rest and revive him, and these two will not be in a hurry to retake their places, nor with the best will in the world, is it easy to regain a place in a moving column.

Water was desperately important but sometimes impossible to find in certain areas of the country. Theodore Upson found that much of the water in Mississippi was not fit to use and very scarce. It was mostly pond water and the "Johnny's had killed hogs and cattle in the ponds and thrown dead dogs and cats in the cisterns and shallow wells, and I actualy [sic] saw men marching along through the awful dust with thier toungues [sic] hanging out of thier mouths."

Clean water was rare in eastern Virginia as well. In June 1862 Sergeant Stearns and his comrades looked for good water near a swamp. Coming to a pool deep in this swamp he found it filled with more bullfrogs than water:

I commenced to dip it up using my drinking cup, trying to fill my larger dish. The frogs, anticipating my intentions, tried to prevent me by saying "aint fit to drink, aint fit to drink." I was one of the first to invade their dominion and they tried to scare us away, but after a little, seeing their water disappearing, they showed fight and the boys had to arm themselves with sticks to keep them back;.... After giving the water a good boiling, I drank some made into coffee. In the morning after our two hours march, I found more water, that to strike it with a stick it would crack clear across, the scum was so thick.

Clouds of cloaking dust were not the only complaints heard from troops. Water, mud, rain, snow, and ice were all factors that could turn any normally easy trek into an exasperating experience. Various bodies of water had to be crossed, from small brooks to full-fledged rivers. These crossings could be difficult, or sometimes even pleasurable or humorous. Captain Hough witnessed one funny scene in Alabama:

We have had one most striking and at the same time ridiculous spectacle also; it was the crossing of Elk river.... We were ordered to take off our pantaloons, drawers and stockings but to keep on our shoes [as the bottom was covered with sharp stones]. Now just imagine a string of men a mile long, 4 abreast with their pantaloons off and shoes on marching along the bank of the river, and when in the river it was too funny, from bank to bank this string of men extended, one arm holding the cast off clothing and musket, the other holding up their coattails; further remarks are unnecessary.

Pennsylvania chaplain J.W. McFarland was struck by the same sight while wading Cedar Creek in Virginia one early May morning: "I have never witnessed a scene in which the sublime and the ludicrous were so completely blended as in this undress parade of crossing with fixed bayonets, each one holding up high and dry sixty rounds of cartridges eight days rations and one suit of clothes. About ten thousand crossed in this manner...."

On rainy days when, according to Lee Stillwell, the dirt roads would be "worked into a loblolly of sticky yellow mud," he and his companions would "take off our shoes

Confederate infantry fording the Potomac River. (BL)

and socks, tie them to the barrel of our muskets a little below the muzzle and just above the end of the stock, poise the piece on the hammer on either shoulder, stock uppermost, and roll up our breeches to the knees. Then like Tam O'Shanter, we 'skelpit on through dub and mire, despising wind, and rain, and fire' and singing 'John Brown's Body,' or whatever else came handy."

But during a heavy storm, the men were not often so merry, as related by a member of the 21st Virginia:

> Now the rain commences and soon pours down. Poor fellow! He pulls down his hat, buttons up his jacket, pulls up his collar, and tries to protect his gun. In a short while he feels the water running down his arms and legs; but he is defiant yet, and the same good old Confederate! Now the water is slowly felling its way down his back. As it gradually covers him, the courage goes out; and when his back gets completely wet, he for a few minutes forgets that he is a Confederate soldier! The thought only lasts a few minutes; yet the storm within him breaks loose, resulting in his cursing the Confederacy, the generals, everything in the army, and even himself! Then, with a new inspiration, he commences [cursing] on the Yankees.... He is [soon] all right....

Night marches brought not only discomfort but accidents as well. Sergeant Stearns confessed that one such march was "terriable." "[T]he mud was deep, and cobble stones were plenty, adding to a pitch dark night. Henry Vining, hitting his foot against a stone, fell full length into the mud, and on regaining his feet..., he called out to his brother in a most pitiful tone. 'Albion, I'm all mud;' this served for a by-word during our entire time of service whenever we saw anyone laboring under circumstances that was not at all favorable for them."

Kentuckian Johnny Green once had to slog for miles well into the night in four inches of snow during very cold weather. Near ten o'clock p.m. some cavalry rode by, kindly dismounted, and "we mounted their horses to ride but the snow had wet our feet & we almost froze on those horses & before we had ridden five miles we were shouting for the cavelry [sic] men to come & get their horses. Their feet by this time had gotten wet & cold in the snow so we both suffered more than we would if we had stuck to our own arm of the service from first to last."

Severe marching could damage the infantryman's body. Sergeant Fitzpatrick once marched so much that "it wore the ends of my toenails down to the quick, blistered my feet, and [made] them sore generally...." Another poor infantryman observed by Wilbur Fisk had "one boot in one hand, and the other stuck on his gun, while his stockings were nearly worn off his feet by the dirt and hard travelling. His feet were swelled and he had several large blisters on them. He was a new recruit, and one of the veterans asked him how much of his town bounty he had paid for that day." Now and then, a soldier just ignored the whole ordeal, as was the case of Walter Clark who attested:

> The roads were very muddy, the march was obstructed by wagons in front and we made only 2 1/2 miles in four hours. There were frequent halts and at one of them Will Daniel and the writer, standing side by side in the mud, both fell asleep. After a time the company moved on, but neither of us awoke until jostled by other troops in passing us. This incident recalls the fact that on a forced march in Tennessee afterwards, I slept walking. The nap must have been a short one, but that I lost consciousness was proven by the fact that I dreamed of a young lady three hundred miles away.[112]

William and Charles Issermoyer, 153rd Pennsylvania. These two appear ready for the march carrying knapsacks, blankets rolled up in rubber ponchos, and with rain covers on their kepis.
(GNMP)

FIGHTING THE BATTLES

Ther is no fun in fighting I do asshure you.

Pvt. James Graham
62nd Pennsylvania Infantry

The test of one's mettle in battle is of paramount importance in the minds of all who take the oath to serve as infantrymen during wartime. It was no less so in 1861-1862 when regiments were being filled to capacity by eager volunteers from states both north and south of the Mason-Dixon Line. Ironically, most infantrymen who enlisted for the average of three years were probably under fire, that is, in actual combat, for only a total of several hours to a few days, at most, during their whole time in service. Naturally these durations varied. A soldier belonging to a unit fighting at the sieges of Port Hudson, Vicksburg, or Petersburg might tally considerably more hours in contact with the enemy than Civil War regiments operating against guerillas in Tennessee, or guarding railroads somewhere for most of its service. Others saw more than their share of action if they were involved with Lee's or Meade's armies during the spring and summer campaign of 1864 in Virginia, or in the Atlanta Campaign under Sherman or Johnston in Georgia.

Using the diaries, letters, or post-war memoirs of any veteran who left such materials, it is easy to determine almost the exact hours and days spent enduring cannon and musket fire. Army of the Potomac Infantry Private Roland E. Bowen, 15th Massachusetts, makes a good subject for speculation. He served three years with the Second Corps, but like many soldiers, he missed some time in the ranks, (although he was never absent due to illness) once on leave for 30 days, and twice captured. Deleting his seven months in captivity and one at home, he spent 28 months in the ranks. Totaling his time under fire, he was in light or heavy combat for approximately 40 hours: during 10 major battles and several dozen skirmishes.

In battle every soldier was part and parcel of a giant machine which sometimes worked well and other times did not. Even in smaller engagements a soldier saw little of the fighting except in his immediate neighborhood. Terrain, weather, foliage, and especially rifle and cannon smoke often obscured the battlefield even from the view of brigade and division commanders. It was rare for a company line officer or a private in the ranks to see entire fields of fighting, and a description of a battle written by a participant very often sounded a lot like this:

> I encountered the enemy in an unbroken forest, rendered the more difficult of passage by the dense undergrowth which for more than two hundred yards extended along my entire line; and the difficulties were still further enhanced by the smoke of battle and the burning of the woods, rendering it impossible to distinguish objects twenty paces in advance.

Even on Cemetery Ridge at Gettysburg, with an open space extending about one square mile in front of them, the average man in formation there saw almost nothing of the famous Pickett-Pettigrew assault of July 3, 1863. Only once in a lifetime, if fortune favored, could the entire battlelines of two armies about to engage or locked in combat be visually comprehended. The fight at Mansura, or Avoyelles Prairie, on May 16, 1864 was such an occurrence. Major John Becht, 5th Minnesota, described the field as "a splendid one for a fair and equal contest, a smooth, clear prairie, slightly descending to the south 3 or 4 miles in extent, and surrounded by heavy timber." There the army of General Banks, about 20,000 men, met the forces of General Taylor who had at least 6,500. Becht called the scene, "a splendid sight; our whole force and every movement could be clearly and distinctly seen.... the numerous banners [of the regiments] glistening in the clear morning sunlight,..." A member of the 114th New York said the "marshalling of forces was transcendently imposing a sight at once grand and inspiring. As far as the eye could reach, or aided vision extend, serried ranks, bristling bayonets, burnished guns, glittering sabres, waving banners, and battle flags all tattered and torn every where met the view."[113]

Imposing as these descriptions may sound, to the private soldier most Civil War battles, large or small, were close brutal contests which brought together fear, excitement and exhaustion all in the small personal context and scope of an infantry company, regiment or brigade. Written commentary on the feelings of men before, during and after combat is plentiful, as are their experiences and recollections of the fighting itself. Lieutenant John H. Lewis for one, believed that there "is no place better than a field of battle to test the higher qualities and the nobility of man."

Wilbur Fisk claimed that newspaper articles were nearly always composed with the premise that infantrymen on the eve of combat "were in the best of spirits, and eager for a dash at the enemy." Fisk agreed that he and his comrades were in the "best of spirits," but only when they could get the best of spirits to "put into us;" but as "for being eager for a dash at the enemy, perhaps it is all true; I can speak for but one, but there was certainly a fellow there [prior to battle] about my size that felt no such eagerness at all."

Maine Lieutenant Abner Small believed the real test of courage comes "before the battle—in the rear line, under fire waiting." He acknowledged that the "true perspective of danger is observed and comprehended by the man attached to the edge of a battle— not in it, but near enough to feel its fierce pulsations and get an occasional shock of its power." Making light of books like *The Red Badge of Courage*, Small called it "absurd" and "sheer rot" that any man "analyzed his feelings and marked out any specific line of conduct while under fire, or even thought for five consecutive minutes of the past, present, or future, or measured out or acted upon any theoretical course of conduct irrespective of the arbitrary law which held him in obedience...." For Lieutenant Small, anyone who had been in battle could barely describe their feelings and emotions, while "young authors with a boyish fancy," who had not participated in mortal combat lacked any claim to that rare perspective.

One Massachusetts private conceded that "the most of humanity,...when confronted with actual danger,...have less fear than in its contemplation,...[and that] the actual dangers of war [are] always less terrible face to face than on the night before the battle." General John Gibbon came to a similar conclusion when he said that:

> One contemplating going under fire has suffered all the pangs one experiences when actually under fire for the first time, & a good many more...the imagination always magnifies before hand...,[and] the anticipation of danger is far more formidable than

the realization of it, and I believe that no one ever completely recovers from this anticipated dread....[M]en do become anxious & restless in the contemplation of approaching danger...there is not much talking...when a halt is made...some will take a pull at a canteen, some will light their pipes, & a large number will drop out of ranks...to obey what is perhaps a fanciful prompting of nature...."

An officer of the 121st Ohio, Lieutenant Milo Lewis, remembered the actions of his men upon receiving the word that they would lead a forthcoming charge near Kennesaw Mountain, Georgia on June 27, 1864. A short announcement made to the officers—"Have your men fall in without knapsacks"—was enough to forewarn the rank and file of what awaited them. The lieutenant had the opportunity to "note the effect of these words; how the silence was only broken by company commanders repeating the order; how the men arose from their reclining positions with compressed lips and a faraway look of the eyes, each busy with his own thoughts of home and loved ones, and [then] proceeded to lay aside such articles as must be left behind and might never be needed again." Similarly, Confederate Surgeon Spencer Welch, 13th South Carolina, testified about the eyes of men moving into action: "Upon looking around I at once noticed in the countenance of all an expression of intense seriousness and solemnity, which I have always perceived in the faces of men who are about to face death and the awful shock of battle."

A Yankee doctor, Francis Wafer, 108th New York, saw infantrymen on the way to the front at Gettysburg, "their glistening eyes and firmly compressed lips bespeaking their fearful and earnest purpose." And Confederate Walter Clark was impressed by and never forgot the look of the infantryman while in the heat of the contest:

[A member of our regiment]...stood loading and firing as rapidly as his teeth could tear the cartridges and his hands could ram them home. His face was cold and pallid and bloodless, but not from fear. Blackened with powder stain, through which the perspiration trickled in streams, his eyes flashed defiance with every flash from his gun,...he stood there a perfect demon of war, with no thought save to kill.

While also at Kennesaw, Sergeant John Brubacker, 86th Illinois, recalled a chilling event which occurred as his Company A was ordered to assault the Confederate earthworks ahead:

As we made the first step in the forward movement I shall never forget the act of two of the boys who had been chums. They reached behind one of the men that separated them and clasped hands as though bidding each other goodbye. I thought it meant a pledge of succor in need or distress and that neither felt hope of surviving the attempt [of taking the works]. Both fell, sealing their devotion with their lives.

A 55th Illinois veteran, Captain H.S. Nourse, felt he could sense the changing personalities of his command before an assault:

[My] comrades could read in each other's faces signs not always to be seen there; in those of the prominent officers sterner and more rigid facial lines, indicating the load of responsibility they felt resting upon them; in all countenances a more quiet and fixed expression, almost amounting to a slight pallor. The laugh sometimes heard had no heart in it, the arguments no vivacity, the sportiveness rare or spasmodic, and often a faraway look in some eyes told of thoughts wandering to a distant Northern home, perhaps never again to be seen. A few handed to one of the guards, or to the chaplain, a valued watch or keepsake,.... A few wrote brief notes and placed them in their knapsacks.

Edmund Patterson, 9th Alabama, proclaimed that pre-combat moments brought on "a feeling that cannot be described that takes possession of one,...[a] restless, feverish feeling...[where] the breath comes thick and short, and it is only when there is a momentary lull in the fearful storm that you draw a long breath.... [And] while you watch the progress of the conflict you become weary, and great drops of perspiration will stand upon your forehead." The tendency to make oneself scarce, claimed Private Fisk, was great at moments like these. He believed that soldiers:

> ...when they are not in the ranks armed and equipped and under the influence of discipline, and not directly under the control of a leader, feel just as other people are supposed to in times of danger,...[and] it is the most natural thing in the world for even soldiers to feel inclined to run, and to anyone who would attribute this inclination to cowardice, I would say it is a great pity, [that the army] should be deprived of their services.

When engaged in battle, some infantrymen found themselves too busy, confused, or determined to comprehend the intense danger surrounding them. Discipline and the comforting behavior of comrades, or the settling influence of officers and non-commissioned file closers often brought a sense of purpose and direction to what would otherwise have been utter chaos. Leander Stillwell of Illinois, for one, knew the true emotion of a man in combat. He wrote, "a soldier on the fighting line is possessed by the demon of destruction. He wants to kill, and the more of his adversaries he can see killed, the more intense his gratification!" And this from a man, who after the war, refused even to kill a chicken.

A soldier of the 19th Iowa, E.C. Condit, had a hard time explaining how a person felt in battle but recalled that the "nerves are strung up to the highest pitch." Condit assessed too the difficulty of clearly seeing the enemy; "but you know where they are," he stressed. "[A]fter you have shot three or four rounds your nervousness passes away, and it becomes a matter of doing the most execution you can. If any of the boys are acting or shooting wild, you will hear the company officers saying, 'Steady, there!' 'Get back in your place!' 'Shoot low!' etc., and all are working like a machine." All the while, said Condit, men are praying or cursing, and it seemed strange to him that during these moments men would swear venomous oaths. "Standing there in the face of death, yet they would curse their Maker until it would make the cold chills run over a person to hear them, and you could almost smell brimstone around them."

Infantry officers carried swords into battle to guide and direct their men. This weapon was worn by Capt. J.G. Rodgers, 12th Georgia, in 18 engagements. He was holding it and encouraging his comrades when he was killed at Antietam. (GAC)

Officers had the greatest responsibility in combat situations. In his first encounter with the enemy, Captain Alfred Hough felt "as cool and collected as ever I did in my life and for the time was as strong. I felt a great work was in my hands and I must execute it. I had 50 men who looked to me for their every action, and almost for their every thought. I knew they had confidence in me, and if I did my duty they would do theirs."

Approaching his first engagement, another officer, William Spencer, 61st New York, felt almost gay and declared at that time that he "wouldn't have exchanged places just then with any man north of Mason & Dixon's line." Later, he remembered these unusual emotions, saying, "I never knew them again in battle." Afterward, Spencer was overcome with a "sickening dread" and the normal sense of fear. The effect of actual combat on him was "neither exhilarating nor infuriating, but depressing and almost sickening. I wondered why I was not hit, and was dreading the expected bullet nearly all the time, while trying to look as if I didn't care. I clearly remember thinking, as I stood there in the midst of that storm of bullets, 'Well, this then is a battle and I'm in it' but I didn't like it all the same." He summarized that "war and all its miseries, had to my mind in the midst of that battle the hellish aspect that it has always had for me since that day."

The commander of the 5th Vermont, Colonel Lewis A. Grant, unlike Captain Spencer, asserted that the feeling of trepidation before combat never lasted very long for him once he met the enemy: "It never extended through a battle. As soon as actually engaged all fear was gone and it generally disappeared while making an advance. The roar of cannon and the rattle of musketry had no terrors for me. I accepted the chances of personal injury and thought only of the proper exercise of my command and of the result. On two occasions I actually enjoyed the fight." And Confederate Officer D. Augustus Dickert left a fine account of men before and during an engagement:

> Some men, on the eve of battle, the most trying time in a soldier's life, will stand calm and impassive, awaiting the command, "forward," while his next neighbor will tremble and shake, as with a great chill, praying, meditating, and almost in despair, awaiting the orders to advance. Then when in the heat of the conflict both men seem metamorphosed. The former, almost frightened out of his wits, loses his head and is just as apt to fire backwards as forwards; while the latter seems to have lost all fear, reckless of his life, and fights like a hero. I have known men who at home were perfect cowards,...and become fearless and brave as lions in battle; while on the other hand men who were called "game cocks" at home and great "crossroads bullies" were abject cowards in battle.

Dickert believed that no man wants to die, and that the truth is all men are basically cowards in the face of death. "Pride, ambition, a keen sense of duty, will make differences outwardly, but the heart is a coward still when death stares the possessor in the face.... I write so...to controvert the rot written in history and fiction of soldiers anxious to rush headlong into eternity on the bayonets of the enemy."

The nervousness of soldiers prior to combat and the composure regained in battle, is a main theme throughout the war literature of the 1860s. Sergeant Hamlin A. Coe, 19th Michigan, experienced this firsthand when he commented in his diary on his actions near Tunnel Hill, Georgia, May 8, 1864: "Although I have heard the balls often before, I must confess I was a little unsteady, but I soon gained control of myself, and now I am afraid I should shoot if I could see a Rebel."

Others held to a different theory for bravery in action. Stonewall Brigade member, John Casler, knew a sergeant in Company F, 33rd Virginia, nicknamed "Doggie" who believed that "if a man was born to be killed he would be killed anyway and there was no use in trying to protect himself from bullets." On one occasion during a skirmish someone warned the sergeant to get behind a tree or he would be killed. He replied that if he was "to be killed the tree wouldn't save him." In a few moments he was shot dead. Fortunately, the majority of infantrymen chose not to believe such nonsense, or relatively few would have survived the slaughter of Civil War battlefields.

Once engaged, the terror of the prospect of fighting diminished and the majority of soldiers did their duty. Simon Bolivar Hulbert noted this phenomenon after surviving an infantry assault against Fort Wagner, South Carolina on July 18, 1863: "I do not want to see another charge in the night.... The grape & canister from the enemies guns dealt death & Destruction in our ranks, but I marched forward with a firm & steady step. When the canister shots came I would stoop over & rush forward while many others would fall flat to ground. But I did not so much as get a scratch while many others around me were falling, screaming with pain & crying to God to forgive their sins."

Georgian Marion Fitzpatrick implied that he too was more steady once in combat, telling his wife that after almost six months in the army he had "changed much in my feelings. The bombs and balls excite me but little and a battlefield strewed with dead and wounded is an everyday consequence." Another Rebel, Floridian Washington Ives, agreed: "[I]t would have surprised anyone to see how cooly we all went into the hottest fire and there were only one or two men in the regiment who showed any sign of fear.... I did not mind seeing human blood anymore than animals,...."

In a two-hour fight during the Battle of Second Manassas, Charles Barber's regiment lost 37 men killed and wounded and 100 missing, but he "stayed perfectly cool[,] loaded and fired my gun as coolly as if I was shooting squirrels but I had many narrow escapes." At Antietam three weeks later, Barber had not changed that opinion of himself, saying:

> I was not born to be killed in battle but it seemed as though the rebs was trying to see how near they could come to me and not hit me[,] probably 50 bullets come in a few inches of me while my comrades fell right and left[.] I was not a bit afraid in battle but now the battle is over and I look back and see the many chances I had it makes me almost tremble now[.] a man feels and acts strange in battle when the danger is the most his fear is the least.

This similar explanation to his Aunt Ellen Lee was written by James Graham, 62nd Pennsylvania who fought at Spotsylvania, Virginia in 1864: "You asked me how I felt when I was going into the charge and how I felt while in and how I felt after I came out. I felt just as cool as I do now, When in I felt like as if I could take Richmond myself. After I came out...it was then I thought about it. I thought how good God has ben [sic] to me in sparing my unprofitable life while many of my comrades have fallen around me."

To David Thompson, the truth about serving in an infantry regiment in battle was that "when bullets are whacking against tree-trunks and solid shot are cracking skulls like egg shells, the consuming passion in the breast of the average man is to get out of the way. Between the physical fear of going forward and the mortal fear of turning back, there is a predicament of exceptional awkwardness from which a hidden hole in the ground would be a wonderfully welcome outlet." Sergeant Walter Clark, 1st Georgia, confessed that although the "excitement produced by the crack of the rifles and the hiss of the minies did in some degree lessen the sense of personal danger, I have been able, even in my limited experience as a traveler, to find quite a number of places that were to me equally as pleasant as being under fire.... I only claim that while I had been curious to know how I would feel under such circumstances, my curiosity was satisfied in a little while, in a very little while." In his humorous, understated way Clark added that he had known men who at such times suffered from "nervous chills and on one occasion it brought on a member of the regiment an attack of cholera morbus [diarrhea]. As when such result was produced, I am not prepared without further evidence, to recommend it to the medical profession either as an emetic or an aperient."

When asked how he felt upon the eve of battle or while employed in its midst, an officer of the 9th Virginia clarified that when he heard the clash of musketry and the roar of artillery, along with the screeching of shells, he "was not quite as anxious as some of the boys seemed to be to get there." But as time passed, Lieutenant John Lewis noticed a change in the demeanor of his men, saying: "Soldiers are not heathens; but the life of danger seems to cause them to forget the past. They take no thought of the future, and nothing but the present lives with them and they make the most of it."

One 35th Massachusetts officer never got used to combat. Lieutenant Albert Pope confided to his diary on October 4, 1864, after several years of army life: "I am perfectly willing to admit that I do not like fighting. I dread going into a fight, but when I am there no one can accuse me of not doing my duty."

The physical and mental terror of battle took its toll before, during, and even long after the experience. A 25th Wisconsin private, Chauncey H. Cooke, spoke of one incident where the emotions of his comrades were totally out of control. After an engagement in July 1864, he told his father that "[m]any of the boys were crying like children, running back and forth without hats or guns cursing the rebels for killing their comrades. The whole army seemed to be turned into a mob. I never saw such a mixup."

Some men could never recover from their first battle experience. These individuals either deserted or looked for clever ways to avoid combat. A small number took more drastic action and found a permanent solution to the nightmare, as here recorded by an Alabama soldier named Steele on June 23, 1862: "I forgot to tell you in my last that one of our recruits (Thrasher) killed himself[,] he committed the act a few days after the battle of the 'Seven Pines' he was in the battle and acted very coolly[.] when he got back to camp he said he never intended going into another so he shot himself in the bust with his own musket. He left a wife and several children...."[114]

The skirmish line. (BL)

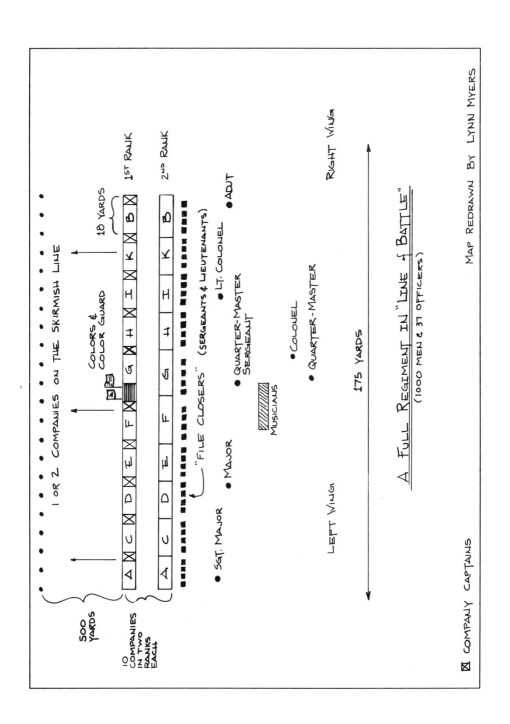

A FULL REGIMENT IN "LINE of BATTLE"
(1000 MEN & 37 OFFICERS)

MAP REDRAWN BY LYNN MYERS

⊠ COMPANY CAPTAINS

CONTINUING COMBAT

"Like the boiling cauldron of hell."

Sergeant Daniel Crotty
3rd Michigan Infantry

The basic experiences of infantrymen in battle which have been recorded by the participants both during and after the Civil War run almost into uncounted volumes. As was pointed out by Alabamian E.D. Patterson, some slight knowledge about war is gained through these recollections, but in reality, "one knows...nothing at all about it until he has participated in it." Inside the realm of combat, throughout the 1860s, as in all of the previous and even in recent military actions, very little beyond the limited scope of an individual's environment can be clearly seen. Thomas Galwey wrote:

> The soldier on the battlefield who is doing his duty knows but little of the general movements of the battle. These he is anxious to know, of course, but only finds them out or begins to understand them when the battle is over, or he has a chance to talk to men or officers of other regiments, or to prisoners captured.... The soldier advances or retreats, or marches by the flank to the right or left, as his command goes. To him, his regiment or at least his brigade, is the whole army. And generally he cannot see far even when he has time to look. He fights in a cornfield where the tall stalks wave above, or where hedge fences and clumps of trees, houses, barns, and even chicken coops limit his view.

Wilbur Fisk agreed, exclaiming: "You never need to ask a private soldier for general information. He is the last man to get that. His circle of observation is very limited. He sees but little of what is going on, and takes part in still less." And during the Seven Days' Battles in 1862 Val Giles called attention to the fact that a "soldier of the line in a great battle...looks quick and thinks fast. He doesn't see much except what is occurring immediately around him,...." After his first action, Perry Mayo was hard pressed to know what he had just been involved in. "The fact is I could not...see the enemy except occasionally between the volleys of their musketry when the smoke would clear off a little. I fired four rounds and had to guess about the right h[e]ight and fire away trusting to providence for the effect, but I didn't shoot over." Abner Small, as usual, cut right to the bone on this subject:

> Any member of a regiment, officer or private, can have but little knowledge of movements outside of his immediate command. In all engagements with the enemy he has his special duty to perform, and no time to look with a critical eye upon his comrade's conduct; he has all he can do to obey orders and keep from running—many failed even in this....
>
> The idea that a soldier, whose duty it is to remain in the ranks and move in geometrical lines, has an opportunity to view a [battle] as he would a panorama, is absurd.... The inequalities of the ground, the wooded slopes and deep ravines, the fog, the dense smoke, and the apparent and often real confusion of troops moving in differ-

A battle was often a confused and bewildering experience. (BL)

ent directions under different orders, utterly preclude the possibility of a correct detailed observation of a battle of any magnitude.

The major obstacle to a wide-range view of most battlefields, other than terrain, was the thick smoke from thousands of muskets and dozens or even hundreds of cannon. The gunpowder of the 1860s was not "smokeless" and when burned it created voluminous clouds of a grayish, heavy smoke. As an illustration, Lieutenant Richard Tuthill of Michigan said that in battle, the "smell of powder was everywhere. The smoke from the guns was so dense that though a July sun was shining, there was the appearance of a dense fog. Only as the breath of a passing breeze blew the smoke away could the movements of the enemy be discerned clearly...." A Texan who had just been through several engagements, and was corresponding to a friend at home on July 12, 1862, pronounced that "[a]fter the fighting I was surprised to learn how little of it I had really seen and participated in.... We privates look only to our immediate front, right, and left, and are not permitted to stand on eminences which overlook the whole field of battle."

Although very little of the conflict could be seen by the average private, a Southerner from the 9th Alabama once announced that he could hear almost everything said around him even in the great tumult of a fight: "It is strange how one can hear the human voice amid the roar and confusion of the battlefield, but when John Childress fell, [at Frayser's Farm] shot through, he said, 'I am killed, tell Ma and Pa goodbye for me' and I heard it as distinctly as if everything had been still."[115]

❖ ❖ ❖

The sound of battle was unquestionably one of the sensations most often recalled by infantry veterans. At the Battle of Fredericksburg Lieutanant Galwey recalled streaks of fire coming from "every gun, cannon, and bursting shell," which painted the valley around the town lurid with flames from the flashes of light from, "the burning fuses of coursing shells. The roar of artillery, the awful crash ('rattle' is too weak a word for it) of musketry volleys, and the cheers and yells of the two armies, made an excellent representation of Hell." The sounds at Gettysburg moved Lieutenant Edgar A. Burpee, 19th Maine, who commented that at one moment shot, shell, and other projectiles were coming at his regiment "like a hurricane." "You cannot conceive," he pronounced, "the terrible shriek and noise of shell and the appalling report grape and canister make when it strikes the ground. It almost makes a man shudder and cringe to be a listener to it."

Similarly, Wilbur Fisk was impressed by the noise and action of "grape and canister." Calling the effect "grand," he attempted to define it more closely: "At every discharge the grape could be heard rattling against the trees like throwing a handful of pebbles against the side of a building." Fisk, like many Civil War era soldiers often confused grape and canister. Grape, which came in "stands," were large balls fired from naval and siege guns rather than field artillery, which rarely used grape. Canister balls came packed in tin cans and were much smaller in size.

Fisk even tried to depict the characteristics of the Minie balls which constantly tormented the men who were besieging Petersburg, Virginia in 1864:

These bullets have a peculiar sound. Some of them come with a sharp "clit," like striking a cabbage leaf with a whip lash, others come with a sort of screech, very much such as you would get by treading on a cat's tail. Then there are others, the sharpshooter's bullets we suppose, that whistle on a much higher key, and snap against a tree with as much force as if the tree had been struck by a heavy sledge hammer. Some strike in the dirt with a peculiar "thud," others fly high in the air and make a noise similar to a huge bumble bee.

Like Fisk, Captain Albert A. Pope spent days in the trenches near Petersburg, and on March 8, 1865 commented that the "minie balls are flying around like bumble bees in June." These "spiteful missiles" as Lyman Widney, 34th Illinois, called them, were a great danger and annoyance to the men of his regiment "six miles from Atlanta." Each one that went "cracking through the tree tops," he said, was "pitched to a different tune:"

We have a splendid opportunity for noticing the different notes sounded by them. Some go over with a short "whisp" as if well greased and sliding through the air.... Others come like a young thrashing machine, whirling end over end. They have struck something on their course which has deranged their original motion. They are generally battered into different shapes and emit a sound that is varied according to the form and speed of the ball. The consequence is that there are just as many different sounds as there are different shaped balls. Every hour or so some new note is struck, and is generally greeted by a laugh that runs through the regiment.

Robert B. Davidson, a lieutenant in Company B, 35th Ohio, in his diary entry for June 23, 1864, categorized each cannon projectile by its unique consonance:

The sound of a parrot gun on being fired is something similar to the crack of a rifle. It is keener and shakes the ground more than a brass piece of larg callibre [sic]. A shell from a (10 lb.) parrott gun, in passing through the air, sounds something like the plaining of a board. The sound of a 20 lb. parott shell is deep, between a buzz and a groan. The shell or ball from a smooth bore brass piece makes a hissing nois [sic]. The nois caused by the discharge of a brass piece sounds more like an explosion than the discharge of a parrott gun. The sound caused by grape or canister passing through the air, sounds very much like that caused by the working of a wind mill but not quite so loud.

Other infantrymen, like Davidson, were constantly improving on their own definitions. Louisianian H.E. Handerson who once "hugged the earth while shell and shot tore the air above me" explained the sound was like "the hasty ripping of stout canvas, only intensely magnified." To Austin Stearns, grape and canister made a "sch'w's sch'w's" as it flew by; and to Warren Goss, musketry was like "a pack of Fourth of July fire-crackers under a barrel magnified a thousand times." Lt. H.W. Jackson, 4th New Jersey, hearing the rifle balls, said they were "never-to-be forgotten" and made a "ping" as they flew over.

According to Private Goss, some of the Minie' balls seemed to get personal. A soldier he knew named Spinney ran away during one of the battles of the Seven Days'. Afterwards when asked why he had so cowardly departed his comrades, the man replied that "every bullet which went by his head said 'Spinney' and he thought they were calling for him." But one of the most defining accounts, which brings a creepy and sinister personal quality to being under fire, is this quote from G.N. Galloway who remembered the murderous rifle balls at Spotsylvania: "I cannot imagine how any of us survived the sharp fire that swept over us [that day (May 10, 1864)]—a fire so keen that it split the blades of grass all about us, the minies moaning in a furious concert as they picked out victims by the score."[116]

Civil War era projectiles were heard by all infantrymen in battle, but sometimes they could even be seen in flight. Lieutenant Henry Handerson, 9th Louisiana, claimed that at the Battle of Malvern Hill he saw for the first time, "a shell in its course from the mouth of the cannon until its explosion. Coming directly towards me, it appeared as a small black object apparently changing its position very little from moment to moment, but gradually enlarging as it approached, until it burst perhaps a hundred yards in my front." And during one bombardment on March 25, 1865 at Petersburg, George Kilmer commented that the "air was full of shells" from both sides. On glancing up, Kilmer said one could see, "as it were, a flock of blackbirds with blazing tails beating about in a gale." Chesley A. Mosman, an Illinois officer, in a strange encounter while passing along his regiment's line on May 14, 1864, "happened to look up and I saw a black spot in the air coming directly towards me and I ducked my head, and heard it strike the brush above me. So I am certain that by mere chance I had seen a canister shot in the air before it reached and passed me. My dodging did no good for it was too high to hit me." Oddly, a lieutenant next to Mosman saw the same ball and confessed, "I dodged just like you."

One shell, fired at the 38th Wisconsin, became intimately acquainted with an officer in that regiment. Writing "from the field" on August 24, 1864, Lieutenant Frank Phelps stated:

The rebel shell began to fly fast.... I never saw them fall so thick as they did there [on August 19].... I was laying just behind my company so I was next to the rear rank. One shell came over I saw it coming with lightening speed right for my head (so I thought). I could not dodge could do nothing but remain motionless—in a second—less time than I can think of—everything was dark before me. I turned my head & heard the shell strike with a dull sound in my company & burst. I looked—& oh what a sight[,] shall I describe it as I saw it for a minute—and then everything was as blank to me. I saw one man next to me, the first the shell hit, with his head taken off as far as the lower jaw, his brains & blood splattering me full in the face; next was one of my company (the first one belonged to the 15 New York) it struck him in the left breast & burst litterally tearing him to pieces—the poor fellow never knew what hit him. one piece of the shell hit one of my sergeants in the side cutting his back clear across. he lived about half of an hour. other pieces hit my men but only one proved fatal.

Like Phelps, John Gould, 90th Pennsylvania, recalled the destruction of one shell that hit a companion in the torso: "[W]hen it exploded [it] tore the whole top part of his body off. You could see nothing but his legs. His head, arms, and breast was nothing but a lot of mashed bones and torn flesh."

Large mortar balls falling to the ground always warranted comments, like this one from William Chambers on duty in the trenches protecting Vicksburg, Mississippi: "[At] night we watched these mortar shells. From the flash of the [muzzle blasts we] beheld them rise, go streaming across the sky like a flying meteor, describe a great curve and pitch head-long to the earth, gathering momentum as they fell. Sometimes they bursted high in mid air with a detonation like thunder, sometimes exploding near the ground, and they buried themselves in the earth and tore out great holes when the explosion came."

After so much experience, infantrymen became adept at predicting the path and contact point of fired shells. On March 20, 1865, Lieutenant Albert Pope wrote: "Our men all got up close to the works, and watched the shells, and by paying particular attention both with eye and ear, one could tell pretty near where the shell would strike. Today nine struck and burst within fifty yards of me in one minute; the shells were eight and six inches in diameter."

Almost eerie and certainly unsettling was the "sight," of Minie balls striking near a soldier while under heavy musketry fire. Explaining this phenomenon is Lieutenant Thomas Galwey, 8th Ohio at Antietam:

The fight goes on with unabated fury [opposite the "sunken lane"]. The air is alive with the concussion of all sorts of explosions. We are kneeling in the soft grass and I notice for a long time that almost every blade of grass is moving. For some time I supposed that this is caused by the merry crickets; and it is not until I have made a remark to that effect to one of our boys near me and notice him laugh, that I know it is the bullets that are falling thickly around us! It is wonderful how a man can live through such close danger. I have made up my mind that I shall not, cannot, escape. Strangely the idea causes me no nervousness nor the least bit of inward excitement. I contemplate the prospect of sudden death without flinching. It is not heroism, but cool reason which actuates me.[117]

Under severe battle conditions, shells flew over and exploded, and uncountable bullets whizzed by. The uncomfortable sounds of iron and lead striking and smashing and crushing delicate human bodies were a never-to-be-forgotten, jarring reality, horrible to contemplate, but nevertheless difficult for an infantryman not to record. Referring to the demise of his friend, Hardy Allen, who was fatally injured during the Antietam Campaign, John Stevens, 5th Texas, remembered vividly how Allen was shot through the breast: "He was standing close to my side. I heard the death mizzle [sic] as it hit him, making a sound as though he had slapped his hands together."

One Confederate actually saw the missile strike that killed a Federal soldier. During the Battle of Chickamauga, Private Val Giles was caught in a wooded area that was being bombarded by "shells, grapeshot, canister, shrapnel and Minie balls," which were tearing through the trees, "while dirt, leaves, limbs, and bark were falling and flying all over and around," making the position, he said, "a veritable hell on earth." Giles called it the "meanest, most unsatisfactory place I struck during the whole war." Giles' lieutenant ordered a group of recently captured Yankee prisoners to move quickly to the rear so they would not be killed by their own artillery. As they did, a Union battery opened fire, "and one of the men was hit in the back. He was so close to me," recalled the Texan, "that I distinctly saw the dust rise from his shoulders where the grapeshot struck him. He fell forward on his knees,...then gradually sank to the ground."

Thirteenth New York Volunteer Samuel S. Partridge declared that when "a bullet goes into a man's head it makes a crash among the bones that can be heard distinctly for some feet." Edmund Patterson watched his friend Perkins Pool die instantaneously, the bullet making "the peculiar sound...when it strikes a man (and which does not resemble any other sound either in nature or art)...."

Bullets sometimes killed more than once. According to William Chambers, two men in Company G, 46th Mississippi, "were struck by the same minie ball. It passed through one's loins and entered the abdomen of the other, inflicting a fatal wound in each. The men were brothers-in-law." While fighting near the "Dead Angle" at Kennesaw Mountain, Georgia, Major James Holmes, 52nd Ohio watched men give up their lives everywhere. "You could not say or think who would die or be maimed the next instant. I shall never forget the thud of a minie ball through human flesh; it is a sickening sound...." And 15th Ohio Sergeant-Major A. J. Gleason, while on the firing line in Georgia on May 27, 1864 saw a man near him hit by a Minie ball in the temple. Gleason was deeply impressed "with that peculiar 'spat' which once heard is at once recognized as the passage of a bullet through flesh and bone. It killed him so suddenly that he never changed position, and had I not heard the shot strike and been splattered by his blood and brains I might have believed him still untouched."

An 82nd Ohio officer at Gettysburg on July 1 left an account of how he felt upon being struck by a flying missile on the retreat from his regiment's position north of town. "A moment or two later [after seeing a Union soldier near him fall] I too felt the sting of a bullet, and fell benumbed with pain. It was an instantaneous metamorphosis from strength and vigor to utter helplessness." Lieutenant Davidson, 35th Ohio, went even further, compiling this interesting information on the sensations of being hit in combat:

> Feelings of wounds received in different parts of the body. A wound by a minie ball in full force through the bow[e]lls feels like a read [red] hot wire run through instantly and does not become painfull immediately. A ball in full force passing through any part of the body and hitting no bones has a similar feeling. A ball in full force, hitting a bone or bones in any part of the body, causes a numbness as though you had been hit by a heavy bar of iron, and causes pain sooner and more severe than a flesh wound. A wound by a cannon ball or piece of shell causes intense pain immediately. A wound in the hand or foot is never [as] painfull as a general thing than in other parts of the body.

In almost the same vein as Lieutenant Davidson's observations are these from George Kilmer, 27th New York:

When felt at all, bullets through the flesh usually produce a burning sensation more or less acute. When bones are hit but not broken, there is a numbing sensation in the whole region involved in the shock, followed very soon by severe and sometimes intense pain. When muscles and tendons are involved, there is a tugging sensation, sometimes very slight, and shell-wounds produce feelings similar to those by bullets, more or less exaggerated, according to the size of the missile and the degree of velocity. Bayonet wounds I never saw except upon corpses...and as for cannon-balls, they do not, as a rule, leave anything behind to exhibit feelings.

Experts affirm that a cannon-ball having velocity to keep it in the air will make a clean cut of flesh, bones, and ligaments, and not simply tear them, or push them aside as with a punch;...

Relating to the above, Kilmer gave a unique example.

On the 17th of June [near Petersburg], a sergeant of the Fifty-seventh Massachusetts leaped upon the parapet, and, with his cap in his left hand and his musket in his right, stood cheering and gesturing with his arms to incite his comrades to come on. Suddenly a shell took his head off as completely as a knife could have done, but the tall form continued erect for some seconds, the arms still waving frantically, but with ever-lessening sweep and power, until the forces of the body collapsed, when the headless trunk toppled over to the ground.

The effects of bullets on the environment could be astounding and terrifying. For instance, at Spotsylvania one artillery battery was riddled by heavy fire; 27 balls passed through the lid of the limber-chest, 39 shots went through one of the sponge-buckets (which was made of one-eighth iron); and elsewhere the head logs of the breastworks "were cut and torn until they resembled hickory brooms. Several large oak-trees, which grew just in rear of the works were completely gnawed off by...converging fire,"

Breastworks, barricades, and walls afforded extra protection to the soldiers. These Confederates took full advantage of this wall at Fredericksburg. (BL)

and later fell with a loud crash. And near Kennesaw, Georgia, Captain John Gillespie, 78th Ohio, remarked on "a furious barrage of bullets cutting the limbs and leaves from the bushes so that they looked as naked as though a furious hailstorm had passed over them. I never heard balls come thicker or faster...."

On June 20, 1864, Lieutenant Andrew Neal reported his unit's flag was struck by infantry fire 31 times; the flagstaff, no larger around than a thumb, was hit seven times. Recalled Neal: "The trees...were riddled with balls. On one little sapling I counted about 80 balls on the body." The artillery pieces in the earthworks had hundreds of bullet marks on them, and canteens, blankets, etc., he said, "were shot to pieces."

Chaplain G.W. Pepper, 80th Ohio, near Ezra Church, Georgia saw in one length of rail fence over 100 bullet holes; likewise a Southerner, W.H. Swallow, resting just south of Gettysburg after the battle counted 836 holes in a wooden fence plank which measured 16 feet long. After the Atlanta Campaign, John Green, 9th Kentucky, "walked over the ground in front of the position we defended & there was not a twig which had not been cut down by bullets & there were trees as big as my leg which were actually whittled down by minnie balls. It seemed a miracle that any living soul could have survived that hailstorm of lead."

"As to musketry fire," recounted Robert Stiles at Cold Harbor, "I remember counting ninety odd bullet holes through a 'dog tent,'...and the bronze guns of a battery looked as if they had smallpox, from the striking and splaying of leaden balls against them. Even the narrow lips of the pieces, about their muzzles, were indented in this way. One of the guns,...was actually cut down by musketry fire, every spoke of both wheels being cut."[118]

"Close calls" in battle were a normal occurrence to Civil War riflemen. Finding that musket balls had pierced the clothing was a fairly "everyday" event in combat, and bullets were constantly being turned aside or stopped by a variety of objects. Perry Mayo, who was in the thick of it all during the First Battle of Bull Run, wrote to his parents claiming that he "was in the field during both the engagements and escaped with no other injury than a sprained ankle and two ball holes in my clothes, one in my cap and the other in my blanket which was done up in a roll and passed over my right shoulder."

In the Battle of Gettysburg, Frank Jennings, 90th Pennsylvania, commented that a "cannon ball whizzed past my legs between the 1st Sergeant of the next Company and myself. If I had been 4 or 5 inches ahead of the spot I was then I should most asuredly have had both my legs taken off, in fact...the ball [was] so close to me [it] almost [took] me off my feet. I can tell you it scared me for a few moments." During the Atlanta Campaign William Chambers, 46th Mississippi, heard a shell approaching, "which by its peculiar noise I knew it was about to explode." Chambers dropped to the ground with his face a few inches from a rock. When the shell detonated a large fragment of the shell struck the rock just under his face with great force and "glanced off with a loud whizzing sound." And in the same campaign Private Washington Crumpton, 37th Mississippi, reported that his "old haversack had a half dozen bullet holes through it." Continuing he said: "For ten days my body was not safe from the passage of bullets, some through my clothing and some that barely made my clothes threadbare as they passed, but leaving a sore place on the flesh as if scorched by fire. My case knife in the bottom of my haversack turned two bullets off me, and my tube wrench and screw driver in my cartridge box was broken by another."

Infantry fighting at close quarters at Gettysburg. (BL)

After the engagement at Chancellorsville in May 1863, Wilbur Fisk wrote:

Bullets play curious freaks sometimes, and every battle has its hair-breadth escapes. One fellow had his gun shot out of his hands, and another close by had his life spared because his gun intercepted the bullet. Sergt. Davis of Company E, was struck in the breast with a ball, but an account book in his pocket was his life-preserve. Capt. Ballou, Company H, had the skin scratched off his nose by a rebel minnie, and that is shooting a man almost within an inch of his life.

In an engagement near Cat Creek, Georgia, Sam Watkins declared: "A minnie ball passes through my Bible in my side pocket," while in a similar case, a lieutenant of the 4th Texas was struck during the fight at Chickamauga on the left breast above the heart by a Minie ball. Immediately, Val Giles saw the officer's sword fly from his grip and "he fell heavily to the ground, apparently dead. But he was not killed," said Giles, "[t]he bullet never entered his body, but embedded itself in his bundle of love letters. When the battle was over he took pride in showing his mutilated letters to his intimate friends.... The bullet passed through eight or ten of them, and they were big, fat ones too! The bullet lodged against the last one received. He was the merriest soldier in that weary army."

A "close shave" was recorded by Theodore Upson on May 17, 1864 near Resaca, Georgia. "We had a hard battle.... Sam Allbright of my company was struck with a peice [sic] of shell, and I was hit on my belt buckle with a spent ball which knocked me out for a while. The boys thought I was done for and dragged me behind a tree, but I come to after a while. I was sick at my stomach and am pretty sore."

In his first battle, Johnny Green had a close call soon after he lifted his own weapon to kill the man who had shot one of the captains in the 9th Kentucky. "[J]ust as I had loaded & was raising my gun to fire I fell from a bullit [sic] which struck me just over the heart. I felt sure it had gone clear through me & it flashed through my mind that I would live until the arterial blood started back to my heart, when I would drop dead,..... I felt my breast to learn the extent of my wound when I found one piece of the bullit laying against my skin inside my clothes just over my heart. The ball had passed through the stock of my gun, split on the iron ramrod of my gun, and the other piece had passed through my jacket & burried itself in a little testament in my jacket pocket. The force of the blow knocked me down but nothing more serious had befallen me."

Cannon projectiles had to be the most frightening "near misses" of all. After the bloody fight at Spotsylvania, Charles Barber penned a letter to his wife and children telling them of his good fortune, claiming he was well "except a slight wound on my hip.... [O]ur whole line was ordered to charge on the rebel breastworks[, and] we had advanced about two rods when a cannon ball brushed my left hip and knocked me full ten feet against a pine tree.... I fainted away twice."

One of the last actions of the Civil War was at Bentonville, North Carolina, on March 19, 1865. Sergeant Clark, 63rd Georgia, was hit by a musket ball in his cartridge box "which had been drawn to the front of my body for convenience in loading as well as for protection...." Clark gave an involuntary grunt, which alerted his comrades to believe he was hurt. But in fact the ball, "passing through the leather and tin had struck the leaden end of a cartridge and being in that way deflected had passed out the right side of the box instead of through my body."

Stories of the antics of Minie balls are endless. For instance, in the space of just a few days during the desperate fighting for Atlanta, a bullet "singed" the mustache of Lieutenant Robert M. Collins of Texas; another struck the forehead of Colonel H.R. Feild, 1st Tennessee "at the edge of the hair and ranged over the skull," knocking him unconscious. Nearby, Sergeant Slasher, 74th Ohio had a bullet graze his back leaving a red streak, but no blood, and Captain Isaac Rogers, 27th Alabama "had four holes Shot through my clothes and one through my cap...." Weeks later, in August, Corporal Erastus Winters, 50th Ohio, watched as a Minie hit a tree, glanced down and "thumped" his lieutenant on the head. It did no harm but to draw a few drops of blood. That same day a bullet came into the Union works, passed through three or four tents and hit his friend Henry Shepherd on the chest. Shepherd yelled and grabbed his chest, but upon removing his hand saw the flattened missile fall to the ground. It had not penetrated his clothes, but left a black and blue lump on his breast "the size of a hen's egg."

One of the most unusual of these events was described by Major James Holmes, 52nd Ohio, when a sharpshooter fired at a group of eight officers and non-commissioned offisers of his regiment. The bullet flew between two logs of the breastwork and "missed Sergeant Major Freeman's arm about three inches, Capt. Barnett's knee two inches, Lieut. James four or five inches, Col. Clancey's head one inch, Adjutant Masury's thigh six inches, grazed my boot leg, cut Lieut. Duff's pants and drawers on the calf of the leg and plunged through Capt. Sturgis' right leg, entering just below the knee in front, and passing between the two bones came out half way down toward the ankle. It was a remarkable shot. Six inches lower and to the right would have sent it through the whole row of men."

The story of Oliver Norton, 83rd Pennsylvania at Gaines's Mill, Virginia beats all odds when it comes to close calls and pure luck. With his colonel shot, and his regiment in danger of being outflanked, Norton and a few men rallied on their flag and advanced up a hill:

I returned to the fight, and our boys were dropping on all sides of me. I was blazing away at the rascals not ten rods off when a ball struck my gun just above the lower band as I was capping it, and cut it in two. The ball flew in pieces and part went by my head to the right and three pieces struck just below my left collar bone. The deepest one was not over half an inch, and stopping to open my coat I pulled them out and snatched a gun from Ames in Company H as he fell dead. Before I had fired this at all a ball clipped off a piece of the stock, and an instant after, another struck the seam of my canteen and entered my left groin. I pulled it out, and, more maddened than ever, I rushed in again. A few minutes after, another ball took six inches off the muzzle of this gun. I snatched another from a wounded man under a tree, and, as I was loading kneeling by the side of the road, a ball cut my rammer in two as I was turning it over my head. Another gun was easier got than a rammer so I threw that away and picked up a fourth one. Here in the road a buckshot struck me in the left eyebrow, making the third slight scratch I received in the action. It exceeded all I ever dreamed of, it was almost a miracle.[119]

Although trained and motivated to destroy their enemies, something they did with skill and even relished at times, Union and Confederate infantrymen did not often write about that aspect of warfare, especially to their families. Rare is the find in a diary or letter where a soldier gloats or brags about slaying an individual opponent. To many, the whole dirty business was repugnant both when it was being carried out, and later when thinking it over. More commonly found is a general portrayal of combat where "Yankees or Rebels" are destroyed as a group, such as this description by Private Roland E. Bowen, 15th Massachusetts at Antietam, who fired at both the masses and a solitary officer nearly 300 yards away. Entering the woods near the Dunker Church, Bowen and his brigade were instantly engaged by the Southern Infantry. There they saw,

...the Rebels a distance of perhaps 30 or 40 rods in strong force. We halted and at it we went. I never had a better chance at them in my life. Well, I guess the bullets flew for about 18 or 20 minits [sic] just as fast as we could get them in and out of our guns. I saw a Confederate Officer sitting on a horse up on a knoll. I thought I could fe[t]ch him off that horse, but after trying 3 or 4 times, I give it up thinking I might do better to fire at the crowd. So I don't know wither I hit any body or not.

Earlier in the war, Private Bowen mentioned an encounter with an enemy soldier in a more personal way. The act occurred at Ball's Bluff, Virginia on October 21, 1861 and was recorded in a letter to a friend which was nearly 40 pages long. For content it is one of the finest Civil War battle accounts in print. Late in the action, the 15th regiment was ordered to "fall back a little," and Roland Bowen wrote:

Before we fell back I could see the Devils guns stick up all along behind the ridge. We were within 5 rods of each other [88 feet]. One of them came up so that I could see his breast. He had neither gun nor sword, but had his hat in his hand which he waived and seemed to say, hold. Yes I did hold. On to the trigger of my gun so tight that it went off and down he went. Now I don't pretend to say I know I killed him, but that I had a fair shot at 5 rods and did shoot. There is hardly a man in our Regmt but what knows he killed One and thinks 2 or 3 which, of course is not true. Don't know as I wounded a Secesh during the whole day.

A splendid example of a soldier showing delight in the killing of an enemy is in the diary of Samuel T. Foster of the 24th Texas. Speaking of the Federal troops at Missionary Ridge on November 25, 1863, he said:

They reform and come again—and just to see them blue coats fall is glorious. We can see them dropping all along their lines, sometimes great gaps are made, they can't stand it, and away they go to find shelter from our bullets.

In a little while a fresh set comes. They have a flag. I told my men to go in for that flag and down it came, another one picks it up and down he went, then another—until away they all go leaving three dead in trying to carry that flag. They got in nearly 100 yds of us before they broke—and there are a great many dead men left on the ground, and wounded ones crying for help—One man is helping another to get away and they are both shot down together. Now the fun of all this is that we are behind these logs and are not getting hurt one particle....

Here they come again for about the sixth time.... Now we give them fits. See how they do fall, like leaves in the fall of the year. Still they advance, and still we shoot them down—and still they come. Oh this is fun to lie here and shoot them down and we not get hurt....

This is business, we can see what we are doing here, when we kill a man we know it, we see him fall.

Unlike Foster's happiness at what clearly amounted to murder, John Green recalled one of his experiences on the fighting line with a grim, determined attitude. At one point during the battles for Atlanta he remembered it was, "now sullen give & take. The enemy however were lying down & fired only when one of our men loaded & rose to fire & if our man was not killed he took the best aim; indeed we were now placing our guns against the man we fired at,...."

Sam Watkins, 1st Tennessee, held back very little when he composed his memoirs in 1882. During a discussion of the crushing, maddened fighting at the "Dead Angle" near Kennesaw Mountain on June 27, 1864, Watkins admonished:

I have heard men say that if they ever killed a Yankee during the war they were not aware of it. I am satisfied that on this memorable day, every man in our regiment killed from one score to four score, yea, five score men. I mean from twenty to one hundred each. All that was necessary was to load and shoot.... The ground was piled up with one solid mass of dead and wounded Yankees. I learned afterwards from the burying squad that in some places they were piled up like cord wood, twelve deep.

In Watkins' version of that day's events, every other battle he had seen paled into insignificance:

The sun beaming down on our uncovered heads, the thermometer being one hundred and ten degrees in the shade, and a solid line of blazing fire right from the muzzles of the Yankee guns being poured right into our very faces, singeing our hair and clothes, the hot blood of our dead and wounded spurting on us, the blinding smoke and shifting atmosphere filling our eyes and mouths, and the awful concussion [of the cannons and exploding shells] causing the blood to gush out of our eyes and ears, and above all, the roar of battle, made it a perfect pandemonium. Afterward I heard a soldier express himself by saying that he thought "Hell had broke loose in Georgia, sure enough."

On a lighter note was the experience of Perry Mayo. In the fight for Jackson, Mississippi in July 1863, Mayo was in a charge into the enemy rifle pits where he said there was no time to fix bayonets, "so we took the but[t]s of our muskets and made a clean sweep, killing two, wounding four, and taking two prisoners. Here I shot my first man that I am sure of. When we came up I saw one of them making good time for safe quarters and fired. The shot went through his right ankle. When we came up I asked him if he wanted any water. He said his canteen was full and remarked that I made a 'd___d good line shot but a little too low for comfort.'"

Infantrymen normally directed fire toward the far off hazy figure of a person and hoped their aim was true. Such was the case with Private Stanard Harley of an Arkansas regiment who once saw an enemy color-bearer in the distance. Harley was posed safely behind a large hickory tree and the man was within his range:

> I brought my gun down, and as I lowered it I noticed that I had my sights raised to 200 yards, so I lowered my gun correspondingly and fired, and he fell—whether killed or not I never knew.
>
> Elledge, who was sent out with me [on the skirmish line] and who always called me "Stanley," even though that was not my name, cried out: "There, Stanley, you got one!"

In letters he wrote from near Port Hudson, Louisiana in 1863, Private Eugene Kingman, 12th Maine Infantry, who was acknowledged as one of the bravest in the regiment accentuated Harley's words. On June 1, he told his mother: "Tell Charley that I think I knocked over one Sesech in good shape and shall do the same by another if I get a good chance." And on June 14 he confided, "I shot one Rebel I think." Later, on June 29, he wrote to his brother Charley: "I have been in another charge since I wrote you last and to all appearances I knocked over another Reb if not two. He kept showing himself and firing at us and I fired at him several times and the last time he threw up his hands and went over, pretty badly hurt anyhow and I think he has fired his last bullet."

On May 23, 1862 Henry Handerson, 9th Louisiana, took part in an engagement at Front Royal, Virginia. Writing to his father almost two months later he revealed that he was still innocent of taking a human life, which seemed important to him at the time. Looking back on that action, Handerson "rendered" that the encounter "was memorable to me [because] in it I fired my first shot at the enemy. I can, however, say safely that, if my shooting since has not improved upon my first shot, my conscience is free from every stain of blood. The only visible effect was a slight acceleration of a gait already headlong. In Yankee parlance my man 'skedaddled.'"[120]

Infantrymen often found themselves face to face with an enemy. Such close encounters were rare, usually sudden, and almost certainly not calculated. Veteran soldiers dreaded such man to man personal encounters. They were sharp, vicious and deadly. As Lieutenant Henry Dwight, 20th Ohio corrected:

> We hear a great deal about hand to hand fighting. Gallant though it would be, and extremely pleasant to the sensation newspapers to have it to record, yet, unfortunately for gatherers of items, it is of very rare occurrence.... When men can kill one another at 600 yards they generally would prefer to do it at that distance than to come down to two paces....
>
> This war is not one between mere military machines as soldiers are in Europe, but of rational, thinking beings, fighting with the highest of motives.... When such men are thrown in deadly personal contact with each other the strife is deadly indeed.

Hand to hand combat made a lasting impression on Confederate Major Robert Stiles at Sayler's Creek, Virginia on April 6, 1865. He testified that the battle "degenerated into a butchery and a confused meleé of brutal personal conflicts."

> I saw numbers of men kill each other with bayonets and the butts of muskets, and even bite each others' throats and ears and noses, rolling on the ground like wild beasts. I

saw one of my officers and a Federal officer fighting with swords over the battalion colors,...each having his left hand upon the staff. I could not get to them, but my man was a very athletic, powerful [person], and soon I saw the Federal officer fall....

I could not let myself degenerate into a mere fighting brute or devil, because the lives of these poor fellows were, in some sense, in my hand, though there was nothing I could do just then to shield or save them. Suddenly, by one of those inexplicable shiftings which take place on a battle-field, the fighting around me almost entirely ceased, and whereas the moment before the whole environment seemed to be crowded with the enemy, there were now few or none of them on the spot,...

The quickness with which these close combats began and ended was underscored by John Green at Stones River:

Their line wavered; the command came to us, "Charge bayonetts! Forward march!" We rushed fo[r]ward, their line broke & we pressed them hard; here & there some gallant man in blue half hidden behind a tree or rock would stubbornly hold his position & fire at us.

One man raised his gun to fire at Jim Burba running towards him while placing a cap on his gun. Jim called to him, "Surrender or I'll kill you!" The fearless hearted Yankee heard his threat with scorn & fired point blank at Jim; by some mysterious intervention he missed him, though not ten feet from him. Jim at once executed his threat & sent that poor fellow beyond all cares of the world.

Amidst the slaughter near Spotsylvania Court House, Lieutenant Charles Denoon calculated that on May 12, 1864, "[w]e were charging the Yankees all day. Our Regt. took three stands of colours and about 300 prisoners. We had a rough roll and a terrible fight at one time. I got hold of a Yankee's musket while he was trying to shoot me and whacked him over the head with my sword until [he] cried out for quarter. The Yankees fought to the last."

Private William E. Bevens, 1st Arkansas, recalled a charge made by four of his comrades toward a Union trench line containing about 100 enemy riflemen on July 22, 1864. Finding they were alone the four Southerners still kept going:

It was death anyway so they ran forward firing on the troops with terrible accuracy. One man had a bead on [George] Thomas when [Jim] Murphy shot the fellow. One hinged for Murphy when Thomas bayoneted him. So they had it—hand to hand. Poor [Jim] Hensley was killed, Murphy terribly wounded, [John] Baird wounded, but Thomas would not surrender. He bayoneted them until they took his gun, then he kicked and bit until they finally killed him there. Four men had killed 25 Yankees, but only one of the four lived to tell the tale. To question the morale of such men is farcical.

On the same day at another point on the Federal front, General Pat Cleburne's Texans made an attack on the U.S. held trenches. A Yankee eyewitness conceded that "[m]any of the enemy reached our line; some got across it; many were bayoneted, many killed with clubbed muskets; hand to hand conflicts were frequent. But not one inch did [we] give way. The boys obeyed [General Thomas] Logan's well-remembered command to them at Champion Hill—'Give them the cold steel! Give them hell!'" In the same campaign, Lieutenant Dwight saw a man almost dismembered during a pitched hand to hand fight:

[It was a]...free-for-all, the rebs pulling his feet to take him prisoner, and our boys pulling his head to save him. Men were bayoneted, knocked down with butts of muskets and even fists were used in default of better weapons in that deadly strife.

Officers used their dress swords.... A rebel colonel, who had laid hold of the colors of the 20th Ohio Regiment, was bayoneted by the color-guard.... Men begged for more cartridges as they would for bread and made every one count, as the horrible sight in the ditch testified the next morning.

At Utoy Creek, Georgia, a private in the 14th Ohio Infantry confessed that his brigade became a bit uncontrollable in the midst of an attack over rough ground and on into the Rebel line:

If our boys were half crazy before, they were frantic now, and as we got out of the entanglement of the brush we raised a fearful yell and ran at the works. We climbed the sides, fired right down into the defenders and then began with the bayonet and sword. For a few minutes it was simply awful. On both sides men acted like infuriated devils. They dashed each others' brains out with clubbed muskets; bayonets were driven into men's bodies up to the muzzle of the gun; officers ran their swords through their opponents; and revolvers, after being emptied into the faces of the rebels, were thrown with desperate force into the ranks.

There was at least one comical moment in all of this. Lieutenant Frank Fleck had been a butcher before the war. During the frey, Fleck, described as a "stout German, threw down his sword and rushed among the rebels with his bare fists, knocking down a swath of them. He yelled to the first rebel he met, 'Py Gott, I've no patience mit you!' and knocked him sprawling. He caught hold of a rebel officer and snatched him back over the works by main strength. Wonderful to say, he escaped unhurt but the boys will probably not soon let him hear the last of 'Py Gott, I've no patience mit you!'"

This same private related that in this particular fight two of the regiments who opposed each other were the U.S. 10th Kentucky and the 9th Kentucky, a Confederate unit. Said he: "The commanders of the two regiments were brothers-in-law, and the men relatives, friends, acquaintances and schoolmates. They hated each other accordingly, and the fight between them was more bitter, if possible, than anywhere else on the line."[121]

Infantrymen were frequently injured or even killed as a result of their own companions' weapons, through carelessness, excitement, or confusion. Today the term for this tragic situation is ironically called "friendly fire." While in the engagements known as the Second Bull Run Campaign in August 1862, Captain James G. Rodgers, 12th Georgia, both boasted and complained to his wife Lucretia in a letter dated August 31 about his experience with self-inflicted casualties: "We have had hard, continuous fighting for five days and have whipped the Yankees every time—last night completely routed the whole army.... I have been in every fight and got not a scratch, except a few holes through my clothes.... We had balls flying around us like hail and, worst of all, we were fired into by two brigades of our own.... Our regiment lost seventy five killed and wounded."

During the attack on Fort Fisher, North Carolina in January 1865, Union naval guns destroyed some of their own forces on the night of the 15th, as mentioned by Hermon Clarke, 117th New York in a letter to his father:

The fight was no doubt the closest and longest of the war. It was hand-to-hand for nearly six hours....

The fire of our gunboats [which supported the infantry] after dark killed more of our men than the enemy. We had gained ground and they couldn't see where our advance was. Just before the surrender [of the fort] I was with Capt. [David] Magill when a piece of one of our own shells took off his left leg. It seemed too bad after leading the Regt. so nearly through the fight to be so badly wounded by our own fire.

Near Cheat Mountain, Virginia very early in the war the 12th Georgia was shot into by their own friends in the 1st Georgia and retaliated, inflicting several casualties. The event occurred at night on difficult terrain. Sergeant Walter Clark of the 1st remembered that his regiment charged the 12th Georgia up a road with both sides firing until the frightful discovery was made that the regiments were on the same side. Soon order was restored; but the result of that collision was three men killed and a number wounded. Clark noted with some relief that one of his own companions named Hitt had "drawn a bead...on my anatomy, and was in the act of firing when Col. Ed Johnson,...[commander of the 12th] road directly between us and possibly saved him the horror of having killed a comrade and messmate."

Sergeant Charles Leuschner, 6th Texas, recorded in his diary on May 27, 1864 that at New Hope Church, Georgia during an evening battle, three Texas regiments ran forward into the Union lines and became "so mixt [sic] up that they could not tell wich [sic] was a rebel or wich was the Yankey's." Leuschner said that the men resorted to calling out "what Regiment do you belong to" in order to correctly identify an opponent. He wrote in his own quaint spelling: "We coud not see that affel sceine. It was to dark in front of our line that night, but next morning evry body opent his ey's with astonishment. We have bin in many a battle it is true, but never dit we see such a sight before as it was before our ey's then."

The "Orphan Brigade" suffered a few of these injuries at Jonesborough, Georgia. After being captured by the Federals, several Confederates of the 9th Kentucky were hurried to the rear of the Yankee line. In doing so they came under Southern artillery fire. Private Green finished the scene:

Our batteries which were directed against the enemy were now bursting shells in the midst of our men who were prisoners as well as amidst our captors. One shell which burst right amongst us almost tore Ed Hagan's arm off. He cried out, "They got me that time instead of getting a Yank." The blood spirted over all of us showing that an artery was ruptured. Booker Reed & I took a hankerchief,...tied it around the arm above the wound, took a little stick &...twisted the hankerchief tight until we stopped the flow of blood & Booker helped Ed back to the Yankee hospital....

One of the most singular of these cases on record concerns what happened to several soldiers as a result of the carelessness of their superiors at Fort DeRussy, near Marksville, Louisiana, one night in March, 1864. This Confederate fort on Red River had been captured two days earlier, but on the evening of the 16th the men bivouacked around the fortifications after having worked all day to destroy the strong earthworks. Between 9 and 11 p.m. someone under General Smith's orders blew up the fort's magazines which were full of powder, shot, and percussion shells. "Dirt, timbers, shells, and other debris rained down from the sky during the indescribable explosion," injuring several men. A few minutes later two captured iron cannons were detonated. Heavy chunks of the guns flew in every direction, killing Lieutenant Jerome Bishop, 81st Illinois, and another man in the 95th Illinois. Several more men were wounded as well. An eyewitness said he "handled the piece of cannon [that crushed the skulls of the two dead men] soon afterwards with the brains still on it. Capt. Young was spattered with the brains, and in that condition went to Gen. A.J. Smith, to show the commander his work."

A recovered piece of one of the 6-pounder iron cannons destroyed at Ft. DeRussy, which accidentally killed two men. (GAC)

One of the most commonplace of these misfortunes during the war was mentioned by Austin Stearns. It was 1861 and it involved "...the first man of the Regiment hit by a bullet." A soldier of Company K, 13th Massachusetts, was selected to deliver a change in some orders to members of Company D, who were on duty at a picket post atop a mountain near Harpers Ferry:

> He started up the path that ran direct to their post. It was almost dark when he started, and quite dark when he reached there. He went along, expecting every minute to be challenged by "Who comes there?" Instead, he received a volley from their guns and fell, severly wounded.... He lingered about two years, dying from the effect of the wound. No one ever knew which of the four shots [from the picket guard] hit him, and nothing was ever done about it.

Bugler Theodore Birmingham, 23rd Michigan in a gruesome diary entry for December, 1863 at Knoxville, Tennessee, talks of the attack made by the Confederates Fort Sanders on November 29:

> The ditch around this fort is about eight feet deep.... When the Rebs charged they stumbled and fell headlong into the ditch. Some broke their necks and others broke their backs, others fell into their comrades, piercing them with their bayonets. And as soon as this was done our men from inside the fort lit shells and threw them over into the ditch, which cut them down like grass before the scythe.... The slaughter was terrible.... Some say that they lay 15 men deep in some parts of the ditch.

"Purposeful friendly fire" was not particularly uncommon. If soldiers showed cowardice or attempted to "go over," and desert to the enemy, former friends could become very anxious to shorten their lives. G.N. Galloway witnessed just such an event on May 12, 1864 as a "party of twenty or thirty" Confederates attempted to come across into Yankee lines and surrender: "Springing upon the breastworks in a body, they stood for an instant panic-stricken at the Terrible array before them; that momentary delay was the signal for their destruction. While we...shouted to them to jump, their troops, massed in the rear, poured a volley into them, killing or wounding all but a few, who dropped with the rest and crawled in...."[122]

Hermon Clarke, 117th New York, described an atrocity of war after an engagement near Petersburg, Virginia in June 1864. Along with other troops, his brigade was ordered to capture some Rebel works which they accomplished "with the bayonet and [it] didn't last long." After the Confederate earthwork was secured and the prisoners collected, Clarke saw some black soldiers who had assisted in the action come over to his regiment and attempt to kill the Southern captives. "I didn't see but one killed," noted Clarke, "he was a fine looking fellow. A great bushy Nigger came up to him, knocked him down, and ran his bayonet through his heart. Our boys turned on the Niggers and kept them back."

Retaliatory measures such as this were commonplace. For example, at the capture of Fort Pillow, Tennessee on April 12, 1864, the command of General N.B. Forrest had murdered some white and black soldiers after the fort had capitulated. Not long afterward during the Battle of Resaca, Georgia, a private named Strong in the 105th Illinois was among the units which took a Confederate battery there. A Rebel cannoneer crawled out from under a cannon and begged for quarter. Strong described him as a big red-headed man, bare-chested with a tattoo on his arm proclaiming "Fort Pillow." "As soon as the boys saw the letters on his arm," said Strong, "they yelled, 'No quarter for you!' and a dozen bayonets went into him and a dozen bullets were shot into him. I shall never forget his look of fear."

Contempt for the enemy is evident in this letter by W.B. Whitcomb of the 82nd Indiana to his sisters on April 17, 1864 from near Ringgold, Georgia. According to Whitcomb "[The Rebels] are mean enough to do anything. The way they used our dead and wounded at Chickamauga was enough to convince me of that fact. Instead of burying the dead, they would take the clothes off from them and stand them up in the side of the road for people to look at. You may think this to be a hard yarn but I know men that saw them and those that I would believe too. When we had driven them back from Mission Ridge, I saw a Yankee's skull stuck up on a stake."

A Confederate named James K. Lewis who fought at First Bull Run with the 16th North Carolina Infantry, C.S.A., claimed in a letter home that he was sadly disappointed in his own army:

> They are well drilled but they are the infernalist set of rascals I ever saw.... I was on the battleground a day or so ago and it presents one of the most horrible sights I ever saw. The dead Yankees who were buried there have nearly all been dug up by our men. Nearly all of them have a bone of some sort hung to his watch chain & they have sent home any number of skulls! Some of them took the rib bones for pipe stems.... I put no confidence in men who won't let their enemies bones rest in their graves. Whoever wars with the dead won't do for the battlefield.

One who would have relished the thought of desecrating the bones of his mortal enemies, if only for a brief moment, was Douglas J. Cater, 19th Louisiana. He found his brother's body on the battlefield of Chickamauga, in September 1864:

> Continuing my search I met my old friend Jack Franks who had found Brother Rufus' body and was looking for me. He led the way and soon I was beside the lifeless form of my dear brother. His blanket which he had folded in the morning and carried over his shoulder [before the battle]...had been unfolded and he was lying on it, cold in death. His watch, his purse, the shoes from his feet, his sword and scabbard had all been taken. His pants pockets were turned wrong side out, and the devils in human form, not yet satisfied, had fired a rifle ball through his forehead. The ball which caused him to fall in the charge had passed through his breast and out at his back through the folds of his blanket, but not near his heart. He might had gotten well of this wound, but the ball through his forehead was sufficient evidence that he was murdered while a prisoner on the battlefield.

In every single regiment in every field army there were men who perfunctorily robbed the dead and wounded bodies that littered Civil War battlefields. Any soldier who kept a diary, wrote letters to his folks and friends back home, or composed a memoir after the war, sooner or later mentioned the work of these ghouls and corpse robbers. The men who practiced this macabre art were not always bad soldiers. Some like John Casler were regular infantrymen who felt, and logically too, that it was merely plunder and they had a right to it as much as anyone else:

> Now, I am not a moralist, nor capable of moralizing, except in a crude way; but my moral training caused me to abhor the idea of taking anything from a dead body,...and I was greatly shocked when I first learned that such things were done. But why try to conceal what is well known by all soldiers of both armies....
>
> It was difficult for a soldier to figure out why a gold watch or money in the pocket of a dead soldier, who had been trying to kill him all day, did not belong to the man who found it as much as it did to anyone else.

Ironically, shortly after making that statement, Casler and a friend were burying an enemy corpse, and his comrade found $40 on the dead body. Even though he refused to go through the pockets himself, Casler argued that his companion should share the money. Afterward, admitted Casler, "[I] searched everyone I helped to bury, but found nothing but a few pocket-knives."

Another of General Jackson's men, John H. Worsham, had no compulsion about searching the dead for valuables. After the Battle of the Wilderness he returned to the corpse of a Federal officer and "removed his sword, and then felt in his pockets to see what he had. I found a knife, a pipe, and a piece of string. In every pocket—even the one in his shirt, he had smoking tobacco." And Captain Sam Foster happily penned in his diary on July 23, 1864 after an engagement: "Our men are getting boots hats &c watches knives &c off of the dead Yanks near us in the woods—lots of them.... We cook and eat, talk and laugh with the enemy's dead lying all about us as though they were so many logs."

In a similar situation, but without the "glee" imbued by Foster, a Union soldier confessed he had "desecrated" the dead to find some little comfort for himself. After the Battle of Gettysburg, Thomas Moon was exhausted and the rain had been falling hard and long: "I happened to be sargent of the gard on duty that night...and we had nothing to guard except a few dead men that we managed to gett off of the field [our lieutenant] among the rest. I slept on top of [his body] all night as it kept me out of the water as it rained all night."

One of the "atrocities" most often claimed by both sides during the war, was the idea that once the enemy was overrun or had surrendered, he had better not attempt to take any further offensive action. Wilbur Fisk explained that once after the 5th Wisconsin had captured a Confederate fort, some of the enemy kept their positions and refused to surrender, even after the Yankees were inside the fortifications:

> One rebel boldly bared his breast and told our men to shoot him, he would never surrender. Perhaps he hardly expected to be taken at his word, but he was; a dozen bullets pierced him at once. Another rebel was seen loading his gun, after our men had charged by him. You G_d d____d son of a B___h, said a sergeant,...I'll learn you to shoot our men after you are within our lines, and he clubbed his gun which he had no time to reload, and placed him hors du combat on the spot, without ceremony.

One of the most horrible pictures of human cruelty was witnessed by Robert Stiles in 1862. After one action Stiles spotted a wounded Federal prisoner shot through the bowels,

...who was rolling on the ground in excruciating agony and beseeching the bystanders to put him out of his misery.... I was in the act of turning away from the painful spectacle when a couple of...Louisiana tigers...came up and peered over the shoulders of the circle of onlookers.

Suddenly one of them pushed through the ring, saying: "Put you out of your misery? Certainly, sir!" and before anyone had time to interfere, or even the faintest idea of his intention, brained the man with the butt of his musket; and the bloody club still in his hands, looking around upon the other wounded men, added glibly, "Any other gentleman here'd like to be accommodated?"[123]

Death was a common occurrence even to civilians in 19th Century America. No one could escape its presence. But for the ultimate face of death, the Civil War period was awash in it. Death by disease was more widespread but less noticeable or forceful. To the Confederate and Union infantrymen who fought the thousands of battles, actions, skirmishes, and engagements, death on the battlefield was the one scene the senses could never forget. The crushing futility of war and the uncertainty of death at any moment was summarized by Abner Small:

At first it shocked him immeasurably that his old life should have become a far-away, indistinct thing of memory....

There was something singularly shocking to him in the stiff disorder of the dead lying where they fell; in torn clothing; in the waxy arm yet hugging a gun. Some men lay as if asleep, with a smile of peace and contentment on their faces. Others showed the lingering agony of their death, their very attitude one of protest and unreconciliation. Never before had our soldier been brought so near to the unseen, the unknown, and now it was always surrounding him, and possibly for months and years to come there

A halt in line of battle amid the debris of battle. (BL)

would be endless repetitions of these horrors which stirred him to the depths. Yet the time came, and soon, when he was indifferent to the sight of thousands dead.

He resented it all, and at times his resentment grew into a hatred for those who forced the whirlpool of war—a whirlpool that had so soon engulfed him. He hated his surroundings and all that war implied; it was drudgery, it was cruelty; yet he forced himself to resist whatever was inimical to the interests of a hated service. If he had at times any longing to lay down his arms, he carefully concealed it. [And] [a]llways in front of him was the enemy,...

A scene which would have affected even the most hardened veteran was described by Robert Stiles. It concerned two brothers, Judson and Carey Smith of the 21st Mississippi. During the Battle of Savage Station, Virginia, Carey the youngest, was mortally wounded:

Judson Smith went almost deranged; Yes, I think altogether deranged. He bore his dead brother out of the woods [where he had died].... He kept the body folded to his bosom, and all through the night his comrades heard Judson kissing Carey and talking to him and petting him, and then sobbing as if his heart would break. Next morning he consented to have his brother's body sent to Richmond.... When the regiment moved he kissed Carey again and again, and then left him, following the column all day alone, allowing no one to comfort him or even speak to him. So that night he lay down alone, not accepting the proffered sympathy and ministrations of his friends, and resumed his solitary march in the morning.

That was [the Battle of] Malvern Hill day, and when the regiment, on its first charge, stopped ascending that fearful slope of death and turned back, Jud. Smith did not stop. He went right on, never returned and was never heard of again.

This story has an even more pathetic ending. Living in Mississippi was the father of the boys, who was then an old man. Hearing of the loss of his two sons he joined the army as a private soldier. At the fight near Iuka, Mississippi, he "did just as his eldest son had done at Malvern Hill, which was the last ever seen or heard of him, and the family became extinct."

An even more tragic event tore apart a family during one of the assaults against Port Hudson on July 14, 1863. There the color-bearer of the 91st New York, Private Samuel Townsend, a Southerner by birth, attempted to plant the national flag he carried upon the Confederate parapet. While struggling to accomplish this act he was shot down by a 49th Alabama defender, who recognized too late he had just killed his own brother. Almost as morose was this scene indicated by Theodore Upson while on the "March to the Sea" in Georgia. "We went down on the line where lay the dead of the Confederates [after a sharp skirmish]. It was a terrible sight. Some one was groaning. We moved a few bodies, and there was a boy with a broken arm and leg—just a boy 14 years old; and beside him, cold in death, lay his Father, two Brothers, and an Uncle. It was a harvest of death."

Battlefields were cruel, grotesque places, with death and agony present in all its ghastly forms. Infantrymen vividly remembered these heartless and melancholy scenes and many recorded them. Robert Stiles, after the fight at Savage Station, crossed over a section of the ground and saw a place where the bodies of the dead had been carried out of the woods and laid in rows for burial. "Almost every man struck," he said, had been "shot through the brain...[their] eyes wide-staring. A sickly summer rain had fallen in the night and the faces of the dead were bleached with more than death's pallor. Every eyeball was strained upward toward the spot where the bullet had crashed through the skull, and every forehead stained with ooze and trickle of blood."

After the First Battle of Bull Run, Edmund Patterson, 9th Alabama, forced himself to walk over the field, even though the smell of the blood made him sick. He was amazed at the sights of horror that he had only read about before:

Here are mangled human bodies on every side, some pierced by a rifle or a musket ball— others almost torn to fragments by shell—.... Some have a look or expression on their face as mild and calm as if they were only sleeping, others seem to have had a terrible struggle with the monster death and only yielded after having suffered such pain as has caused their faces to assume expressions that are fearful to look upon, their features distorted, their eyeballs glaring, and often with their hands full of mud and grass that they have clutched in their last agony. I noticed one who had striven vainly to staunch the flow of blood from a wound through the body by stuffing mud into the wound.

Corpses often excited notice and comment. Leander Stillwell, 61st Illinois, remembered two unusual bodies on the field of Shiloh, and said that the contrast between the pair was remarkable:

One was a full grown man, seemingly about thirty years of age, with sandy, reddish hair, and a scrubby head and mustache of the same color. He had been firing from behind a tree, had exposed his head, and had been struck square in the forehead by a musketball, killed instantly, and dropped at the foot of the tree in a heap. He was in the act of biting a cartridge when struck, his teeth were still fastened on the paper extremity, while his right hand clutched the bullet end. His teeth were long and snaggy, and

Collecting remains of dead on the battlefield after the war. (USAMHI)

discolored by tobacco juice.... His eyes were wide open and gleaming with Satanic fury. His transition from life to death had been immediate, with the result that there was indelibly stamped on his face all the furious rage and lust of battle. He was an ill-looking fellow, and all in all was not an agreeable object to contemplate. The other was a far different case.... He was a mere boy, not over eighteen, with regular features, light brown hair, blue eyes, and, generally speaking, was strikingly handsome. He had been struck on his right leg, above the knee, about mid-way the thigh, by a cannonball, which had cut off the limb, except a small strip of skin. He was lying on his back, at full length, his right arm straight up in the air, rigid as a stake, and his fist tightly clinched. His eyes were wide open, but their expression was calm and natural. The shock and the loss of blood doubtless brought death to his relief in a short time. As I stood looking at this unfortunate boy, I thought of how some poor mother's heart would be well-nigh broken when she heard of the sad, untimely fate of her darling son.

On the Shiloh battleground lay several more corpses which caught the eye of John Green of Kentucky:

Many a mother's darling lay stark & cold. I shall never forget the face of a young Lieut from Louisiana with smoothe face & the bluest blue eyes, as he lay with his revolver in his right hand, a most peaceful smile on his face & a great big Yankee laying across him cold in death with his musket still firmly grasped in his hand. The Yankees gun was empty & the Lieutenants pistol had two empty chambers. The Lieutenant had a death wound made by a musket ball & the other man had two pistol ball holes clear through him; neither face had any expression of pain or anger.... I dont know but what we should have put them both to sleep in the same grave, but we did not.

The strange positions of the dead fascinated many infantrymen. In July 1862, Virginian John Casler described one of these macabre sights:

While on this skirmish I saw a man in a kneeling position, as if in the act of firing; but upon closer examination he did not appear to have any gun. As no one was firing just then I thought strange of his position; but as I went up to him I found him dead. He had been killed the day before, and so suddenly that he remained in the same position as when living—one knee and one foot on the ground, his arms in position of taking aim, but the gun had fallen and his head was thrown a little back.

Color-sergeant Daniel Crotty visited a battlefield on May 6, 1862 and found:

Horrid sights meet the eye everywhere. The dead are in all possible shapes, some on their backs with their eyes wide open, others on their faces, others on their sides, and others in a sitting posture leaning against some brush or tree. One dead rebel I never shall forget. He was in a ditch leaning on his elbows the face turned up the very picture of despair and fright. He holds his right hand pointing up ready, as it were, to grasp at something. His head and face are swollen to an unnatural size, and is of a dirty, greenish hue, positively the worst sight of a rebel I ever saw, and I am sure that a good many of my comrades will remember the same. Our regiment file by, and each one turns his head with loathing at the horrid sight.

One of the most bizarre images imaginable was seen on the field of Seven Pines by W.L. Goss, along with "men suspended in the positions in which they had been shot" while in the act of climbing over a fence. Nearing Fair Oaks, Virginia, Goss visited a swamp where some of the enemy had been killed while attempting a crossing. They were found still standing in the mud and had "decomposed so rapidly that the flesh had partly dropped from the bones."

Portrayed as "the worst looking sight I ever saw," was a Union soldier's body that had fallen in an attack at Port Hudson, Louisiana on June 14, 1863. Isaac Blake of the 12th Maine was called over by a comrade to view the dead man. The deceased had toppled onto a bag of cotton near the Rebel earthworks and the cotton had caught fire. "All that was left of the carcass," said Blake, "was the back part of the body and bones of the head. The limbs were entirely consumed. It was a horrid sight, enough to appall even a soldier."

The seemingly heartless Captain Foster of the 24th Texas once met a scene that may have affected him. On May 28, 1864, he had just passed over a part of the battlefield at New Hope Church, Georgia, near a place where 703 dead had been collected for burial. Foster recalled that those killed:

[M]eet the eye in every direction, and in one place I stopped and counted 50 dead men in a circle of 30 feet of me. Men lying in all sorts of shapes just as they had fallen, and it seems like they have nearly all been shot in the head. A great number of them have their skulls bursted open and their brains running out, quite a number that way.

I have seen many dead men,...but I never saw anything before that made me sick like looking at the brains of these men did. I do believe that if a soldier could be made to faint that I would have fainted if I had not passed on and got out of that place as soon as I did.

Two months later and a little closer to Atlanta, Major James Connolly, 123rd Illinois, experienced a similar scene when he crossed the battlefield of Ezra Church:

I was over the ground next morning, and the dead lay just where they had fallen, festering and decomposing in the hot July sun. I rode over a space about 400 yards long by about 75 yards in width, and in that area scanned the faces of 225 dead rebels, and then had seen [no] more than one third of those who lay there, but that number satisfied my appetite for blood, and I returned feeling very thankful that I was not a rebel and especially a dead rebel. Colonels, lieutenant colonels, majors, captains, lieutenants and privates lay mingled together on that field of blood, all reduced to the same rank.... Poor fellows! They fought manfully, like Americans, and I honor them for their valor, even though they fought for a bad cause.

William Whitcomb, 26th Indiana, documented the brutality of the Stone's River battleground in Tennessee, in a letter to his brother on January 12, 1863:

We came through the battlefield where the last charge was made. The dead had not been picked up yet. You had better believe it was a hard looking sight, men lying in the mud, torn to pieces by musket and cannon ball. I don't see how civilized people can perform in such a way but I see they do, and don't know how much longer they will keep it up. I saw many a poor fellow with his head entirely torn from his shoulders, others with their faces all shot away. Some with their bodies torn and mangled in a thousand pieces by the booming cannon.

After the Battle at Cedar Mountain, Virginia, Charles Barber underscored just how quickly dead men and animals began to decompose and become truly foul: "[W]e marched the whole length of the late battle field it was an awful sight[.] some of the men was only half buried[.] the stench was awful[.] none of the horses was buried and bushels of maggots was on them. the feet and legs of dead men was sticking out of their graves they was not buried deep enough."

The color of the dead often intrigued sightseers who chanced to examine a recent field of battle. Austin C. Stearns, the 13th Massachusetts sergeant, and a friend named Henry Gassett, described one encounter:

> [We]...stole over to view the field, [of Cedar Mountain] for we had great curiosity to see how a battlefield would look. Details of men were there burying the dead; in the centre of one field was a long trench filled with Union dead; in a stubble field we saw several bodies that were still unburied. At first I thought them Colored, they were so black and swollen [sic], and I woundered how Negros should be wearing the blue coat of a soldier, but I soon discovered my mistake; the stench of the bodies were fearful.

Private Marshall Dye, 121st New York, reported something curious when he viewed corpses during the Antietam Campaign. "One thing I cannot account for is that the Rebs after being killed, will turn black and smell bad in six hours, while our men will remain fresh for at least 24 hours."

To some infantrymen, especially those who were superstitious, it was unsettling to visit or pass across an old battlefield where the dead had been quickly and incompletely buried, and where the scenes of strife were still apparent. While visiting his brother in the vicinity of the Chickamauga battlefield, a battle which had been fought eight months before, Theodore Upson decided to take a short cut through the area to return to his regiment. It was night and he rode under a full moon:

> When I reached it I could see by the broken Artillery wheels, fallen limbs of trees, scattered remnants of arms and caissons that I was on the ground where a short time before two great Armies had met in a death grapple. Thousands of dead hastily buried were around me. The winter rains had in many places washed off part of the thin covering, and arms and legs protruded from the ground. It was a ghastly, ghostly sight, and I should not have been surprised if I had seen ghostly forms around me, but nothing disturbed the stillness of the night but the hoot of an owl or the distant firing at Dalton miles away....

While in bivouac near Falling Waters, Maryland around the middle of July 1863, Lieutenant Galwey's company took time to do some foraging for much needed supplies. Galwey reminisced:

> Late in the night a party consisting of some men of my company and some others of the regiment returned to camp with cider, whiskey, chickens, and other plunder. They had been almost to Sharpsburg and told with a superstitious horror of a luminous haze [the gas from the graves of thousands of decomposing bodies] which they said overhung the field of Antietam. All concurred in saying that but for the terror which this strange misty light had caused them they would have brought back more that was good to eat and drink.

A 10th Indiana Volunteer Sergeant Samuel McIlvaine had occasion to see parts of the old Shiloh battleground a few weeks after the fight. For a newly enlisted soldier, this "baptism" was quite unsettling:

> As we passed out today, a short distance from our camp, [at Pittsburgh Landing] I witnessed a sight I had little thought of ever seeing even on a battlefield. Seeing little mounds of earth scattered through the woods, I approached one and observed a bit of cloth or blanket lying on one end of a pile of dirt. One of my comrades directed me to raise it up. To my horror it disclosed a man's skull, the skin had decomposed and slipped off and his hair lay around his half uncovered skull on the dirt as the rain had

beat or washed it down. Another one's head and face I saw projecting from the slight covering of earth. A third one's whole breast was exposed, and in which the worms were working a speedy destruction. They had just been laid upon the ground upon their blankets...and [a] little dirt was thrown over them. They were of the enemy.... My feelings were much shocked....

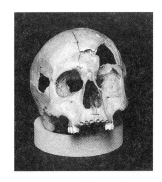

This skull, with bullet hole, was found on the Wilderness battlefield. (NMHM)

Texan Val Giles, spent some uncomfortable hours with a friend on the field of Second Manassas, tending to the sad duty of hunting for lost comrades: "I will not record here any of the horrors that came under my observation as John Wheeler and I, hand in hand, groped our way over that dark and bloody field. I still see those dark forms and pale faces, those dim and flickering lights as they moved slowly over the grounds in the hands of anxious soldiers as they looked for lost friends and brothers."[124]

When Major Stiles wrote that "for months and years to come there would be endless repetitions of these horrors which stirred him to the depths," or when Val Giles admitted that "I still see those dark forms and pale faces...," their deeper meaning can be appreciated. From a time when people knew little about psychology and rarely spoke in public about the intense mental anguish they had experienced in war, little evidence exists in the written record on this important subject. Only now and then does a sentence or two break the silence, allowing for a glimpse into the darker world of the mind of the Civil War infantryman. The trials they long endured made constant and unpleasant memories of their experiences a logical fact of life. After one particularly hard fought engagement Sam Watkins knew that to forget such images would be virtually impossible:

> When the Yankees fell back and the firing ceased, I never saw so many broken down and exhausted men in my life. I was sick as a horse, and as wet with blood and sweat as I could be, and many of our men were vomiting with excessive fatigue, over-exhaustion, and sunstroke; our tongues were parched and cracked for water, and our faces blackened with powder and smoke, and our dead and wounded were piled indiscriminately in the trenches. There was not a single man in the company who was not wounded, or had holes shot through his hat and clothing.

In a strange confession showing the subtleties of this dilemma, Lieutenant Ralsa Rice, 125th Ohio, described the changes that had occurred physically to his men: "We were not yet aware that our physical condition had underwent that change as to make us barbarious, a class to be feared—dreaded—by the peace-loving citizen at home; that those stains of battle and the wild life in camp would beget lawlessness, and make of us a dangerous element to turn loose in society." One wonders if he was speaking for the mind as well as the body?

Dreams and nightmares are common to almost every combat soldier. Take the illustration of three officers who met in a conference to discuss the plan prior to making an assault on a portion of the Confederate lines in Georgia on June 27, 1864. While sitting there, Lieutenant Colonel Allen Fahnestock, 86th Illinois, and two other regimental officers compared the dreams they had had the night before, all containing visions of fighting, death, and wounds. Fahnestock dreamed of a terrible battle; Colonel O.F. Harmon had the same type of morbid night vision and Captain Charles Fellows had dreamed his left foot was cut off by a cannon ball; all indicative of intense emotional distress. Harmon and Fellows did not survive the charge.

This continuous stress eventually caused some men to go literally "crazy" as in the case of a soldier who, during a desperate fight picked up a bucket and calmly walked openly over to the Rebel fortifications. According to Colonel Fahnestock, he had gone insane. After being discharged and while recovering from the hardships of military life, William Keesy was nursed back to health by his mother. In the process which took six months, he said he "often dreamed of tented camp, the weary march and gory field. Oh, how natural the musket rattle or cannon roar would be to my weakened brain in my dreamy flighty slumbers." Similarly Mississippi Private William Chambers wrote during the Siege of Vicksburg:

> None save those who were there will ever fully comprehend our experience during those monotonous days. There was an unrest, a fever of the mind, intensified by the pangs of hunger that utterly baffles my poor powers of description and makes the whole seem unreal. Was it any wonder that the heart grew callous as to the things of eternity. And yet I did not feel condemned in the sight of God, and in order to turn away His wrath I strove to lead a better life. I read the New Testament a great Deal, but its gracious promises were not for me and the condemnation still remained.

In a letter home in July 1864, Indiana Private A.W. Brown spoke simply: "I am troubled considerable with dreams...." But Lieutenant James M. Williams, 21st Alabama, who professed the same problem, gave better detail to his wife Elizabeth: "I've had great and exciting times at night with my dreams since the battle; [of Shiloh] some of them are tragedies and frighten me more than ever the fight did when I was wide awake."

The recurring visions and mental anguish caused by so much physical abuse due to bad food, severe weather conditions, constant marching, plus the death and mutilation of comrades, the horrors of the battlefield and its burials, also disease, and grim, bloody, pain-filled field hospitals, took a heavy toll on many infantrymen. These scars followed veterans to their peaceful homes at war's end, and even to their graves. In his last diary entry on June 15, 1865, 6th Texas Lieutenant Charles A. Leuschner conceded this after almost four years of wartime service:

> I expectat [sic] to be happy, [now that he was home] and I was for a little while; but it is not so now, my heart has a whegd [wedge] thrown upon it wich cannot so easily be taken off. It pains me. I may forget it a minute or two, but it will come in my mind again; I try all in the world to be happy and others that see me think so, but there is something that works in me which I dare not to explain.... When I am in presence of Ladie's, I forget for a little while; but while I am speaking my troubles come into my mind, where at other times I would have killed myself a laughing. I could not now make a laughing [sound?] if I was to try my hartest.[125]

The battlegrounds of the Civil War were a constant reminder of how unstable and unpredictable life could be. But to the historian, the oddities, humor, and unusual scenes enacted on these fields which are often described by the participants, present a wealth of interesting and useful information to be located and catalogued. In their writings, infantrymen recorded for posterity many out-of-the-ordinary circumstances and events.

In the 4th Texas at Chickamauga, Captain Bob Bassett of Company G was struck by a huge piece of red oak tree which was split by a shell, causing permanent injury and discharge; he later died from the effects of that freak occurrence. The body of Captain Peter Schneider, 52nd Ohio, was found after the Battle of Peachtree Creek, Georgia, with a revolver in his hand with one chamber empty. "A rebel major lay dead within a few feet of him. The hole in the major's head, was made by a .32 caliber, the same as the captain's revolver, and the major's bullet had struck the captain in the temple."

During the continuous skirmishes which went on during the long, murderous Atlanta Campaign, someone was killed or wounded almost every minute. Soldiers on the line would then raise a ramrod tied with a piece of white cloth up onto the breastworks, and call out, "Cease firing on this pit!" That area would thus become a "no-fire zone" until the litter bearers would come by and recover the injured or dead man. Then the shooting would begin again. Both sides constantly honored these informal truces, but only on particular parts of the field.

Once after a narrow miss by four shells which exploded over or around him as his men lay prone on the ground, Major James Holmes, 52nd Ohio, stood up with arms folded and gazed at the Rebel battery which had sent over the projectiles, "without a feeling of fear" until they slackened their fire. "What possessed me to do it I cannot tell..." said the major. And lying between the battle lines, a wounded captain of the 90th Pennsylvania, George Watson, was caught in the crossfire between Union and Confederate sharpshooters on May 5, 1864. Seeing a "Johnny Reb" behind a tree whose position was drawing a heavy and dangerous fire toward the spot where the captain and several other companions were sequestered, Watson called out to him to kindly "change his position." The Reb, "responded with a hearty assent, and I was gratified to see him take another tree to the right."

During the Gettysburg Campaign Colonel Alfred Belo, "in showing the character of the men who were serving as privates in the Southern army," made interesting remarks about the 11th Mississippi, a regiment which had a large number of black servants in the ranks. These slaves usually foraged food for their masters, among other duties, but on one occasion when Belo saw the 11th drawn up in line, "their servants all fell in behind the regiment in their regular place...," a most unusual and unmilitary sight indeed. And at the Battle of Cold Harbor on June 2, 1864 Colonel Belo told of another curious incident. One of his men was killed by a cannon ball. They laid the body on the bank of the earthwork on its back. Shortly afterwards "a ball came from the other direction and turned him on his face."

The feeling of self-preservation beats strong in the human breast, and infantrymen would go far to protect their lives. Lieutenant Albert A. Pope, after Antietam, purchased a set of iron "breastplates" or body armour. On November 2, 1862 he wrote in his diary: "When we started [on the march] I put on my armour and all my equipment over it. Besides that I had two blankets and an overcoat strapped upon my back, and all pressing on the armour, hurt and tired me so much, that after I had marched half the distance I was obliged to take the armour off, and carry it in my hands." Eventually Pope threw away the heavy iron breastplates and took his chances like everyone else.

The 19th Louisiana was present in the siege lines around Jackson, Mississippi in July 1863, with Private Douglas Cater among them. A piano was found by one of the Confederates in an abandoned house owned by the Cooper family near their position. Carried to the breastworks, it was used by members of a nearby artillery unit, commanded by Captain Slocumb. Cater, who could play, was sent for, and amid the sound of the shells and Minie balls banged away for awhile until the Federals made an attack on their front. Cater recalled, "After the firing ceased I went back to the piano and we had more music." After the war, Mr. Cooper gave the piano to the ex-members of Slocumb's Battery.

At the Battle of Arkansas Post on January 11, 1863 Captain S.T. Foster commented on the destruction caused by Yankee shells, including this heartbreaking drama:

> The next [shell] goes nearly in the same place in that company, [of the 24th Texas] killing one man and cutting off both legs of his brother. The one that has his legs shot off turned his body about half way to speak to his brother, not knowing he was dead. As soon as he saw his brother was dead, he takes his pistol (a 6 shooter) puts it to his head and killed himself ——

In the confusion of battle, infantrymen sometimes made mistakes in loading and firing their weapons. Often the ball was put in before the powder, or the percussion cap was forgotten, or even the ramrod was not removed from the barrel before the discharge of the piece. The latter happened quite often, sometimes with weird consequences. Near the "bloody angle" at Spotsylvania, a soldier wrote that on May 12, 1864, "Major William Ellis, of the 49th New York,... was shot through the arm and body with a ramrod...." Ellis died three months later as a result of this bizarre wound.

Battle and disease losses in some regiments were terrific. After Antietam, the 13th Massachusetts was reduced to so few men that a corporal was in charge of the regiment for some time. Austin Stearns specified that for a while the corporal signed all the regimental papers as simply, "Corp. Jones," and then sent them up to brigade headquarters. Brigade commander Colonel Richard Coulter, seeing these documents so frequently, once remarked: "Who in hell is this Corp. Jones that I hear so much about." Stearns noted that Jones "did not remain long in command, for another commissioned officer was soon appointed."

The Siege of Petersburg was a long, drawn out and deadly affair that lasted for many months. Danger was everywhere, as millions of bullets and thousands of shells were thrown back and forth between the Union and Confederate lines. For one officer this daily warfare must have become almost routine, as mentioned by Albert Pope: "This evening [December 20, 1864] a rebel bullet struck Lieut. White's cabin, next to mine. He very cooly called out. 'Come in, you needn't stop to knock.' It hit one of the logs in the center, or would probably have come through."

General Edward McCook reported an outlandish attack on the enemy by "undressed" Federal troops, July 9, 1864 at the Chattahoochee River in Georgia:

> I had ordered a detachment to cross at Cochran's Ford. It was deep, and [Colonel Brownlow] took them over naked, nothing but guns, cartridge-boxes and hats. They drove the enemy out of their rifle-pits, captured a non-commissioned officer and 3 men, and the two boats on the other side. They would have got more, but the rebels had the advantage in running through the bushes with clothes on. It was certainly one of the funniest sights of the war, and a very successful raid for naked men to make.

At the Battle of Franklin, Tennessee, many Union troops were captured as they tried to get to their reserve positions after losing their first defensive lines. Some had close calls and narrow escapes. One such fellow was Jake Wilt, an older volunteer in the 64th Ohio, nicknamed "Uncle Jake." William Keesy and others in the regiment thought Jake was a prisoner for sure. But soon they spied the unmistakable form and "waddle" of Jake slowly making his way back to his comrades, "puffing like a steam engine." Keesy leaped over the breastworks, greeted him, and saw that Jake was, "loaded down with a mule load of military paraphernalia. He had his camp-kettle and frying pan strung to his knapsack, canteen, haversack, gun and accouterments in as ship shape order as if just emerging from an orderly camp...."

'Why in the world, Uncle Jake, don't you throw away part of that mule load of yours, so that you can keep up? The Johnnies will get you sure, loaded this way.'

'Well, I'll tell you, Al, I handt godt anysthing more 'an wat I need.'"

Duels between individual soldiers during regular campaigns have been documented by a variety of eyewitnesses. Colonel Belo, 55th North Carolina, tells of one that he and three other officers in his own brigade fought in early May 1863. The weapons used were double-barrelled shot guns and Mississippi rifles at forty paces. Fortunately, after firing only a few shots, the contest ended when several of the parties apologized.

Sergeant Clark of the 63rd Georgia said that he knew the fate of two unknown opposing pickets who were posted on the same line during the summer of 1864 and had been taking shots at each other across the "gurgling waters of the Chattahoochee." These antagonists finally agreed on a challenge. They left the protection of their rifle pits and declared a fight to the finish. Clark continued: "Standing on either bank, in full view of each other and without protection, they loaded and fired until one was killed." The frustrations of a long and dangerous campaign had finally gotten to them.

Such was the case in the story of two mounted officers during the Battle of Fredericksburg on December 13, 1862. A Confederate from Tennessee found his regiment positioned directly across the battle lines from a New England unit. John Stevens, 5th Texas, who was stationed nearby, wrote that in the Federal regiment (both units were posted at Hamilton's Crossing about one-and-a-half miles below the town), was an officer who had attended the same school up north and was an intimate friend of the Tennesseean. They recognized each other from afar and began to taunt and menace each other until one charged toward the other and was met with a counter charge. Each was armed with a revolver and "begun circling and maneuvering, each shooting; and cursing.... This lasted for only a minute or two, but to the troops...it seemed as many hours. Finally the Confederate hit the horse of his antagonist a death shot, and then dispatched the rider. The Federal's horse—a large gray—lay there all during the winter. I saw it once every week for two months, as I went on picket duty. A member of the 7th Tennessee regiment,...told me that it was the most exciting scene one could possibly imagine, and such as he hoped would never be seen again. He said his entire command felt sympathy for the slain antagonist, but—such is Civil War."

Sharpshooting along the fortified lines around Petersburg, Virginia, was an every day, every minute affair during the siege of 1864-1865. The earthworks provided protection from most shots, but an infantryman knew never to take unnecessary chances, and to keep his head and body covered.

In the 3rd Michigan there was a brave soldier who was being discharged after three years of diligent and faithful service. His papers for home were snugly in his possession as he began to make the rounds of his old regiment, which was stationed in Fort Hell, to bid adieu. After this courtesy was completed, an eyewitness confirmed what happened next:

A thought strikes him, and he turns back and tells his comrades that he must have one more look at the Johnnies before he leaves. His comrades expostulate with him not to go near the port holes again; that now he has his discharge in his pocket and ought to be satisfied with what sights he has seen. But all to no purpose; he must have one more look, and goes to the port hole and looks through, but it is his last look on this earth, for he falls back a corpse in the arms of his weeping comrades.

While on picket securing the front of his 9th Kentucky regiment, Irishman Mike McClarey and a companion were fired on when a Yankee force began to drive in the picket line in preparation for an assault. In return the Confederates shot back, rounds flying dangerously close to the Irishman from both sides. It was December 28, 1862 and only two days prior to the battle at Stone's River, Tennessee. When the shots were exchanged, McClarey's friend was wounded. According to John Green:

[T]o bring [the injured man] home through a corn field where the stalks had not been cut down & take care of his gun at the same time was a difficult task, but with this comrade on his back Mike came swearing at us most vociferously. "Sure are you trying to kill your own men?" But his disgust was immense when upon laying his wounded friend down he discovered that a second ball had gone through his head & killed him, where upon he remarked, "I thought you said it was your leg you were shot in."

During the fighting around Chattanooga, Green's regiment was in line of battle on November 28, 1863 when the Union army made a major attack on their position. Forced to retreat, all hands fell back through an open field, crossing at a run. Green gave a humorous account of what happened next:

We had to climb a high staked & rider fence. George Granger, a fat short leged [sic] boy in Co. H who was a good deal handicapped by a big supply of sugar & hard tack which he had just gotten..., was pressed pretty hard & had a close shave when he had to climb the fence. Before he had gotten well over a mr[.] Yank fired at him but missed him. He was making his best speed across that open field when an other [sic] yank blazed away at him which helped Granger along a good deal & enabled him to increase his speed by about double. When the second yank fired & missed him he yelled at him, "Run you scoundrel of a rebel!"

Granger called back at him, "You blamed fool you, dont you see I am doing my best."

Shortly afterward, Granger was transferred to the navy.

On the night of October 28, 1863, on a hill in the Raccoon Valley near the Tennessee River, Val Giles and his 4th Texas were pushed out of their position by an assault made by a strong Union column. For a while everything was confusion as his colonel ordered a retreat, and Giles recorded it was,

...the night the boys made a pontoon bridge of Old Man Reece. When Colonel Bain gave the order to fall back the old man was the first to light out. There was a gully at the foot of the hill, not very wide, but about three feet deep. The old fellow was obeying orders, gallantly leading the whole push. Just as he got to the bottom of the hill he stumbled and fell, spanning the gully, his hands on one side and his feet on the other, bowed up like a mad tomcat. The fellow immediately behind him planted his foot squarely on the old man's back, and the next, until they crushed him down and bent him the other way. Like a flock of goats, crossing a footlog they all followed the same track. Afterward, he took pride in saying he was the last man to leave the battlefield in Racoon Valley.

There are numerous documented accounts throughout Civil War literature of friends and relatives on opposing sides meeting in the strangest situations, but usually when one or the other had become a prisoner of war. Following the Battle of Cedar Mountain a member of the 13th Massachusetts, Mike O'Loughlin of Company K told Sergeant Stearns,

> ...that he was standing looking at some rebs [prisoners] when one of them says "Hello Mike what brought you here?" and going up to them he found an old acquaintance, one he use to work with in the coal mines of Penn. Together they sat down on a log and each tried to convince the other that his side was right. After an hour of pleasant conversation they seperated and each went to his command; [the rebel] belonged to a New Orleans regiment.

The Battle of Resaca, Georgia was fought on May 14 and 15, 1864. Corporal Joseph Gaskill, 104th Ohio, recalled an amusing incident regarding his Irish colonel and that officer's "plug" horse, who was a worthless, worn out old animal, but was still used in combat. Gaskill describes the scene during the fighting of the 14th:

> Col. [James] Reilly leads the charge mounted on a plug horse and dressed in the uniform of a private soldier. The colonel does not want to lose a good horse or draw any more than his share of the enemy's fire, but he loses his cap and with his hair and galways [sideburns?] standing out like porcupine quills he reaches the enemy line with his command. The plug horse, unable to leap the works, lands with his front feet in the ditch and balks, leaving the colonel in a very uncomfortable position. He dismounts and finishes the advance on foot, for he could not coax or swear the animal out of the ditch. The boys think it was the sight of the charging Reilly that frightened the enemy out of their works.[126]

An infantry regiment advancing at Winchester. (BL)

INJURY, DEATH, AND BURIAL

We are continually surrounded by danger.

Pvt. Theodore Birmingham
23rd Michigan Infantry

Infantry service could be deadly to its participants in many ways. Disease, we know, killed many times more men than bullets or shells ever did on the battlefields of the war. But what is often discounted are the additional thousands who died in drownings, by sunstroke, in accidental shootings, those murdered by comrades, or as a result of other misfortunes. Accidents, then, accounted for a much larger number of deaths and injuries than is first supposed.

Moving troops via the antiquated rail lines of the South was always dangerous. Washington Ives recounted a train accident between Pollard, Florida and Montgomery, Alabama on August 22, 1862. At 2 a.m. the engine ran off the rails, but luckily it broke away from the cars carrying the infantrymen. The boxcar, however, left the tracks and crashed into a deep cut, causing injury to about a dozen men in the 4th Florida, including two broken legs and a skull fracture. Ives believed that if the engine had held on to the cars it "would have killed us all."

William Pitt Chambers, while serving in the 46th Mississippi, witnessed several calamities. One involved his friend Private E.A. Easterling who had laid down his musket to take a brief rest during the Battle of Port Gibson, Mississippi. When he was ready to move on he grasped the gun by the muzzle and drew it to him. According to Chambers, "The hammer struck the tree, the cap exploded and the whole charge struck his right arm, literally tearing it to fragments from the wrist to above the elbow. Never will I forget the horror-stricken face as he cried, 'Oh! Pitt, I have ruined my arm!...'" He was placed on a litter, borne to the rear and I never saw him again." In a sad finale to the story, Easterling was soon discharged, but fortune was against him. While at home he cut his knee with an ax; it became gangrenous and soon killed him. In another freak accident, Lieutenant Colonel W.E. Ross of the 39th Mississippi went to the regimental surgeon in June 1864 requesting a stimulant for his illness. William Chambers recorded: "By some mistake chloroform instead of whiskey was handed him. He swallowed the draught and fell like a dead man. An incision was made in the trachea and an air pump was inserted, by which life was preserved till the effects of the drug could be counteracted. He is still in a helpless condition, [at his home] and some express the conviction that he will never leave his bed again."

Unintentional weapon discharges were notoriously frequent and responsible for large numbers of deaths and wounds between 1861 and 1865. Will Stannard, 64th Ohio, was killed on duty in Tennessee while guarding a railroad trestle. Private Keesy wrote that Stannard was,

> ...standing with the butt of his gun on a tie and his hands on the muzzle and allowing his head to rest on his hands. In weaving around in this way the gun slipped off the tie,

130

and the hammer coming in contact with the tie in the fall, the gun was discharged. The ball tore the bone from the thick flesh of one of the thumbs and going into the head under the jaw came out at the crown of the head. It could not have done its work more thoroughly had it taken the head completely off.

Keesy came close to death himself while strolling along on a railroad line near Huntsville, Alabama in March, 1865. He explained his close call:

I was walking on the railroad here one day in a thunder storm when there came a flash of lightning, clap of thunder, ball of fire, sulphuric smoke and electric shock which came near ending my career on earth,...A guard [nearby] received a lightning stroke that welded the bayonet and every band on his gun solidly to the barrel. The hammer and [percussion] tube were welded as though they were one. A quarter of a dollar in his pocket...had a hole melted through it. Of course, the guard was killed instantly.

When the end of the war came in 1865, joyous demonstrations were common. On one occasion whiskey had been given out. The unhappy result was recorded by William Keesy:

Only three times while I was in the army did I know of whisky being issued, and that was just three times too often. This time it proved to be a serious affair. We were camped in a wood. The drunken men began firing their guns. The balls were glancing in every direction through the timber. My diary says that in this drunken spree three men were killed and fifteen were wounded in our own camp.

The 35th Massachusetts Regiment lost three dead during the week of January 15 to 19, 1863. One in particular was noted by Lieutenant A.A. Pope: "One of the men of Co. A of our regiment shot a part of his hand off this morning. He was taking his gun out of his tent to go on guard with, when it discharged itself, taking away part of his hand. He died a short time after from the effects of chloroform which the doctor gave him."

John Casler's 33rd Virginia organized a pioneer corps of 100 men in the spring of 1863. Principally mechanics, these men were capable of building roads, bridges, pontoons, and the like. Casler said one of these men was a shoemaker. One day this fellow, along with the others in the pioneer detachment, were cutting down some trees that would be in the way of the artillery. A limb from one of the trees fell, hit the ax of the shoemaker and "drove it into his leg, making a fearful wound. He was sent to the hospital and soon died."

A gun accident was chronicled by John Stevens, who agreed that "[i]t was not uncommon for similar casualties to occur—the only wonder is that they were not more frequent." This situation involved Dennis Rowe, 5th Texas, who was moving forward in line of battle near Suffolk, Virginia one day and came to a fence. In crossing over the fence he placed his gun over the rails with the breech "on the ground and his hand over the muzzle, and as he climbed over the fence his gun went off and shot him through the palm of the hand which resulted in the loss of the middle finger of his right hand."

Perry Mayo illustrated an involuntary misdeed in September 1861 near Arlington Heights, Virginia: "A couple of Company G's men [2nd Michigan] were going through with the manual of arms. One was giving orders and the other going through with the exercise (not thinking the gun was loaded), when the orders were given, ready—aim—fire. The gun was aimed at the breast of the person giving orders and the whole charge went throug[h] him killing him instantly, but such things are so common here that I hardly ever make note of them."

A 10th Alabama infantryman recorded in his 1901 memoirs that within the span of a few days, while camped near Centerville, Virginia, two men in his regiment were lost as a result of foolish accidents. The first was a lieutenant who was hit by a stray musket ball while lying on his bunk in his tent. The bullet "made a lodgment in his forehead," said B.G. McClelen, "from which he soon died without being able to speak after he was hit. I don't think it was ever found out who fired the ball. The fellow doubtless shot at a squirrel with no intention of hitting a man." Shortly afterwards, in bivouac at Cub Run, "a private soldier got the top of his head blown off by the discharge of a musket in the hands of another comrade. The two were sporting with each other in a friendly play, not knowing that the gun was loaded and the carelessness caused the life of one."

A strange and curious incident began when two privates of the 13th Massachusetts, Pat Cleary and Warren W. Day, shot an old ram near Middleburg, Virginia in March 1862 and then dressed the hindquarters. The meat was distributed throughout the camp, but it was so tough most of the men could not eat it. Eventually Cleary boiled a piece all night, and the next day ate what he could get down. During the succeeding night Cleary was taken fearfully ill. He was brought to the surgeon, and then to the brigade hospital, but to no avail. He lived but two days. His body was sent home where it lay for 15 years in a paupers' graveyard. Cleary's old friend W.W. Day took up a collection and moved the body to a fitting grave in the Day family plot. Austin Stearns called Cleary "a good soldier, [who] was Mourned by the whole company."

The early days of the war saw many infantrymen carrying weapons they would never use and would soon dispose of, such as large "bowie" knives and small personal revolvers. New recruit Samuel McIlvaine remembered how one of these basically useless instruments took the life of a member of the 10th Indiana in late March of 1862: "Another unfortunate accident happened in our camp today. One of the men in Company K of our regiment accidentally shot himself through the breast with his pistol, which fell out of his belt or pocket while stooping for something, and striking on the rock with muzzle up went off. It did not kill him immediately, but he will hardly live." And James L. Graham, 62nd Pennsylvania, was awakened during the evening of February 1, 1862 near Camp Black, Virginia by a similar situation:

Last night about this time I was sitting just where I am now writing a letter when I heard the sharp report of a revolver and just after it a groan. I jumped up and ran in when I discovered the dead body of a young friend of mine. He had taken the pistol from the holster not knowing it was loaded, commenced swinging it around when one barrel was discharged, the ball striking him on the temple and passing through the brain on a diagonal course and lodged in the skull in the back of his head. His brother, who is a lieutenant in the company, was sitting close to him at the time.

Two years later Graham wrote to his aunt about a "sad accident." One of his company, "Mike Daugherty...yesterday was halling [sic] polls to build a corderoy road [sic]. He was throwing out the load and the mules took fright, started to run. He jumped, caught the saddle mule. After running for some distance he fell, the wagon running over his right leg above the knee. It was so badly mangled up that they had to take it off up close.... Dr. Wishart...said he was afraid Mike's time in this world was short, he did not think he would live till morning." A similar misfortune occurred in the ranks of the 9th Pennsylvania at the Battle of Cedar Mountain when exploding shells landed among the ammunition and baggage wagons, creating a stampede. The teamsters were frightened and ran away, and several men were killed in the confusion as the runaway teams and heavy wagons crushed soldiers under the wheels. These men were buried where they fell beside the road.

During the winter of 1864-1865 infantrymen in the siege lines around Petersburg and Richmond suffered from the extreme temperatures. A soldier in the 117th New York, Hermon Clarke, told his father in a January 22 letter that while "we lay in our old camp before Richmond the weather was very cold. One man in [the] 3rd N.Y., the regiment next to us, froze to death on the night of the 31st [of] December."

On May 9, 1864 in an attack on some Confederate works, Captain John Tuttle claimed he received "a painful stab in my right leg from a bayonet of one of our [men] during the scramble on the charge. In the retreat I with some others...went back down the hill on the west side. Being crippled in both legs, I could not have got along very well had my retreat not been facilitated by some rebel sharpshooters in trees who made the balls sing about my ears."

With evening approaching on January 5, 1865, Lieutenant Colonel Columbus Sykes, 43rd Mississippi and two other officers bivouacked with their regiment in Itawamba County, Mississippi. Their bedding was placed under a large dead oak tree. During the night the tree's roots gave way and the oak fell and crushed all three officers. In the few minutes before he died Sykes cried out: "Oh, why should I have to die this way. If only I could have died in battle, like my brother...Oh, it is too bad, too bad. Tell my dear wife and children I loved them to the last."

One of the most unusual and bizarre accidents ever recorded was inscribed by Sam Watkins while in camp near Dalton, Georgia where a religious revival "sprang up." In the center of the meeting place an old tree had been set afire while brush was being burned in the pre-revival clean up. It had been smoking and burning for several days and according to Watkins, "nobody seemed to notice it." During the sermon given by Reverend J.G. Bolton of the 50th Tennessee, a "mourner's bench" had been placed in position for as many as ten men to kneel on as they poured out "their souls in prayer." In the middle of the service, without warning, the burning tree fell with a crash right across ten kneeling mourners, crushing them to death. Watkins chided that, "God had heard their prayers. Their souls had been carried to heaven."[127]

Whether an infantryman died from battle wounds, disease or by accident, he deserved and expected a proper burial. Overall, very few deceased soldiers received regulation military funerals during the Civil War. The great majority of corpses, however, did get some type of basic interment, simple and poor though it may have been. And lamentably, a very large percentage of these dead were placed in mass or trench graves without any identification rendered whatsoever, while hundreds got no burial at all, and were left to decompose above the ground. Battlefield interments were discussed in most memoirs, letters, and diaries. Sergeant Hamlin A. Coe of the 19th Michigan illustrated a universal thread associated with battlefield burials, i.e., that the victor of the engagement, or the army which held the ground after the contest, usually took the greater care with its own dead:

The worst sight I saw [on the field of Chickamauga] was the dead that had been buried, particularly upon the ground the rebels occupied. They buried their own men decently, putting a board and inscription at the head of each, but the Union forces they covered so slightly that their hands, feet, and their skulls are now uncovered and exposed to the open air. They burned a great many and their bones are now lying with the ashes above the ground. This I saw and examined for myself. We found one that was buried with the leaves of the forest. One whose feet and legs were unburied was actually petrified; but enough. I shall always remember the scene....

Some battlefield graves presented the viewer with memorable sights. Warren Goss took a poetic yet realistic viewpoint on the subject in May 1864 on the old Chancellorsville battleground. There he encountered "bleaching bones and grinning skulls" nestled among "weather-stained remnants of clothing, rusty gun-barrels and bayonets, tarnished brasses and equipments." "In the cavity of one of these skulls," wrote Goss, "was a nest with three speckled eggs of a field bird. In yet another was a wasp-nest. Life in embryo in the skull of death! The sting of the wasp and the song of the bird! One, as it were, defending the skull of the battle's victim; the other singing the hopeful paeans of a nation redeemed by their death."

After a battle, details from infantry regiments were called for to assist the pioneer corps in burying the corpses. Often these squads came from both sides and Union and Confederates worked together to accomplish the unpleasant task. After the Fredericksburg battle in December 1862, Lieutenant Galwey said that some soldiers from his 8th Ohio, "one man from each company" went out under a flag of truce and joined Rebels from the 16th Mississippi. When they returned that night Galwey reported that the men were "full of stories of how they had passed the day...," and all had "parted on good terms and bade one another a sincere goodbye."

One private who did not recall his grave digging chores so fondly was Robert Strong, 105th Illinois. He and the rest of his brigade were assigned this duty near Resaca, Georgia, on May 19, 1864, and he called it the most disagreeable job he had ever undertaken:

It was our first experience, and to carry men to a hole and dump them in was almost too much for me. Some had been dead for three or four days, and the flesh would not hold together to lift them. So we put them in blankets or tied the legs of their pants and their coat sleeves together and gently dragged them to their last resting place....

On one part of the battlefield the leaves had taken fire, I suppose from shells, and we found a few of the dead who had more or less burned. It is all truly horrible, and if you tell me you don't want anything more on battle scenes, why all right. But so many things come to mind, some worse than these.

When properly interred by friends or relatives, a deceased infantryman might receive a more kindly burial than most dead do today. The comrades of the soldier who had been killed prepared the remains tenderly with their own hands. Modern society simply shifts that once precious responsibility to strangers. A case in point was that of Douglas Cater who buried his brother, Rufus, on the field of Chickamauga with the help of a friend, Private Gus Hendrick who had also lost a sibling in the battle:

[We] obtained a spade and pick and he and I dug two graves, one for his brother and one for mine. It took a long time and much hard work to get these graves ready. We wrapped blankets around the bodies of our brothers and placed them in these crude graves. There were no caskets, no flowers, but there were loving hands that filled in the earth on these blanket enshrouded forms and cut their names on the rough boards, which marked "the place where they were laid." There were sad bleeding hearts and there were falling tears which helped us to bear the pains of loss and separation.

For the majority, however "[t]he burial of the dead is a very common-place business affair," said the chaplain of the 62nd Pennsylvania, J.W. McFarland, who presided at many of these simple military funerals. After the Battle of Chancellorsville he claimed that he officiated only,

> [for]...those who were brought off the field. Of these, I with three or four to assist me buried thirteen in one day in one place—eleven of our own and two of the enemy.... Spread his bloody blanket lightly over him, it is all the shroud he had. Bring some small cedar twigs and lay on those dirty rags that are to be his last pillow. There are no attendants but those who carried him here from the place a few rods distant where he died. No tears are shed here;.... For them and for ourselves we offer a brief prayer. The workmen take off their hats but keep on smoking while the prayer is said, now they cover them with their two feet of clay and the ceremony is over.

Barbarous things sometimes occurred in the burial duties. In one instance, a grave had been dug for five men, all to be laid closely side by side. One corpse was too tall for the space he had been allowed. When the grave diggers were told to lengthen the space for the taller man, an Irishman refused, and at once raised an ax and cut off the lower limbs of the body. The officiating chaplain quickly drew back his fist and knocked the Irishman into the grave. As McFarland remembered, "[a]ll this was only a momentary interruption of the burial ceremony."

Correctly marking a grave, and "mapping" its location was an important step, not only in respect for the dead comrade, but especially in the event the government or family ever returned to take up the body for reinterment. William P. Chambers took special pains to indicate the gravesite of his "messmate," Stephen Robertson, 46th Mississippi, who was killed on August 14, 1864 near Atlanta:

> He was buried as decently as possible under the circumstances. His grave is about a mile southwest of Atlanta on the farm of Mr. Jett. It is about two hundred and fifty yards south of the dwelling and is on the east side of the road. I marked the spot by putting up a durable board, with full name, company, regiment, and date of death upon it, and upon the center of the grave I placed a white stone about as large as a man's head. His brother, W.C.R., was present at the burial and Brother Lattimore made a talk....

An unusual show of respect for a friend, was described by Theodore Upson. Private Aaron Wolford, shot through the head and instantly killed on November 24, 1864, was buried near Savannah, Georgia:

> That night after the Johnnys had gone we buried our dead. We had no coffins, but I could not bear to think of putting my old friend into his grave in that way. I remembered that at a house a short distance away I had seen a gum or hollow sycamore log of about the right length and size. We got it, split it in halves, put one in the grave dug in the sandy soil, put his lifeless body in it, covered it with the other half, filled up the grave and by the light of the fire we had built with the rails, marked with a peice [sic] of lumber pencil his name, Company, and Regiment. I took his well worn Testament, his watch, his little store of money, and if I am spared shall send them to the wife who will see him no more.

In one particularly sad case, a true disservice was done to a dead enemy. Not just the usual unidentified trench burial, which both sides were forced to resort to; this was plain cruelty and meanness. Warren Goss explained that the incident happened on the Gaine's farm in 1862 right before the Battle of Seven Pines. Visiting a field hospital there, he had discovered an old friend from his college days lying wounded in the barn of that farm. The friend was a North Carolina lieutenant who had been unceasing in his criticism of the Union while under the care of the Federal medical personel. After the visit with his former acquaintance Goss left, and returned two days later only to find the lieutenant gone. Asked about the North Carolina man, the attendants replied, "That cock is done crowing." Goss asked where he had been buried and was told, "[h]e isn't buried; they carried him out!" "I stepped into the barn-yard," finished Goss, "and found him thrown upon a heap of dirt. It was impossible to express all the indignation I felt; I emphatically said that none but cowards would have been guilty of such an act.... Undoubtedly he had been very bitter, but that was no excuse. I mention this as the only instance I ever knew where a dead enemy, or even a prisoner, was insulted by our soldiers. No soldier would have committed such a foul act. It was reserved for some miserable 'skulker' who, to avoid the active duties of a soldier, had taken refuge in a hospital."

Periodically, families made attempts to recover the remains of their sons, brothers or husbands from the old battlefields and return the bones to a hometown cemetery. Captain Richard B. Wood, of Bellevue, Ohio, was killed leading a charge in a skirmish on February 24, 1864 near Buzzard's Roost, Georgia. His father, Bourdette Wood, commissioned the services of James B. Wood (who was no relation), to "invade the enemy's country" and bring back the body of the captain. "This was a serious undertaking for a country boy but 20 years of age and who had never been away from home," noted C.R. Callaghan, a friend of Bourdette Wood. "However, he successfully accomplished his work and in spite of the many dangers and obstacles, located [the] grave near Tunnel Hill, Ga., and brought the body back."

In 1867 James Archer was sent on such a quest. His mission was to go to Petersburg, Virginia and attempt to locate the grave of J. Smith Graham, 140th Pennsylvania, who had fallen in the fighting near Fort Stedman on March 25, 1865. Graham had died in a nearby U.S. hospital. The grave was dug in an "enclosure [graveyard] at Patrick's Station." The body was placed in a coffin with the feet toward a large stump. In addition to a headboard containing his name, rank, etc., a large stake was driven in next to the head of the grave, and all was recorded by a hospital steward. Even under these ideal conditions, Archer was unable to procure the remains. He accepted the kind services of a Union general officer and a medical doctor who were stationed in the vicinity, but still to no avail. Archer spent two days in the exact area, opened ten graves, which he stated was "by no means a pleasant job," and had to admit defeat in the end.

Even if a soldier's remains were located, preparing them for transportation home was a challenge. Private Hermon Clarke explained how his comrade Andrew Rowell's body was readied for such a trip. In a letter home dated November 13, 1864 near Richmond, Virginia Clarke said he had been in contact with Andrew's father, J.P. Rowell in regard to the condition of the corpse, but "didn't expect it would be embalmed; it couldn't be, it had been buried too long [since October 27]. But there is a disinfecting process which is used in such cases and we contracted for it in Andrew's. It costs more than embalming. We paid the parties for taking up the body, cleaning it properly, disinfecting it, putting it in a disinfecting case, and sending it to Utica [New York]."

In 1865 the U.S. government began a wholesale effort to find and reinter several hundred thousand Union soldiers' remains into national cemeteries. It was an enormous task, and although a large majority of these bodies have remained unidentified, at least many ended up with a better and more permanent fate. Some Confederate dead were eventually removed from field sites, but these activities were limited and mostly carried out by state or local level authorities or by private organizations. A former Rebel major, W. Roy Mason, reported:

> In 1865-66 some shrewd Yankee contractors obtained government sanction to disinter all the Federal dead on the battle-fields of Fredericksburg, Chancellorsville, the Wilderness, and Spotsylvania Court House. They were to be paid per capita. When I went out to see the skeletons [being taken up], I found the contractor provided with unpainted boxes of common pine about six feet long and twelve inches wide; but I soon saw the scoundrel was dividing the remains so as to make as much by his contract as possible.[128]

Wounded soldiers needed more immediate attention. Unlike the present day when less than one percent of wounded die of their injuries, a soldier during the Civil War had only about a 70-75% chance of surviving shell fragment or gunshot damage to the body. And if the wound was especially serious, his chances became slimmer still. So many combat casualties during the 1860s were of a horrendous nature, and the medical techniques and knowledge of the day were still quite primitive. The men who chronicled the lives of infantrymen never hesitated in describing some of these wounds, even in the most graphic language. J.W. Emerson, a member of General John Geary's Brigade, gave an unusually faithful portrayal after a battle in Virginia of the grievous type of injuries encountered on Civil War battlefields:

> At Cedar Mountain...I went out to the front.... We found about every body [corpse] stripped and black from mortification and stinking. We noticed down on the left of our regt. a man who proved to be of the 7th Ohio. He was wounded over the eyebrow and one eye [was] gouged out by the bullet. This eye had fallen out and was hanging down. This man was nearly dead and perfectly blind in the other eye from filth and swelling. He was lying against a dead man who had had his shoulder and chest blown open by shell or grape, and was maggoty and rotten. The 7th Ohio boy's head was lying in this wound of the dead man and the whole sight was one of the most revolting I saw during the war.

On the Chickamauga battlefield shortly after that terrible contest of arms, Washington Ives of the Florida Brigade saw "a wounded Yankee[,] an Irishman with his back broken and laying on his face, he begged us not to touch him and we built him a little fire (for it was a freezing cold night) and covering him up[.] when we left him he was praying for his mother." Simon B. Hulbert inscribed in a homebound letter a very different sort of injury to a fellow soldier in the 100th New York on Morris Island, South Carolina: "One man, Bernard Smith, which we supposed was dead, has turned up. He was wounded in the head, [on July 18] went to Beaufort & now is with the Co., but has a hole in his forehead. The Bullet would have killed him if he had not stood with his side to the enemy. It struck him right between the eyes & on the forehead."

Pvt. Jefferson Coates, 7th Wisconsin, who was blinded by a bullet at Gettysburg. He is wearing the Medal of Honor he won there. (GNMP)

During the September 1, 1864 fight at Jonesborough near Atlanta, Johnny Green watched two Federal colorbearers who had crossed over into the Confederate trenches and were battling hand to hand with the Rebels there. He saw both bayonetted to death. At that moment, a comrade by the name of Fourqueran cried out, "Oh I am killed! what shall I do?" Green looked at him and "he was sitting down in the trenches trying to pull a bullit [sic] out of his forehead. I said, 'Fourquin (for that is what we called him) I will pull it out & you then run to the rear & go to the hospital.'"

"Just then he got it out & said, 'Never mind now, I have it out.'"

Another peculiar wound was not soon forgotten by Robert Stiles. His brother, nicknamed "Skipper," was shot square in the left temple near Cold Harbor, Virginia in June 1864. His companions immediately bent over him, thinking him dead, when Skipper raised his head and made a request: "If you fellows will stand back and give me some air, I'll get up!" Stiles is quoted as saying, "[w]hich he not only did, but walked out to the hospital camp, refusing a litter. He also refused to take chloroform, and directed the surgeons in exploring the track of the ball, which had crushed up his temple and the under half of the socket of his eye, and lodged somewhere in behind his nose. After they had extracted the ball and a great deal of crushed bone, he declared there was something else in his head which must come out. The surgeons told him it was more crushed bone which would come away of itself after awhile; but he insisted it was something that did not belong there, and that they must take it away immediately. They remonstrated, but he would not be satisfied, and finally they probed further and drew out a piece of his hat brim, cut just the width of the ball and jammed like a wad into his head; after that he was much easier. I omitted to say we never found his hat, either." According to the major, after several months, Skipper made a "wonderful recovery."

Near Kernstown, Virginia, just south of Winchester, on March 23, 1862 General Jackson and General Shields met in a sharp clash. John Casler, 33rd Virginia, admitted that the Confederates under "Stonewall" lost the battle, and "darkness was all that saved us." He also documented the wounding of one of his company:

Mart Miller was shot in the back of the neck as we were running down a hill, and the bullet came out in front, near his windpipe; but he kept on running, when a spent ball struck him in his overcoat collar and lodged there. He turned a complete somersault, and we all thought he was dead; but he said he was all right, and was helped up and escaped. He was sent to the hospital, but came back to the company in about six weeks, perfectly well and ready for duty.

Lieutenant Thomas Galwey was wounded by a shell splinter in the calf during May 1864 near Spotsylvania, Virginia. Assisted to an aid station, he lay down near John Quinn of his company. According to the lieutenant, Quinn had a particularly nasty injury and Galwey rendered him all the assistance in his power. "I called to a surgeon of the Irish Brigade who was passing and induced him to care for his compatriot. Quinn's bowels were hanging out, and the surgeon, having pushed them in with his hand, set a handful of lint against the big hole and tied a big bandage around his body. He told me there was no hope for Quinn, but seeing a First Division ambulance, [we] put him in it. I was sure that Quinn would die enroute [to the field hospital]."

Describing his wound in almost surreal terms is Sergeant James Cooper, 20th Tennessee, who was shot "in the middle of the throat by a Minie ball which passed through his neck and emerged on the right rear side narrowly missing the spinal cord and jugular vein." Cooper was then in action near Resaca, Georgia on the 14th of May, 1864:

I was sitting down, closely wedged in by my companions on every side, [behind the fortifications] for the position was very exposed, when all at once I felt a terrible shock and with a sinking consciousness of dying, became insensible. In an instant I recovered my senses, and found myself with my head fallen forward on my breast, and without power to move a muscle. I could hear the blood from my wound pattering on

the ground, and thinking I was dying, almost thought I saw eternity opening before me. I felt so weak, so powerless, that I did not know whether I was dead or not.

The noise of the battle seemed miles away, and my thoughts were all pent up in my own breast. My system was paralyzed, but my mind was terribly active. My head was full of a buzzing din, and the sound of that blood falling on the ground seemed louder than a cataract. I finally recovered the use of my tongue and still thinking I was dying, told the boys that it was no use doing anything for me, that I was a dead man. All the time I could hear remarks around me, which although very complimentary, were not at all consoling. When first shot one man exclaimed, "By God they killed a good one that time," another "My God! Cooper's killed!" and several others equal to these.

His captain quickly ordered a man who sat nearby to try to stop the blood by "catching hold of the wound." This remedy succeeded and in about half an hour Sergeant Cooper was able to walk to the

Pvt. Rowland Ward, 4th New York Heavy Artillery, was hit by a shell fragment.
(NMHM)

rear to an ambulance one half mile away. After reaching the field hospital he went to Atlanta where he recovered and rejoined the 20th in early July. This was his second wound in less than six months.[129]

Within the "military machine" which operated during and after a battle, a wounded infantryman went through certain steps after the bullet or fragment tore through his flesh. The first action was to leave the firing line quickly, for as Major Holmes asserted, the soldier "is not afraid to die, but after being disabled in the fight he wants to live; [therefore]...you know how eager the wounded man is to get off the field without being killed,...."

If the injured soldier could walk, he made his way to a regimental surgeon at an aid or dressing station close to the scene of action, usually a few hundred yards behind the regiment in a sheltered location. When unable to move on his own, the wounded party waited for the assistance of comrades or a litter team. The stretcher bearers then carried the man to an ambulance collecting area where these conveyances completed the process by hauling the soldier to a field hospital. No operations were performed at aid stations; the surgeons who "operated" plied their trade in less exposed locations one to three miles to the rear of the fighting lines, usually in a village, near a group of farm buildings, out in the open, or shaded by a grove of trees. The men were cared for in these field hospitals (called brigade, division, or corps hospitals) until they could be transported to permanent general hospitals in large towns or cities.

Ambulance rides had to be unforgettable experiences, and memories of them were all bad. During the aftermath of one of the Seven Days' Battles near Richmond, a newspaper reporter described the trip he took in an ambulance trying to get to the rear with six severely shot up men through twenty miles of hilly, woody countryside. The journey, he reiterated, "was like Dante's excursion into the Shades.... The wounded occupants [were]...compelled to ride for hours...their screams frightened the hooting owls and put to silence the whirring insects in the leaves and tree tops...in the awful stillness of the dark pines...."

Michigan Lieutenant A. B. Isham vividly recalled his injury and the harrowing transport after having received a gunshot wound on May 14, 1863 near Warrenton Junction, Virginia. The first sensation of the bullet, he explained, is "not one of pain. The feeling is simply one of shock, without discomfort, accompanied by a peculiar tingling, as though a slight electric current was playing about the site of injury. Quickly [there] ensues a marked sense of numbness, involving a considerable area around the wounded part." Isham, in mentally revisiting the scene of that awful day, said that several soldiers (one with a spinal injury) along with himself were placed in the ambulance on blankets spread over the floor:

> The vehicle was the old style, with high flexible springs, and the road was a corduroy of the roughest variety, tree trunks and saplings being arranged together haphazard, without any regard to evenness. Nowhere had dirt been thrown over the timber. The jolt that resulted from the rebound of the springs when the wheels rolled off a large log to a sapling, or vice versa, threw the invalids half way to the top of the ambulance. Sometimes one was thrown higher than the other, and in falling down again landed on top of his fellow, so that they were falling and sprawling all over each other. The agony of such a ride to one wounded in the hip, unable to move a muscle without pain,...may be imagined. It beggers an adequate portrayal by the pen.

The driver was implored by those within the ambulance to shoot them through the head, or to drop them by the wayside to die of starvation and exposure, rather than to bounce them to death upon a corduroy road.... Prayers, imprecatious shrieks, curses, filled the air until finally unconsciousness supervened, and the rest of the journey was blotted out.

Another account taken from the diary of New York Captain A.C. Brown on May 10, 1864 explained that both ambulances and army wagons,

...with two tiers of flooring, [and] loaded with wounded and drawn by four and six mule teams, pass along the plank, or, rather corduroy road to Fredericksburg, the teamsters lashing their teams to keep up with the train, and the wounded screaming with pain as the wagons go jolting over the corduroy. Many of the wounds are full of maggots. I saw one man with an arm off at the shoulder, with maggots half an inch long crawling in the sloughing flesh and several poor fellows were holding stumps of legs and arms straight up in the air so as to ease the pain the rough road and the heartless drivers subjected them to.

In the ambulances, or on foot, the infantryman eventually reached the field hospital, places, according to Captain Brown, that "climaxed the horrors of war:"

Passing along a little in the rear of the lines,...I came upon a field hospital....,

Under three large "tent flies," the center one the largest of all, stood three heavy wooden tables around which were grouped a number of surgeons and their assistants, the former bare-headed and clad in long linen dusters reaching nearly to the ground, which were covered with blood from top to bottom and had the arms cut off or rolled to the shoulders. The stretcher-bearers deposited their ghastly freight side by side in a winrow on the ground in front of the table under the first tent fly. Here a number of assistants took charge of the poor fellows, and as some of them lifted a man on to the first table others moved up the winrow so that no time nor space should be lost. Then some of the surgeons administered an anaesthetic to the groaning and writhing patient, exposed his wound and passed him to the center table. There the surgeons who were operating made a hasty examination and determined what was to be done and did it, and more often than not, in a very few moments an arm or a leg or some other portion of the subject's anatomy was flung out upon a pile of similar fragments behind the hospital, which was then more than six feet wide and three feet high, and what remained of the man was passed to the third table, where other surgeons finished the bandaging, resuscitated him and posted him off with others in an ambulance. Heaven forbid that I should ever again witness such a sight!

Captain Brown's story does not do complete justice to the devastating and sometimes heartless physical reality that was a "field hospital." This unnamed reporter supplied his newspaper with an adequate description of an infantry hospital:

A dreadful opportunity occurred after the battle of Hanover Court House [May 27, 1862], to look upon wholesale massacre. The wounded of both sides had been hauled from the distant field in and around some old Virginian dwellings. All the cow-houses, wagon-sheds, hay-barracks, hen-coups, negro cabins, and barns had been turned into hospitals. The floors were littered with cornshucks and fodder, and the maimed, gashed, and dying lay confusedly together.... In the first of these, an amputation was being performed, and at the door lay a little heap of human limbs. I shall not soon forget the bare-armed surgeons, with bloody instruments, who leaned over the rigid and insensible figure, while the comrades of the subject looked on horror-struck at the scene. The grating of the murderous saw drove me into the open air, but in the second hospital which I visited a wounded man had just expired, and I encountered his body at the threshold. The lanterns hanging around the room within streamed fitfully upon the red eyes and half-naked figures. All were looking up, and saying in a pleading monotone: "Is that you, doctor?" Men, with their arms in slings, went restlessly up and down, smarting with fever. Those who were wounded in the lower extremities, body, or head, lay upon their backs, tossing even in sleep. They listened peevishly to the wind whistling through the chinks of the barn; they followed one with their rolling eyes; they turned away from the lantern glare, which seemed to sear them.

Soldiers sat by the severely wounded, laving their sores with water. In many wounds the balls still remained, and the flesh was swollen and discolored. There were some who had been shot in the bowels, and now and then these poor fellows were frightfully convulsed, breaking into shrieks and shouts, some of them iterated a single word, as "Doctor!" or "Help!" or "God!" or "Oh!" commencing with a loud spasmodic cry, and continuing the same word till it died away in sighs. The act of calling seemed to lull the pain.... I think still, with a shudder, of the faces of those who were told mercifully that they could not live—the unutterable agony; the plea for somebody on whom to call; the longing eyes that poured out prayers; the looking on mortal as if its resources were infinite; the fearful looking to the immortal, as if it were so far off, so implacable, that the dying appeal would be in vain; the open lips through which one could almost look at the quaking heart below; the ghastliness of brow, and tangled hair; the closing pangs—the awful rest at last!

Within an hour or two he visited another hospital where over thirty Federals lay crowded together on a floor—pale, helpless, hollow-eyed men who were making low moans at every breath:

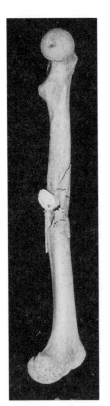

Two or three were feverishly sleeping, and as the flies revelled upon their gashes, they stirred uneasily, and moved their hands to and fro. By the flatness of the covering over the extremities, I could see that several had only stumps of legs. They had lost the sweet enjoyment of walking afield, and were but fragments of men, to limp forever through a painful life. Such wrecks of power I never beheld. Broad, brawny, buoyant, a few hours ago, the nervous shock and the loss of blood attendant upon amputation had well nigh drained them to the last drop. Their faces were as white as the tidy ceiling; they were whining like babes; and only their rolling eyes distinguished them from mutilated corpses....

The most touching of all these scenes was presented in the stable or barn on the premises, where a bare, dingy floor...was strewn with suffering people. Just at the entrance sat a boy, totally blind, both eyes having been torn out by a Minie ball. He crouched against the gable in darkness and agony, tremulously fingering his knees. Near at hand sat another, who had been shot through the middle of the forehead, but, singular to relate, he still lived, though lunatic, and evidently beyond hope. Death had drawn blue and yellow circles beneath his eyes, and he incomprehensibly wagged his head. Two men, perfectly naked, lay in the middle of the place, wounded in bowels and loins....

Femur of Pvt. John Drake, 57th Pennsylvania, shows the Minie ball which shattered it in 1863. (NMHM)

At the railway nearby were some injured Confederates, which invoked this response:

> [T]he rain began to fall at this time, and the poor fellows shut their eyes to avoid the pelting of the drops. There was no shelter for them within a mile, and the mud absolutely reached halfway up their bodies. Nearly one-third had suffered amputation above the knee. There were about thirty at this spot;... Some of them were fine, athletic, vigorous fellows, and attention was called to one who had been married only three days before.

There was a method to the madness of this confusing situation, or so said Lieutenant Galwey who was himself wounded near Spotsylvania in May, 1864:

> After having my leg dressed I was able to look about me. We were some miles from the battle but of course could very plainly hear both the artillery and musketry. There was one noise which seemed to be one continuous sound: The tearing of linen for bandages. The hospital was a vast assemblage of wall-tents or marquees, laid out in sections for the various corps, divisions, and brigades. Men were more or less attended by their own surgeons, and kept in the company of their comrades, thus being more easily identifiable in case of death.
>
> Certain tents here and there were reserved for operations. In them were performed the amputations and most of the probing for balls and shell fragments. Next to our tent was one for operations and, as the walls of the tents were raised three or four feet high for better circulation of air, we could see and of course hear the operations. Still, the surgical business had become something of an old story.

Many infantryman, like Galwey, had recollections of their own wounds, and how they were treated by the constantly overworked doctors. Yankee born Louisiana vol-

A group of Federal officers pose with their "stumps" in view. (NMHM)

143

unteer, Henry Handerson, hit by a musket ball in a retreat of his regiment at Fredericksburg, Virginia in May 1863, initially did not know he was struck. "I had run scarcely more than twenty steps when a dull blow upon my right shoulder knocked me over.... Rising hastily, I shook myself to see if I was all there, and finding nothing apparently materially wrong, I...continued my retreat, but at a slower pace." Lieutenant Handerson stopped to help a wounded comrade as he moved to where his disorganized unit was trying to rally. Within minutes he felt his right arm become stiff and numb, and suspected it was only a spent ball that had caused the problem. But within minutes a fellow officer broke the news that there "was a ragged hole in the shoulder of my coat and advised me to seek the field hospital." After some difficulty Handerson found the hospital in an old dilapidated barn about one-half mile from the field of battle:

> The ball had struck me on the back of the large muscles of the neck and shoulder, penetrated the strap of my haversack, and, ranging inward and forward, had lodged in the right side of my neck close upon the carotid artery. Half an inch further would have inevitably ended my military career! Lying down upon the rough operating table, Surg. Love speedily extracted the ball through a small incision, and sewing up the wound, directed me to dress it and the opening in the shoulder with cold water.

Shortly afterward, the lieutenant was removed to an officers' hospital which occupied a lot on Main Street in Richmond. His wound healed rapidly and within ten days was almost closed. But on one occasion after going to bed Handerson awoke with a sudden start:

> ...[I] involuntarily thrust my hand to my neck. With horror and affright I felt the blood spurting forth in a stream, and found the bed quite soaked with the crimson fluid. Hastily calling to my comrade, who at once turned up the [gaslight] I discovered a small stream, about the size of a knitting needle, spurting out for a foot from my wound, and the house surgeon, who was immediately summoned, found some little difficulty in checking the hemorrhage from a small artery which had opened in the line of the incision made for the extraction of the ball. However, by the simple application of ice he finally succeeded and the wound thereafter never gave me any serious trouble. It was six weeks,...before I ...[returned] to my command.

Sergeant Chambers also received a shoulder injury, but the ball was not the first to hit him at Allatoona, Georgia in October 1864. The first shot penetrated his cartridge box, where the leather and tins saved him from a hip wound, as the bullet went only part way through the box. Next, part of a finger was cut off, then finally a missile bore its way into the shoulder. After the third injury, Chambers lay behind the dead body of a friend who had been struck in the head—the body acting as a shield: "I could hear and feel the [enemy's] balls as they struck the corpse."

As time elapsed, a lull in the firing enabled Chambers to run to the rear, where he reached the brigade surgeon's post. The doctor there ordered him on to the division hospital to have the bullet removed. After grave suffering intermingled with several fainting spells he made his way to an ambulance collection point. For a while he traveled by ambulance, but soon discovered a horse and rode it until nightfall. Delirious with pain, Chambers eventually stopped at an ancient cabin and spent the night. Next morning the sergeant could barely stand. In the pouring rain, he managed to hail someone leading a Mississippi colonel's horse, rode for part of the day, and walked the balance. Still this plucky Rebel had gotten no medical aid. After six more miles, with night approaching, Chambers located a doctor who tried but could not find the ball; however, he did dress the wound for the first time. With permission obtained to head home to recuperate, the worn down sergeant walked, rode, caught a train and a steamboat, and finally reached Montgomery, Alabama, 17 days later. There a surgeon, without chloroform, cut and probed until he found the leaden missile, which was broken into two pieces. According to Chambers, "[i]t was just twenty days after being shot that the bullet was extracted." Two weeks later, in early November, 1864, he arrived home, and by December 30 was again with his regiment in the field.

Texas Captain Samuel T. Foster took a bullet in the right leg, with "the ball going cross ways under my knee, and just over the big leader," at Missionary Ridge on November 25, 1863. At first he disbelieved he was hurt:

It felt like someone had struck my leg with the side of a ramrod, or a stick and benumed [sic] it somewhat.

The boys soon rip[p]ed my pants open and there it was, bleeding very freely.—No mistake I was wounded. The litter bearers are called. I am put on a litter and two men take it up and go in a trot until they get over the hill out of the range of the bullets, where I am put in an ambulance and carried to the field hospital.

When it comes my turn I am put on a table with all the instruments close by like I was to be carved up into soup bones. The Surgeon examined my wound, run his finger in the hole—but could'nt put it clear through so he put the other finger in the other side, then he run his fingers in and out, first one then the other, until as he said there was no foreign substance left in there to hinder it from healing up. Afternight I am put in an Ambulance and carried to the R.R....

Foster was hauled to Marietta, Georgia, where he remained for two months recuperating, mostly, from a secondary infection (erysipelas) which he complained was worse than the initial injury. The limb healed but was crooked and he could walk only on the toe of the lame leg. Captain Foster returned to his regiment where he drilled himself hard all winter, forcing the leg to straighten out. He stayed with the army until the final surrender.

William A. Fletcher, a private in the 5th Texas Infantry, had seen much service in the eastern theater prior to his "meeting with a Minie" at Chickamauga in September 1863. In a memoir of his adventures, he discussed a painful treatment undertaken after contracting gangrene, a condition which affected many thousands of soldiers during the war. Gangrene is the decaying of tissue, and occurs when the flow of blood to a part of the body is obstructed by an injury or wound. When Fletcher was hit in the foot, he first thought it was only bruised, but as "I cast my eyes to my feet, I saw the leather on the left shoe torn near center on inside. I turned my foot and saw a rent on the outside near the heel. I quickly removed the shoe and found I had a bad foot wound made by a bullet." Hopping to the rear he made a temporary stop to rob a Yankee corpse. Fletcher "went through him," acquiring a good filled knapsack before continuing his journey. At this first field hospital he lay bleeding off and on through the night. In the morning the doctor seemed inclined to remove the entire foot; Fletcher refused and pushed him roughly away. This so angered the surgeon that he sent the Texan on a train to Augusta, Georgia without aid. In the earlier hospital, Private Fletcher made a thoughtful appraisal of a subject rarely talked about even now, more than 100 years later: euthanasia. Precipitating his comments was the sight of a suffering and dying soldier who was shot through the head. The brain was observed oozing out from both sides. The man, in great pain and discomfort, would rise, walk a few steps and fall, over and over again. Said Fletcher:

...I thought how brutal human custom was in this particular, and wondered if it was handed down from barbarism and why it was that [a] doctor or friend could not end one's misery, even if done with the best method at hand.... With brutes we sympathize and aid—with man we do not, for death is the only relief. I have often heard the remark: "Poor fellow; he had better ten thousand times be dead." I look upon it as cowardice in time of great need, for true friendship is he who comes in when the world goes out.

After his arrival in Augusta, Private Fletcher was quartered in a large church, his foot was dressed and a fresh bandage was applied every 24 hours. Even so, gangrene set in and the method of treatment there was to burn the wound with acid. He called it a very painful procedure:

The first three applications nearly gave me the horrors and especially the first. If I had been a drunkard I would probably have thought I at least was threatened with delirium tremens, as the worm or snaky feeling would start at the mouth of the wound and make a hurried zig-zag run up near the knee, then would return as though backing out, and running out of the wound. The relief was instantaneous when the sensation had passed out, but was repeated at short intervals for two hours for the first time, the others of less duration. By the time it was through, I was nearly exhausted. This treatment, if I remember correctly, was kept up for seven days, burning each day.

With the arrival of a new doctor in the ward, the acid bath was stopped and a warm poultice applied in its place. To the Texan, this brought "a great expression of relief and joy." In a few days the wounds had sloughed and were healing nicely. After a severe problem with a "crooked foot," Fletcher was discharged from the hospital. Unfit for infantry duty, he secured a place in the 8th Texas Cavalry and resumed his Confederate service.

During the Battle of the Wilderness on May 5, 1864, Captain George Watson, 90th Pennsylvania, was struck by a bullet which went through his right thigh, badly fracturing the bone. Unable to move, he attempted to "check by external pressure, my loss of blood." He made a tourniquet out of a handkerchief, a remedy he had learned at a medical lecture early in 1861 during his first enlistment. Shortly afterwards, he was able, with help, to obtain the straps and wooden frame of a knapsack and the stock of a gun, all in order to fashion a splint for his shattered leg.

For two days and nights the Pennsylvania captain lay on the battlefield without aid. He was robbed twice by Confederate "prowlers" but managed to hide his watch, a few dollars, and a memoranda book. Late on May 7, Watson was picked up and placed in an ambulance and "jolted over rough ground and tortured for a distance of what seemed to be near a mile." Arriving at an enemy field hospital he went through "a hasty and torturing examination" by which the surgeons concluded that the mutilated leg must come off at the thigh. "A sponge charged with ether was used, the tortuous cutting commenced before I had become unconscious." Upon waking, Watson saw around him nearly 800 wounded men, many who were dying each hour. One member of the burial detail went past Watson with his own amputated leg, "which I recognized by the boot on it, [he] carried an amputated arm in his other hand, to a pit dug near by for the burial of the pile of limbs."

From his position on the ground, Captain Watson could see many of the injured parties and "death was making sad havoc among them. Groans and shrieks prevailed, sometimes proceeding from the delirious. Many of the poor-fellows were wallowing in the black mud, soaked by the heavy downpour of rain. I can describe only the horrible as occurring at this time. During the several weeks of sojourn in these woods there was no change of the bandages first put on by the operating surgeons and with flies abounding, I will leave to the imagination the filling up of the sickening picture outlined above."

In time Watson was moved and confined in several military prisons both at Lynchburg and Richmond. By October he was paroled, sent to Annapolis, then home to Philadelphia. There he had to undergo a second operation, "which cut off a portion of my thigh and taking dead bone therefrom nearly to my hip." Watson was still living in 1891 when his memoirs were composed for the edification of the veterans of the old 90th regiment.[130]

The chances of being killed, wounded or taken prisoner in a Civil War battle were very high. For instance, the South lost about 53,000 men killed in battle, approximately 195,000 wounded, (between 21-22,000 died of wounds), and over 215,000 captured. The North's casualties came to nearly 68,000 killed, about 43,000 who died of wounds, and between 200-211,000 captured. If an infantryman was captured, his risk of death was also high, for nearly 50,000 combatants died as prisoners in Union or Confederate States military prisons.

When army positions were overrun, infantrymen became prisoners of war. First hustled to the rear, the prisoner was disarmed. The unarmed individuals were then collected into groups where each man's identity and unit was recorded. Sometimes while near the front a captive might be questioned by an army officer as to his regiment, army commander, or for other military information, however, "interrogation" as it is used in today's armed forces, was rare. From the front line collecting points the prisoners were marched farther to the rear, and during these movements were usually allowed to keep their canteens and haversacks. Most accounts of men captured in regular battles, with some exceptions, acknowledge that their treatment was normally rough but courteous. Rations were issued as soon as practicable or available.

Eventually all captives were marched to a railhead, or to a large town or city where transportation by train or boat to U.S. or C.S. military prison camps was provided. Once the infantryman reached his assigned prison he remained there until paroled or exchanged. This could happen almost immediately, as was normal in the early part of the war, or much later in his confinement; and in some instances, not until the war was terminated. While in prison, and there were well over 150 established in both the Northern and Southern states, conditions and treatment varied, but in all camps the situation was dreary, boring and uncomfortable. In many pens, however, prison life was miserable, as well as brutal, dangerous, and completely unhealthy.

"Prisoner of War" literature was extremely popular after the Civil War and literally scores of accounts exist which cover the experiences of various soldiers in captivity. Also, there are an equal number of good sources in the many diaries, memoirs, and correspondence that have been published in recent years.

MUSTER-OUT

Melt, melt away ye armies - disperse ye blue-clad soldiers, Resolve ye back again, give up for good your deadly arms....

Walt Whitman

Within the mind of each infantryman who patriotically enlisted or had been conscripted during the four year civil war, beliefs, thoughts and memories were stored away of what that service had meant to him. To many it had been just another occupation, a job to be done and finished. Inherently, for these men who felt no sentimentality, even the base and brutal aspects of military life meant little. A significant portion of men who fought the battles were already cruel, callous, and unfeeling.

But, for some veteran infantry soldiers, the training, seasoning, hardships, comradeship, and death-defying ordeals recently survived made an intense and lasting impression on their intellectual psyche. This collective group who kept diaries, wrote letters home, or penned memoirs later in life, were the same men who in the abstract, analyzed all they had witnessed in an attempt to understand what the trials meant to them.

William Keesy, for the rest of his life reviewed the "scenes of the war [that] were so tremendous and its cataclysms so frequent that time cannot dim their recollections of them." Keesy saw the veteran as a person having "meat in his words." And between the old soldier and the modern man there was a difference—one had "seen and done and [the other] has read about it."

The end came almost too quickly for Lieutenant Galwey. One day he and his men were still on the battlelines near Petersburg having barely recovered from a long and arduous campaign; then suddenly they were "relieved from the front," and sent to Columbus, Ohio to be mustered out. Therefore, the very last sentences he wrote about the subject seem oddly anti-climactic:

> Strangely enough the word [of our discharge] had already passed around, but even stranger there was little cheering, little celebration. We had expected to be transported with JOY. Perhaps soldiering in a splendid regiment is not so bad. Where would we find civilian friends to compare with soldier comrades?

The pride of Charles Barber at the time of his discharge gave way to anger, as the government, on a fine point of law, threatened to keep his 104th New York in service two months longer than the legal enlistment papers had called for. The men fought the issue and won, but it made the parting into civilian life a bit less enjoyable, as members of the unit felt used and cheated. Barber said it was a "cruel cruel disappointment" and his companions even spoke of mutiny before the question was settled. As it turned out, they still had to remain three weeks longer than necessary as they waited for a final verdict.

Away from home for four years and five months, Sergeant Valerius C. Giles "bent [his] way slowly and painfully back to Texas, spending three months on the way...." His old dog "Brave" met him at the yard gate and at first didn't know him, but it soon "dawned on him who I was, and he came toward me wagging his tail." Giles remembered that a private soldier in the army "was a very small part of the machine—a mere rivet or bolt or lever to be drawn, or worked at the leisure or pleasure of the chief engineer or his assistants." Then he stated: "It is finished. I have worn my last gray jacket. I have fired my last shot for Dixie."

Simon B. Hulbert poetically rounded out his feelings for the days of military duty:

I am a jolly soldier
As ever you did see,
But as I'm growing older,
I think of Liberty.
O! its no use in talking,
For I know what I'm about,
I don't think I'll enlist again,
For soldiering's played out.

CHORUS -
O! split peas and herring,
Bean soup and rice,
The soldiers in the army
Are living mighty nice;

But I can't see the point.
Salt junk and hard tack
Will give a man the gout;
O! I swear I'll never enlist again,
For soldiering's played out.

O! when I first enlisted
I thought it was but fun
To go out in the army
And follow the fife and drum;
But I soon found out the difference,
When I began to shout
That I never would enlist again,
For soldiering's played out....

Quoting a friend who died at Shiloh, Johnny Green summed up the service of so many thousands of infantrymen who never saw the end of hostilities, and would never relish the sweet morsel of victory or the bitter taste of defeat. Calling William Pope "one of the loveliest boys in our Company," Green watched him suffer two amputations, then slowly die of gangrene as his condition grew steadily worse. Pope "met death with a patriot's spirit," said Green, and his questioning last words could really never be answered: "Johnnie if a boy dies for his country the glory is his forever isn't it?"

At the termination of three long years as an infantryman, Color-Sergeant Daniel Crotty felt that a bit of a lesson was due those who waited in Michigan:

Now that the soldiers are going home a great many ask, what they will do when they get home? I will try and answer. Always take notice in your own vicinity, that when an old soldier settles down, is industrious, keeps sober and makes a good citizen, almost invariably put him down as a good soldier in the field. But let all good people deal lightly with a soldier's faults, for they have been through the mill for the past four years, and will be always glad to see their old comrades and talk over their campaigns and battles, and for a while after they get home very few will blame them for having their time out.

Private John Stevens counseled all ex-soldiers, as well as the people of Texas and of the South generally, not to be ashamed of their history. "Let us be true to the memory of our slain, and be faithful to our country, and as the new problems are presented, let us meet them like men and not as time servers, seeking the spoils of office." Stevens believed that the struggle he had come through was unique and the "coming generations will not look again upon the like, because the world in all coming time will never again behold such a contest for principle by men who, 'holding their conscience unmixed with guile, stood amid all conjunctures true to themselves, their country and their God.' To us is left the inheritance of unsullied and impregnable honor. 'Their's no Judas kiss, their's no traitor's promise, and the pledge so given and so vouched, albeit wrung from them in weakness, has been fulfilled in the gross and in the detail, to the last syllable and the last letter.'"

Writing to his mother late in his wartime service, Henry Prince of the 127th New York wondered aloud if he would be the same son who had left home years before:

Soldiering is a rough coarse life, calculated to corrupt good morals & harden a man's heart.... I could not feel contented if I were not a soldier trying to aid the government. As it is I strive to be a man & a son you will not be ashamed to own. Should I live to return probably I shall be coarse & unrefined but I trust I will be as good at Heart as when I left you & I hope better. I think I will never be ashamed of coarse clothes or plain food. We as a nation have been living too fast. Too much pride & care too much for dress. Methinks I have learned a lesson since I became a soldier.

Virginian Robert Stiles thought that the military existence, "notwithstanding the horrors that often attended it, grew upon me every day I lived it." And he believed that had the Confederacy gained its independence, "and to which...[army service] I should have consecrated myself with whole-hearted devotion." He called to mind also several essential character traits and lessons of "Soldier—Life." They were: service, duty, obedience and command unquestioned, unceasing accountability, and unmeasured responsibility. Stiles found that these elements led to some soldiers exhibiting, "an unrivaled elevation, strength, and perfection of character." He quoted one Southerner who thought very highly of the distinction of having been a soldier:

The sword has developed the grandest natures that the world ever saw. It has developed courage—that sublime energy of the soul which defies the universe when it feels itself to be right. It has developed a self-sacrifice which repudiates the idea that our life is worth more than anything else.... There are thousands among the Northern and Southern veterans of our Civil War who are ninety-five per cent. larger and mightier in soul than they would have been had they not, during the four years of national agony, turned their back on home and fortune, and at the front sacrificed all for a principle.

The journey from veteran infantryman to civilian was a quick one for Abner Small, then major of the 16th Maine. After the grand review in Washington and the muster out, the 16th made an uneventful trip to their home state, there to be disbanded. Upon arrival in Augusta, the word spread and people flocked in to see the returning men of that famous regiment. Small mused:

At the rendezvous [at the State House] we formed in line, but only to break ranks and say good-bye. That was hard; I prefer not to speak of it; I cannot. Neither can I find words for what I saw in other faces; in the

Sharing rations at Appomattox. (BL)

happy rush of our home folk there were troubled fathers and mothers whose sons had gone with us and had not returned, and these unhappy ones had been drawn to us as if somehow we must have brought their dead boys back with us, alive.

[Later]...the officers of the regiment gathered in [the governor's] room in the State House; and there we gave into his keeping the colors of the regiment, the symbols of all that we had dared and suffered and done. I suppose he made a speech, said the expected things; I don't remember. Somehow, everything was suddenly commonplace. Without my knowing when it had happened, I had already taken my leave of war.

Sgt. James Whitehorne, 12th Virginia, who was paroled at Appomattox said of his last day in the army, "The war has been going on so long I can't realize what a man would do now it's over. How can we get interested in farming or working in a store or warehouse when we have been interested day and night for years in keeping alive, whipping the invaders, and preparing for the next fight?"

The conflict between the North and South was already several weeks over when Wilbur Fisk got to his home in Vermont. He remembered soldiering as "a hard life, and a very undesirable one at best." Fisk saw that a "lifetime of experience has been crowded into this fierce term of war." For a man to become a soldier, Fisk believed:

[He]...must lay aside almost everything that makes life worth the having. All the tender endearments of home, and all the refining influence of good society are almost wholly sacrificed for the time being.... Still if a man loves adventure he finds a wide, reckless freedom in soldiering that has a charm for him, and leads him to drop his soberer reflections till a more convenient season.... [T]o become a soldier, simply as a means of earning a livelihood, I say it in all candor, I would only do it to save myself the necessity of begging my bread from door to door.

Now that the war is ended, [however] it is pleasant to reflect that we had the honor of bearing some humble portion in it...[and] I would not exchange such an experience for the noblest fortune in the land.

The Appomattox parole of Pvt. Henry A. Lawson, 49th Georgia. (GAC)

Thinking back on his own experiences, Sergeant Austin Stearns saw the life of a private soldier as "not of much account with some of the officers." He equated its worth with that of the degraded army mule, saying that the military thought it better to "[s]ave the life of a mule for they cost money, but let the soldier be killed for he costs nothing." Or as one old vet cracked: "Two mules and another soldier killed."

But when the time came for disbanding his old regiment in Boston Common, Stearns was more reflective:

> We then...seperated, each going his way to join in his chosen path in life.
>
> The friendships that had been formed and welded through more than twenty battles, long marches, and privations incident to a life of a soldier through three years of service will last as long as life its self [sic], and today after a lapse of twenty years, whenever I see or hear of a 13th [Massachusetts] man, I feel a thrill of pleasure and long to grasp him by the hand and say Comrade.

A few weeks following the final grand military review in Washington, D. C., on May 24, 1865, Sergeant Rice C. Bull and what was left of his 123rd New York were discharged from U.S. service. On that occasion he remarked:

> Our guns that we had carried for so many miles in attack and defense and by most of the boys so carefully handled and so lovingly regarded, were stacked for the last time. Their deadly work in our hands was over....
>
> I realize, far more than I did then, how unprepared we were to meet the life conditions that faced us, not alone from wounds or broken health but from the greater reason that our long absence during the years of life when we would have filled ourselves by education and experience for a successful effort were years gone. Many faced the future with the handicap of physical weakness, ignorance and lost opportunities.
>
> I shall never forget the last meeting our Company had before we separated to go home.... Captain [Alexander] Anderson, gave his last "fall in" command to his men. Without arms or equipment and some in civilian clothes that had replaced their faded uniforms we formed in line. The Captain in a broken voice, for he could not control his emotions, bid us farewell and Godspeed. When he had finished, we men crowded about him to shake his hand and each others.
>
> Surely we all rejoiced that the end had come, that victory was ours and that home was near. But there was after all a sadness deep down in our hearts in this parting hour. We boys had been together for three years; we had formed close friendships; we had slept under the same blanket; we had faced the enemy shoulder to shoulder on the firing line; we had marched side by side; we had borne danger, hardship, and privation alike; thus a comradeship had grown as only such conditions could form. So it was hard to separate and say goodby, one with the other; but we shook hands all around, and laughed and seemed to make merry, while our hearts were heavy and our eyes ready to shed tears.

EPILOGUE

There is at the police station at Woodside, New Jersey,...an aged nomad who gives his name as Martin Schwein, and who is a veteran of the war for the Union. He was brought in near midnight from a tent he had pitched near the edge of the village, and he tells a strange story. Enamored with camp life and a vagabond existence, he has, since his discharge from the army, wandered about the country, pitching his tent literally wherever night overtook him. For seventeen years he has thus tramped over the country from the lakes to the gulf, and from the seaboard to the Mississippi. He retains the weapons he carried when in the army, is provided with a camp kettle, blankets, &c, and seems to be in good health, though somewhat emaciated from lack of a proper commissariat. For a time his presence created some excitement in the vicinity of his camping place. He was held under a charge of vagrancy, and now in a rambling way is expressing his grief over the ingratitude of republics.[132]

Privates E.C. Morrill and Wainwright Cushing, 6th Maine Infantry. (GAC)

NOTES

1. Long, E.B. *The Civil War Day By Day: An Almanac 1861-1865*, Garden City, NY, 1971, 696.
2. *Ibid.*, 709-711, 726-727. A combined estimate is determined from Long's numbers.
3. *Battles and Leaders of the Civil War*, Vol. IV, New York, NY, 1884, 231 (George C. Eggleston). Hereafter cited as *B & L*.
4. *B & L*, Vol. III, 689 (Ulysses S. Grant).
5. Long 701-704, 721-726.
6. *Ibid.*, 704-705. Faust, Patricia L., ed. *Historical Times Illustrated Encyclopedia of the Civil War*, New York, NY, 1986, 24-25.
7. Barton, Michael. *Goodmen: The Character of Civil War Soldiers*, University Park, PA, 1981, 35. *B & L*, Vol. III, 51 (Don C. Buell). Commager, Henry S., ed. *The Blue and the Gray*, New York, NY, 1950, 61.
8. *B & L*, Vol. IV, 232 (George C. Eggleston).
9. Folmar, John K., ed. *From That Terrible Field: Civil War Letters of James M. Williams...*, University, AL, 1981, 81.
10. Fisk, Wilbur. *Anti-Rebel: The Civil War Letters of Wilbur Fisk*, Croton-on-Hudson, NY, 1983, 206, 217.
11. Strayer, L.M. and R.A. Baumgartner, eds. *Echoes of Battle*, Huntington, WV, 1991, 166-167.
12. Jackson, H.E. and T.F. O'Donnell, eds. (Hermon Clarke), *Back Home in Oneida*, Syracuse, NY, 1965, 177.
13. Barton 17-18.
14. Fox, William F. *Regimental Losses in the American Civil War*, Dayton, OH, 1974, 62.
15. Wiley, Bell I. and Hirst D. Milhollen. *They Who Fought Here*, New York, NY, 1959, 7-8.
16. Fisk 5.
17. Nye, Wilbur S., ed. (Thomas F. Galwey), *The Valiant Hours*, Harrisburg, PA, 1961, 80, 126.
18. Prince, Helen W., ed. *The Civil War Letters and Diary of Henry W. Prince*, Southold, NY, 1979, 103.
19. Stiles, Robert. *Four Years Under Marse Robert*, New York, 1903, 363-364.
20. Fox, William F. *Regimental Losses in the American Civil War*, Dayton, OH, 1974, 5.
21. Deforest, John W. *A Volunteer's Adventures*, New Haven, CT, 1946, 35-36.
22. Fox 1-5, 556-557.
23. *Ibid.*, 9.
24. *B & L*, Vol. I, 151-152 (Warren L. Goss).
25. Commager 72.
26. Mason, GA, *Daily Telegraph*, March 7, 1862. Rodgers was killed while commanding the 12th Georgia at Sharpsburg, MD during the Battle of Antietam.
27. Greenleaf, Margery, ed. (George Fowle), *Letters to Eliza from a Union Soldier, 1862-1865*, Chicago, IL, 1970, 8-9.
28. Commager, 89.
29. Kent, Arthur A., ed. (Austin C. Stearns), *Three Years With Company K*, Rutherford, NJ, 1976, 215-216.
30. Marcus, Edward, ed. (Justus M. Silliman), *A New Canaan Private in the Civil War*, New Canaan, CT, 1984, 36, 55.
31. Crotty, Daniel G. *Four Years Campaigning in the Army of the Potomac*, Grand Rapids, MI, 1874, 100. Rieger, Paul E., ed. (James G. Theaker), *Through One Man's Eyes*, Mt. Vernon, OH, 1974, 124.
32. Fisk 209.
33. Hedrick, David T. and Gordon B. Davis, Jr., eds. (John H.W. Stuckenberg), *I'm Surrounded by Methodists*, Gettysburg, PA, 1995, 110-112.
34. Buck, Samuel D. *With the Old Confeds.*, Baltimore, MD, 1925, 15.
35. Tunnard, W.H. *A Southern Record*, Dayton, OH, 1970, 31.
36. Fisk 1-2.
37. Commager 71.
38. Galloway, Richard P., ed. (Simon B. Hulbert), *One Battle Too Many*, 1987, 167.

39. Kent (Austin Stearns) 45.

40. Green, Robert M. *History of the 124th Regiment Pennsylvania Volunteers in the War of the Rebellion—1862-1863*, Philadelphia, PA, 1907, 129-130.

41. *B & L*, Vol. II, 557 (David L. Thompson).

42. *B & L*, Vol. IV, 231 (George C. Eggleston).

43. Billings, John D. *Hardtack and Coffee*, Boston, MA, 1887, 109.

44. Kirwan (John W. Green), Albert D., ed. (John W. Green), *Johnny Green of the Orphan Brigade*, Lexington, KY, 1956, 118, 136.

45. Strayer and Baumgartner 99. Small, Harold A., ed. (Abner R. Small), *The Road to Richmond*, Berkeley, CA, 1939, 197. Strayer and Baumgartner 203.

46. Faust 616.

47. Crotty 164. Fisk 93.

48. Clark, Walter A. *Under the Stars and Bars*, Augusta, GA, 1900, 45. Fisk 194.

49. Stevens, John W. *Reminiscences of the Civil War*, Hillsboro, TX, 1902, 93. Wiley and Milhollen 51.

50. Billings 121.

51. *Ibid.*, 113.

52. Crotty 165.

53. Robertson, Jr., James I., ed. (John H. Worsham), *One of Jackson's Foot Cavalry*, Jackson, TN, 1964, 12.

54. Strayer and Baumgartner 262-263.

55. Scofield, Matthew B. unpublished letter to F.W. Lowe written from "Camp on Red River, Alexandria, LA," March 23, 1864, author's collection.

56. *B & L*, Vol. IV, 134 (Evander M. Law).

57. Page, Charles D. *History of the 14th Connecticut Regiment*, Meriden, CT, 1906, 64.

58. Pettijohn, Dyer B. *Gettysburg and Libby Prison*, privately printed by Harriet P. Crawford, Dayton, OH, 1970, 6.

59. Durkin, James, ed. *This War is an Awful Thing...*, Glenside, PA, 1994, 82. Baumgartner, Richard A., ed. (William Chambers), *Blood & Sacrifice: The Civil War Journal of a Confederate Soldier*, Huntington, WV, 1994, 88. Handerson, Henry E. *Yankee in Gray*, Cleveland, OH, 1962, 82.

60. Strayer and Baumgartner 226.

61. Kent (Austin Stearns) 116.

62. Hodge (Perry Mayo), Robert W., ed. *The Civil War Letters of Perry Mayo*, East Lansing, MI, 1967, 222.

63. Strayer and Baumgartner 196.
Bartosz, Robert C., ed. *Letters Home From Geo. R. White*, Wenonah, NJ, 1991, 26.

64. Kent (Austin Stearns) 22.

65. Keesy, William Allen. *War As Viewed from the Ranks*, Norwalk, OH, 1898, 8.

66. Pope, Albert A. unpublished diary in author's collection, 135.

67. Davis, Jr., Charles E. *Three Years in the Army*, Boston, MA, 1894, 9.

68. Galloway (Simon Hulbert) 271. Strayer and Baumgartner 18. Blackburn, George M., ed. (Thomas N. Stevens), "Dear Carrie...," Mt. Pleasant, MI, 1984, 6, 188 & 196.

69. Hodge (Perry Mayo) 239. Fisk 294.

70. Marcus (Justus Silliman) 23.

71. Prince 52 and 53.

72. Galloway (Simon Hulbert) 42 & 166. Hodge (Perry Mayo) 173.

73. Bartlett, Wm. H., ed. *Aunt and the Soldier Boys*, Santa Cruz, CA, 1970, 11-15. Crotty 36.

74. Hodge (Perry Mayo) 207. Galloway (Simon Hulbert) 72.

75. Fitzpatrick, Marion H. *Letters to Amanda*, Culloden, GA, 1976, 32.

76. Cabaniss, Jim R., ed. *Civil War Journal and Letters of Washington Ives*, Tallahassee, FL, 1987, 27 & 28. Wright, Stuart, ed. *Memoirs of Alfred Horatio Belo*, Gaithersburg, MD, reprint of 1902 edition, 32. Winther, Oscar O., ed. (Theodore F. Upson), *With Sherman to the Sea*, Bloomington, IN, 1958, 26.

77. Couture, Richard T., ed. (Charles E. Denoon), *Charlie's Letters*, Collingswood, NJ, 1989, 35. Mumper, James A., ed. (John L. Holt), *I Wrote Your Word*, Lynchburg, VA, 11, 17, 19, 22, 27, 103.

78. Clark 39. Stevens 8.

79. Lasswell, Mary, ed. (Val C. Giles), *Rags and Hope*, New York, 1961, 23, 38, 50, & 138.

80. Kirwan (John W. Green) 185.

81. Nye (Thomas Galwey) 209.

82. Todd, George T. *First Texas Regiment*, Waco, TX, 1963, 18. Willey, Robert J., ed. (William B. Miller), *I Soldiered for the Union*, privately published by R.J. Willey, no date, 106. Gates, Arnold, ed. (Chesley Mosman), *The Rough Side of War*, Garden City, NY, 1987, 94.

83. *B & L*, Vol. II, 558 (David L. Thompson).

84. Stiles 85. Hosmer, James K. *The Color Guard*, Boston, MA, 1864, 219. Jones, Mary M. and Leslie J. Martin, eds. (William H. Berryhill), *The Gentle Rebel*, Yazoo City, MS, 1982, 80.

85. Strayer and Baumgartner 261. Nye (Thomas Galwey) 109.

86. Hodge (Perry Mayo) 182. Robertson, Jr., (John Worsham), *One of Jackson's...*, 109.

87. Folmar, John K., ed. (James Williams), *From That Terrible Field*, 64-68.

88. Robertson, Jr., (John Worsham) *One of Jackson's...*, 61. Robertson, Jr., James I. (John O. Casler) *Four Years in the Stonewall Brigade*, Dayton, OH, 1971, 96. Kirwan (John W. Green) 57. Nye (Thomas Galwey) 171.

89. Stiles 333.

90. Galloway (Simon Hulbert) 39. Bauer, K. Jack, ed. (Rice C. Bull), *Soldiering*, San Rafael, CA, 1977, 113. Galloway (Simon Hulbert) 121 & 278. Stevens 66-67. Lasswell (Val C. Giles) 190. Clark 176. Fitzpatrick 16 & 33. Keesy 47 & 83.

91. Nye (Thomas Galwey) 32. Winther (Theodore Upson) 27. Fletcher, William A. *Rebel Private Front and Rear*, Washington, DC, 1985, 9. Clark 130. Cramer, Clayton E., ed. (Samuel McIlvaine), *By the Dim and Flaring Lamps*, Monroe, NY, 1990, 79. Robertson Jr., (John Casler) *Four Years...*, 282. Stevens 82-83. Ruddick, Rodger D., ed. *From the Hayfields to the Battlefields*, privately printed, 1986, 117. Kent (Austin Stearns) 206 & 225. Isham, A.B. "The Story of a Gunshot Wound," *Military Order of the Loyal Legion, (MOLLUS) Ohio Commandry*, OH, Vol. IV, 434.

92. Jackson and O'Donnell (Hermon Clarke) 140. Small (Abner Small) 192. Bartlett 146. Winther (Theodore Upson) 25. Davis 9. Kirwan (John W. Green) 121. Lasswell (Val C. Giles) 23-24. Robertson Jr., (John Casler) *Four Years...*, 22.

93. Winther (Theodore Upson) 26. Lasswell (Val C. Giles) 139. Cater, Douglas J., *As It Was*, Austin, TX, 1990, 196.

94. Brown, Kent M. "Virginia County's Civil War," *The Confederate Soldier*, Vol. III, Middleburg, VA, 1985, 30. Lewis, John H. *Recollections from 1860-1865*, Washington, DC, 1895, 55, 57, 61.

95. Barber, Raymond G. and Gary E. Swinson, eds. *The Civil War Letters of Charles Barber*, Torrance, CA, 1991, 74. Nye (Thomas Galwey) 128. Cabaniss (Washington Ives) 42. Fitzpatrick 26. Couture (Charles Denoon) 37. Stevens 41, 95.

96. Keesy 77, 82, 154. Fitzpatrick 106. Barber (Charles Barber) and Swinson 152. Mumper (John Holt) 113. Fisk 112-113. Fitzpatrick 83. Cabaniss (Washington Ives) 74. Couture (Charles Denoon) 7. Robertson, Jr. (John Worsham) *One of Jackson's...*, 2, 8, 9. Watkins, Sam R. *Co. Aytch*, Jackson, TN, 1952, 97. Fisk 71, 88, 133. Crotty 167. Barber (Charles Barber) and Swinson 115. Small (Abner Small) 192. McKelvey, Blake, ed. *Rochester in the Civil War*, Rochester, NY, 1944, 243.

97. Fitzpatrick 23. Strayer and Baumgartner 18. Stillwell, Leander. *The Story of a Common Soldier*, Erie, KS, 1920, 82. Fisk 119, 274. Marcus (Justus Silliman) 25. Kirwan (John W. Green) 147-148. Lappin, Zoe von Ende, ed. (Theodore Birmingham), *Yours In Love*, Grawn, MI, 1989, 89. Winther (Theodore Upson) 35. Kent (Austin Stearns) 65. Nye (Thomas Galwey) 93.

98. *Ibid.*, 70. Kent (Austin Stearns) 70. *B & L*, Vol. II, 556 (David L. Thompson). Fitzpatrick 131. Winther (Theodore Upson) 115. Keesy 46. Nye (Thomas Galwey) 86-87. Fisk 12, 130, 167. Robertson Jr., (John Worsham), *One of Jackson's...*, 90. Cater 168. Wiley, Bell I., ed. (William N. Wood), *Reminiscences of Big I*, Jackson, TN, 1956, 28.

99. Billings 276. Crotty 109-110. Small (Abner Small) 192-193. Fisk 164. Marcus (Justus Silliman) 36. Walton, William, ed. (Edwin Weller), *A Civil War Courtship*, Garden City, NY, 1980, 93.

100. Fitzpatrick 19. Strayer and Baumgartner 261. Fisk 246-247. Keesy 32-33.

101. Spurlin, Charles D., ed. *The Civil War Diary of Charles A. Leuschner*, Austin, TX, 1992, 51. Fisk 172. *B & L*, Vol. III, 205 (James P. Smith).

102. Stillwell 72. Crotty 107. Kent (Austin Stearns) 98, 263. *Ibid.*, 172. Fisk 120-121.

103. Winther (Theodore Upson) 97. Hodge (Perry Mayo) 194. Robertson, Jr., (John Worsham), *One of Jackson's...*, 9.

104. Todd, Frederick P. *American Military Equipage*, Vol. I, NY, 1980, 185-191. *B & L*, Vol. I, 155 (Warren L. Goss). Keesy 30. Prince 122. Robertson, Jr., (John Casler), *Four Years...*, 42. Nye

(Thomas Galwey) 217. Olcott, Mark, ed. *The Civil War Letters of Lewis Bissell*, Washington, DC, 1981, 335. Galloway (Simon Hulbert) 243. Barber (Charles Barber) and Swinson 143, 162. Galloway (Simon Hulbert) 57. War Department, Washington, DC, *General Order 101*, May 30, 1865, by E.D. Townsend, Ass't Adj. General, U.S. Army.

105. Commager 92. Woodhead, Henry, ed. *Echoes of Glory*, Alexandria, VA, 1991, 22-25. Rolph, G.V. and Noel Clark. *The Civil War Soldier*, Washington, DC, 1961, 19. Weller, Jac. "Civil War Minie Rifles Prove Quite Accurate," *The American Rifleman*, July 1971, 36-40. Tucker, Glenn. *Lee and Longstreet at Gettysburg*, New York, NY, 1968, 99-100. Gates (Chesley Mosman) 195. Coco, Gregory A., ed. (Roland E. Bowen), *From Ball's Bluff to Gettysburg...and Beyond*, Gettysburg, PA, 1994, 28.

106. Hosmer 220. Hanie, E.J. (Lt. Col.), *Report on the status of the garrison at Port Hudson, LA, dated Jan. 10, 1863, sent to Inspector General Col. C.W. Fauntleroy*, Jackson, MS, copy at the Port Hudson S.C.A., Zachery, LA. Commager 93. Baumgartner (William Chambers) 18, 25, 47, 100, 206. Commager 94, 99-100. Robertson, Jr., (John Worsham), *One of Jackson's...*, 60. Kirwan (John W. Green) 19. Commager 100-101. Bartlett 12. Marcus (Justus Silliman) 4. Galloway (Simon Hulbert) 76, 174, 228. Winther (Theodore Upson) 27, 34, 43. Clark 122-123. Kirwan (John W. Green) 27. Cabaniss (Washington Ives) 25. Fitzpatrick 43.

107. Fisk 120. Lasswell (Val C. Giles) 128. Warren, Leander H. *My Recollections of the Battle of Gettysburg*, Gettysburg, PA 1926, 12. Thomas J. Knight enlisted in June 1861, was captured once and paroled in 1862, and deserted his unit in July, 1864. Watkins 159. Keesy 150-151. Hodge (Perry Mayo) 171, 183, 199.

108. Galloway (Simon Hulbert) 142. Marcus (Justus Silliman) 23. Hodge (Perry Mayo) 170. Blackburn (Thomas Stevens) 20. Watkins 139-140. Winther (Theodore Upson) 173. Fitzpatrick 123. Cabaniss (Washington Ives) 68. Kirwan (John W. Green) 127. Strayer and Baumgartner 42.

109. Keesy 124. Clark 119. Galloway (Simon Hulbert) 75, 258. Barber (Charles Barber) and Swinson 137. Handerson 45. Kirwan (John W. Green) 160. Cabaniss (Washington Ives) 36. Lasswell (Val C. Giles) 209. Groat, James W. *Pages Clothed in the Plainest of Dress: The Groat Diaries*, Anoka, MN, 1988, 14.

110. Bartlett 85. Wilson, Nicholas G. "Personal War Sketch," Department of Pennsylvania, Grand Army of the Republic, Post #9, Feb. 5, 1896, 73. *B & L*, Vol. IV, 173-174 (G. Norton Galloway). Fitzpatrick 21. *Grand Army Review*, Philadelphia, PA, Vol. I, 11-12. Clark 119. Nye (Thomas Galwey) 236. Gates (Chesley Mosman) 252. Barber (Charles Barber) and Swinson 135, 172. Cabaniss (Washington Ives) 36. Watkins 158. Keesy 124. Hodge (Perry Mayo) 180. Strayer and Baumgartner 216. Commager 92. Winther (Theodore Upson) 107, 157.

111. Moore, Frank, ed. *Rebellion Record*, Vol. 7, New York, NY, 1864, 122-123. Stiles 242. Small (Abner Small) 193. Fisk 142, 321. Commager 65, 67-68. Strayer and Baumgartner 275-276. Barber (Charles Barber) and Swinson 164. *B & L*, Vol. I, 153 (Warren L. Goss). Winther (Theodore Upson) 134, 144. Jackson and O'Donnell (Hermon Clarke) 144. Owen, Harry T. "Pickett at Gettysburg," *Philadelphia Weekly Times*, March 26, 1881. Keesy 154. Galloway (Simon Hulbert) 125. Olcott, Mark, ed. *The Civil War Letters of Lewis Bissell*, 314. Nye (Thomas Galwey) 20. Baumgartner (William Chambers) 197. Stiles 311. Cabaniss (Washington Ives) 49.

112. *B & L*, Vol. II, 557-558 (David L. Thompson). Robertson, Jr., (John Worsham) 97. Harrison, Kathleen G. "A Day Book of the Gettysburg Campaign," July 12, 1863 unpublished manuscript in the office of the Chief Historian, GNMP, Gettysburg, PA. Pope, Albert A., unpublished diary, 66. Galloway (Simon Hulbert) 78. Bartlett 23-24. Fisk 114, 120. Nye (Thomas Galwey) 95. Keesy 36. *B & L*, Vol. II, 532 (Allen C. Redwood). Fisk 229. Kent (Austin Stearns) 285. Fisk 96. Keesy 41. Kirwan (John W. Green) 79. Athearn, Robert G., ed. (Alfred L. Hough), *Soldier in the West*, Philadelphia, PA, 1957, 76-79. Evans, Thomas H. "The Enemy Sullenly Held On To The City," *Civil War Times Illustrated*, April, 1968, 32. Winther (Theodore Upson) 65. Kent (Austin Stearns) 285. Athearn (Alfred Hough) 82. Bartlett 86. Stillwell 27. Robertson Jr., (John Worsham) 96. Kent (Austin Stearns) 136. Kirwan (John W. Green) 55. Fitzpatrick 28. Fisk 196. Clark 124.

113. Coco (Roland Bowen) 31-200. Brown, John C. *Official Records of the War of the Rebellion*, Vol. 30, Part 2, Washington, DC, 1901, 370. Stanyan, John M. *A History of the Eighth Regiment of New Hampshire Volunteers*, Concord, NH, 1892, 466. Beecher, Harris H. *Record of the 114th Regiment, N.Y.S.V.*, Norwich, NY, 1866, 350.

114. Lewis 55. Fisk 171. Small (Abner Small) 185. *B & L*, Vol. I, 152 (Warren L. Goss). Gibbon, John, unpublished 19-page manuscript entitled, "The First Time Under Fire," copy in the author's files. Strayer and Baumgartner 184. Welch, Spencer G. *A Confederate Surgeon's Letters To His*

Wife, New York, NY, 1911, 64. Wafer, Francis M. unpublished diary in the Douglas Library, Queen's University, Kingston, Ontario, 44. Clark 132. Strayer and Baumgartner 180, 166. Barrett, John G., ed. (Edmund D. Patterson), *Yankee Rebel*, Chapel Hill, NC, 1966, 29. Fisk 31-32. Stillwell 62. Condit, E.C. "Battle Experiences," *The National Tribune Scrap Book*, Washington, DC, 1879, 12-13. Athearn (Alfred Hough) 71. Spencer, William H. "How I Felt In Battle And In Prison," MOLLUS Maine Commandry War Papers, Vol. II, Portland, ME, 1902, 124-127. Kilmer, George A. "In Fire of Battle," Gettysburg newspaper clippings file, 1896, GNMP Historian's Office, Book 5, 123. Dickert, D. Augustus. *History of Kershaw's Brigade*, Newberry, SC, 1899, 200, 248. Coe, David, ed. (Hamlin A. Coe), *Mine Eyes Have Seen The Glory*, Rutherford, NJ, 1975, 125. Robertson Jr., (John Casler), *Four Years...*, 208. Galloway (Simon Hulbert) 223. Fitzpatrick 20. Cabaniss (Washington Ives) 36. Barber (Charles Barber) and Swinson 85, 95. Bartlett 136. *B & L*, Vol. II, 662 (David L. Thompson). Clark 28, 34. Lewis 33, 42. Pope 162. Strayer and Baumgartner 140. Siegel, Robert A. *Confederate States Postal History*, Sales Catalogue 772, December 11, 1995, entry 3296, New York, NY, 95.

115. Barrett (Edmund Patterson) 44. Nye (Thomas Galwey) 105. Fisk 218. Lasswell (Val C. Giles) 110. Hodge (Perry Mayo) 180. Small (Abner Small) 184. Strayer and Baumgartner 237. Commager 138. Barrett (Edmund Patterson) 58.

116. Nye (Thomas Galwey) 64. Burpee, Edgar A. (19th Maine Infantry), unpublished letter written on July 12, 1863 from Williamsport, MD, collection of Len Rosa, Gettysburg, PA. Fisk 84, 226. Pope 186. Strayer and Baumgartner 283. Davidson, Robert B. unpublished diary in the collection of "Fields of Glory" Civil War Shop, Gettysburg, PA. Handerson 53. Kent (Austin Stearns) 169. *B & L*, Vol. II, 197 (Warren L. Goss). *B & L*, Vol. III, 225 (H.W. Jackson). *B & L*, Vol. IV, 171 (Lee Galloway). Robertson Jr., (John Casler), *Four Years...*, 45.

117. Handerson 49. *B & L*, Vol. IV, 582 (George L. Kilmer). Gates (Chesley Mosman) 199. Phelps, Frank, (38th Wisconsin Infantry), unpublished letter in the collection of Lewis Leigh, Jr., Fairfax, VA. Durkin 165. Baumgartner (William Chambers) 81. Pope 188. Nye (Thomas Galwey) 42.

118. Stevens 73. Lasswell (Val C. Giles) 203. McKelvey, Blake, ed. *Rochester in the Civil War*, Rochester, 81. Barrett (Edmund Patterson) 35. Baumgartner (William Chambers) 85. Strayer and Baumgartner 329. *Ibid.*, 113. Company Officer, *Reminiscences of the Gettysburg Battle*, Philadelphia, PA, 1883, 56. Davidson, Robert B. unpublished diary, entry for June 24, 1864. Kilmer, George L. "First Actions of Wounded Soldiers," *Popular Science Monthly*, June 1892, 156-161. *B & L*, Vol. IV, 172-173 (Lee Galloway). Strayer and Baumgartner 159. *Ibid.*, 172. *Ibid.*, 264. Swallow, William H. "The Third Day at Gettysburg," *Southern Bivouac*, Vol. 4, 1886, 572. Kirwan (John W. Green) 166. Stiles 302.

119. Hodge (Perry Mayo) 175. Jennings, Frank. (90th Pennsylvania Vols.), unpublished memoir in the GNMP files, 3. Baumgartner (William Chambers) 152. Strayer and Baumgartner 262. Fisk 80. Watkins 129. Lasswell (Val C. Giles) 207. Winther (Theodore Upson) 108. Kirwan (John W. Green) 31. Barber (Charles Barber) and Swinson 172. Clark 193. Strayer and Baumgartner 133, 190, 253, 287, 327. Commager 139.

120. Coco (Roland Bowen) 126. *Ibid.*, 46. Brown, Norman D., ed. (Samuel T. Foster), *One of Cleburne's Command*, Austin, TX, 1980, 62. Kirwan (John W. Green) 161. Watkins 157. Hodge (Perry Mayo) 234. Strayer and Baumgartner 311. Phelan, Helene C., ed. (Eugene Kingman), *Tramping Out the Vintage*, Almond, NY, 1983, 185, 187, 190. Handerson 95.

121. Strayer and Baumgartner 280. Stiles 333. *Ibid.*, 334. Kirwan (John W. Green) 56. Couture (Charles Denoon) 96. Strayer and Baumgartner 233. *B & L*, Vol. IV, 172 (G. Norton Galloway). Strayer and Baumgartner 236. *Ibid.*, 280. *Ibid.*, 305-306.

122. Rogers, James G. letter dated Aug. 31, 1862 to Lucretia Willett Rogers printed in the Macon, GA, *Telegraph* on Sept. 9, 1862, eight days before his death. Jackson and O'Donnell (Hermon Clarke) 185. Clark 26-27. Spurlin, Charles D., ed. *The Civil War Diary of Charles A. Leuschner*, 35. Kirwan (John W. Green) 162. Newsome, Edmund. *Experience in the War of the Great Rebellion, (81st Illinois)*, Carbondale, IL, 1880, 116-117. Kent (Austin Stearns) 23. Lappin (Theodore Birmingham) 73. *B & L*, Vol. IV, 173 (G. Norton Galloway).

123. Jackson and O'Donnell (Hermon Clarke) 142. Halsey, Ashley, ed. (Robert H. Strong), *A Yankee Private's Civil War*, Chicago, IL, 1961, 16. Ruddick (William Whitcomb) 193. Lewis, James K. (16th North Carolina), unpublished letter dated Nov. 25, 1861, in the collection of Len Rosa, Gettysburg, PA. Cater 162-163. Robertson Jr., (John Casler), *Four Years...*, 89, 208. Robertson Jr., (John Worsham), *One of Jackson's...*, 129. Brown, Norman D., ed. (Samuel Foster), *One of*

Cleburne's Command, 115.   Moon, Thomas. unpublished diary in the collection of the GNMP Library, 6-7.   Fisk 87.   Stiles 80.

124.   Small (Abner Small) 194.   Stiles 117.   Cunningham, Edward, *The Port Hudson Campaign*, Baton Rouge, LA, 1963, 87.   Winther (Theodore Upson) 138.   Stiles, 98.   Barrett (Edmund Patterson) 8. Stillwell 64-65.   Kirwan (John W. Green) 33.   Robertson Jr., (John Casler), *Four Years...*, 96.   Crotty 44-45.   *B & L*, Vol. I, 152 (Warren L. Goss).   Blake, Isaac W. "Capture at Port Hudson," *Civil War Times Illustrated*, Dec. 1969, 40.   Brown (Samuel Foster) 88.   Strayer and Baumgartner 122. *Ibid.*, 256.   Ruddick (William Whitcomb) 138.   Barber (Charles Barber) and Swinson 81.   Kent (Austin Stearns) 89.   Dye, Marshall. (121st New York Infantry), undated letter in the files of the GNMP Library.   Winther (Theodore Upson) 107.   Nye (Thomas Galwey) 127.   Cramer (Samuel McIlvaine) 105.   Lasswell (Val C. Giles) 130.

125.   Strayer and Baumgartner 56.   *Ibid.*, 177.   *Ibid.*, 197.   Keesy 67.   Baumgartner (William Chambers) 84.   Ruddick (A.W. Brown) 206.   Folmar (James Williams) 60.   Spurlin (Charles Leuschner) 54.

126.   Lasswell (Val C. Giles) 204.   Strayer and Baumgartner 328.   *Ibid.*, 282.   *Ibid.*, 328.   Durkin 259. Wright (Alfred Horatio Belo) 19.   *Ibid.*, 27.   Pope 16.   Cater 154-155, 157.   Brown (Samuel Foster) 20.   *B & L*, Vol. IV, 173 (G. Norton Galloway).   Kent (Austin Stearns) 133.   Pope 176. Strayer and Baumgartner 132.   Keesy 104.   Wright (Alfred Horatio Belo) 17.   Clark 140. Stevens 90-91.   Crotty 153.   Kirwan (John W. Green) 65-66.   *Ibid.*, 112.   Lasswell (Val C. Giles) 215-216.   Kent (Austin Stearns) 90.   Strayer and Baumgartner 79.

127.   Cabaniss (Washington Ives) 22.   Baumgartner (William Chambers) 64, 184.   *Ibid.*, 151.   Keesy 136, 140.   Pope 43.   Robertson Jr., (John Casler) *Four Years...*, 140.   Stevens, 98.   Hodge (Perry Mayo) 183.   Rourke, Norman E., ed. (Bailey G. McClelen), *I Saw The Elephant*, Shippensburg, PA, 1995, 18-19.   Kent (Austin Stearns) 62.   Cramer (Samuel McIlvaine) 84.   Bartlett 13, 125. Durkin 73.   Jackson and O'Donnell (Hermon Clarke) 185.   Strayer and Baumgartner 73, 124. Watkins 136.

128.   Coe (Hamlin Coe) 120.   *B & L*, Vol. I, 267 (Warren L. Goss).   Nye (Thomas Galwey) 67.   Hakey, Ashley, ed. (Robert Strong), *A Yankee Private's Civil War*, 18.   Cater 164.   Bartlett 87, 88. Baumgartner (William Chambers) 162.   Winther (Theodore Upson) 138.   *B & L*, Vol. I, 47 (Warren L. Goss).   Oddor, Bill, ed. (Richard Wood), *Stories of Old Bellevue*, Sandusky, OH, 1989, 37. Bartlett 166, 168.   Jackson and O'Donnell (Hermon Clarke) 177.   *B & L*, Vol. III, 101 (W. Roy Mason).

129.   Emerson, J.W. extract of unpublished memoir, courtesy of D. Scott Hartwig.   Cabaniss (Washington Ives) 43-44.   Galloway (Simon Hulbert) 236.   Kirwan (John W. Green) 158.   Stiles 296. Robertson Jr., (John Casler), *Four Years...*, 66.   Nye (Thomas Galwey) 213.   Strayer and Baumgartner 84.

130.   *Ibid.*, 329.   Unknown author, "So you would like to see a battle...?" in medical file at the GNMP Library.   Isham, A.B. "The Story of a Gunshot Wound," *MOLLUS Ohio Commandry*, Vol. 4, 429. Brown, Augustus C. *The Diary of a Line Officer*, New York, NY, 1906, 43.   *Ibid.*, 43-44.   Unknown author, "So you would like to see a battle...?", 329-330, 334-336.   Nye (Thomas Galwey) 213-214.   Handerson 59-60.   Baumgartner (William Chambers) 177-184.   Brown (Samuel Foster) 63-68.   Fletcher 74-82.   Durkin 258-268.

131.   Keesy 216.   Nye (Thomas Galwey) 236.   Barber (Charles Barber) and Swinson 194-196.   Lasswell (Val C. Giles) 104, 279-280.   Galloway (Simon Hulbert) 287.   Kirwan (John W. Green) 37. Crotty 193.   Stevens 194.   Prince 103.   Stiles 359, 367.   Small (Abner Small) 183.   Calkins, Chris M. (James Whitehorne) "Final March to Appomattox" *Civil War Regiments* vol. 2, #3, 1992, 248.   Fisk 342-343.   Kent (Austin Stearns) 310-311.   Bauer (Rice Bull) 248-249.

132.   Article in *The National Tribune*, Washington, DC, April 1, 1882.

INDEX

Those soldiers indicated with an (*) are frequently referenced and therefore not included within the index.

Alabama troops
   1st, 66
   9th, 93, 99, 119
   10th, 132
   21st, 39, 124
   27th, 107
   49th, 118
Alexander, E. P., 65, 75
Allan, William, 66-67
Allatoona, GA, 144
Allbright, Sam, 106
Allen, Hardy, 102
ambulances, 140-141
ammunition, 61-62, 65, 99
   extra, 73
   making of, 70
   multiple uses of, 66
   numbers carried, 72
   numbers fired, 72-74
   on the march, 85
Antietam, Battle of, 10-11, 21, 38, 40, 42, 95, 102, 108, 122, 125-126
Appomattox Court House, VA, v, 150-151
Archer, James, 136
Arkansas Post, Battle of, 126
Arkansas troops
   1st, 111
   11th, 66
   12th, 66
   15th, 57, 66
   17th, 66
Arlington Heights, VA, 131
armies
   Northern and Southern, 2-3
   organization, 9-10
   sub-groups of, 10
Army of Northern Virginia, 66
Army of the Potomac, 78, 90
artillery
   damage done by, 101-103, 126
   projectiles, 101
   sounds and sights of, 101
ash-cakes, 30

Atlanta, GA, 25, 49, 71, 74, 79, 90, 100, 105, 107, 109, 121, 125, 135, 138, 140
atrocities, 114-116
Avoyelles Prairie, LA, 91

Bailey, Michael, 21
Ball's Bluff, VA, 108
Banks, Nathaniel, 91
Barber, Charles *
Bassett, Bob, 125
battle
   "close calls" in, 105-108, 124
   hand-to-hand in, 109-112, 138
   smoke of, 98-99
   sounds of, 99-101
   vision in, 90-91
battlefields, scenes on, 118-123
battles
   losses in, 11
   numbers of, 3
Beard, William Harman, v
Becht, John, 91
Belo, Alfred, 36, 125, 127
belts and buckles, 63
Bentonville, NC, 107
Berryhill, William, 38
Bevens, William E., 111
Billings, John, 30, 55
Birmingham, Theodore, 53, 114
Bishop, Jerome, 113
Bissell, Lewis, 64, 80
Blake, Isaac, 121
blankets, 51-53, 80, 84
Blenkers, Louis, 53
Blodgett, Amos C., 16
"bloody angle," 126
boiler (coffee), 28, 29, 31
Bolton, J. G., 133
bounty jumpers, 15-16
Bowen, Roland *
Bragg, Braxton, 38
Brandy Station, VA, 59
breastworks, 104
Brown, A. C., 141

Brown, A. W., 124
Brown, Cyrus, 21
Brubacker, John, 92
Buck, Samuel D., 17
Buell, Don C., 5
Bull, Rice C., 40, 152
bullets
   antics of, 102
   damage to environment, 104-106
   damage to humans, 102-104
   sound of, 100-101
burials, 121-122, 133-137
   incomplete, 122
Burpee, Edgar A., 100
Burton, James H., 65
"butternut" dye, 38
Buzzard's Roost, GA, 136

Camp Black, VA, 132
camp chests, 28
camp fires, 26, 31
camps
   "breaking," 84
   condition of, 42
canteens, 57-59, 85
cap pouch, 61-62
Carroll, John, 71
cartridge box, 61-62, 64
cartridges, 61
Casler, John *
casualties, 1, 137, 147
   "friendly-fire" 112-114
   disease, 117-130
Cat Creek, GA, 106
Cater, Douglas, 46, 55, 115
Cater, Rufus, 134
Cedar Creek, VA, 87
Cedar Mountain, VA, 60, 121-122, 129, 133, 137
Cemetery Ridge, 90
Centerville, VA, 132
Chaffin's Farm, VA, 6
Chambers, William *
Champion Hill, 111

Chancellorsville, VA, 56, 59, 67, 106, 134-135, 137
Chattahoochee River, 126-127
Chattanooga, TN, 36, 68, 128
Cheat Mountain, VA, 113
Chickamauga, TN, 11, 103, 105, 115, 122, 125, 134, 137, 145
Childress, John, 99
chuck-luck, 53
Clark, Walter A. *
Clarke, Hermon, 6, 45, 80, 111
Cleary, Pat, 132
Clem, John, 7
Coates, Jefferson, 138
Cochran's Ford, GA, 126
Coe, Hamlin A., 94, 133
coffee, 30, 31, 56
Cold Harbor, VA, 105, 125, 138
Collins, Robert M., 107
combat
    bravery in, 93-94, 96
    chance of being hit in, 147
    "close calls" in, 105-108, 126
    coolness in, 94, 96
    curious incidents in, 124-129
    emotions before, 91-93
    emotions in, 93, 96, 123
    faces of men in, 92
    fear of, 93-94, 96
    file closers in, 93
    "friendly-fire," 112-114
    humor in, 124-129
    killing, 108-111
    men's actions in, 93, 96, 123
    officers' actions in, 93-94
    psychological injury, 123
    suicide, 96
    time spent in, 90
    vision in, 90-91, 98
Condit, E. C., 93
Confederate strengths and weaknesses, 2
Connecticut troops
    12th, 11
    14th, 29
    17th, 15, 52, 68, 70
conscription, 14-16
Cooke, Chauncey H., 96
Cooper, James, 139
Copperheads, 15
corn-cakes, 29

corn-dodgers, 29
corpses
    color of, 122
    look of, 119-123
    looking for, 123
    robbing of, 116, 130
Coulter, Richard, 126
Crotty, Daniel *
Crumpton, Washington B., 75, 105
Cub Run, VA, 132
Culp's Hill, 74
cups, "boilers, dippers, bailers," 56-57, 59-60
Cushing, Wainwright, 153

Dalton, GA, 133
Daniel, Will, 89
Daugherty, Mike, 132
Davidson, Robert B., 100, 103
Day, Warren W., 132
"Dead Angle," 103, 109
deaths
    by accident, 130-133
    by disease, 117, 130
    in battle, 117-123
Delano, Jesse L., 65
Denoon, Charles, 36, 47, 111
desiccated vegetables, 25, 32
Dicey, Edward, 78
Dickert, D. Augustus, 94
dippers, 59
draft, the, 14-16
Drake, John, 142
dreams, 123-124
dress coat, 34
drill, 18-20
Dry, William C., 32
duels, 127
Dunbar, Elmore, 37
Dunker Church, 108
Dwight, Henry, 79, 110-111
Dye, Marshall, 122
Dyer, Albert W., 67

Easterling, E. A., 130
Echols, John, 57
Eggleston, George, 6, 24
Ellis, William, 126
Emerson, J. W., 137
Evans, Thomas, 86

Ezra Church, GA, 29, 58, 105

Fahnestock, Allen, 124
Fair Oaks, VA, 120
Falling Waters, MD, 41, 122
Farley, Porter, 51
Farrell, Wilson B., 72
Favill, Josiah M., 13
Fellows, Charles, 124
field tents, 53
First Manassas, 45, 64, 74, 105, 115, 119
Fisk, Wilbur *
Fitzpatrick, Marion H. *
Fleck, Frank, 112
Fletcher, William A., 43, 145-146
Florida troops
    4th, 49, 68, 81, 130
forage caps, 44
Forrest, N. B., 115
Fort DeRussy, LA, 113
Fort Fisher, NC, 112
Fort "Hell," VA 127
Fort Pillow, TN, 115
Fort Sanders, TN, 114
Fort Stedman, VA, 136
Fort Sumter, SC, 1
Fort Wagner, SC, 95
Foster, Samuel T. *
Fox, William, 7, 11
Franklin, TN, 126
Franks, Jack, 115
Frayser's Farm, VA, 99
Fredericksburg, VA, 47, 100, 104, 134, 137, 144
frock coats, 36
Front Royal, VA, 110

Gaine's Farm, VA, 136
Gaines's Mill, VA, 107
Galloway, G. Norton, 73-74, 114
Galwey, Thomas *
gangrene, 145-146
Gaskill, Joseph, 129
Gassett, Henry, 122
Geary, John, 137
Georgia troops
    1st, 26, 37, 41, 96, 113
    9th, 11
    12th, 10, 14, 69, 93, 112-113
    13th, v

45th, 36, 41, 51, 68
49th, 151
63rd, 107, 127
66th, 30
Gettysburg, PA, v, 11, 29, 38, 44, 48, 52, 67, 69, 72, 74, 77, 83, 90, 92, 100, 103, 105, 116, 125
Gibbon, John, 91
Giles, Valerius C. *
Gilger, John A., iv
Gillespie, John, 105
Gleason, A. J., 103
Goss, Warren L. *
Gould, John, 102
Graham, James L.. *
Graham, J. Smith, 45, 136
Granger, George, 128
Grant, Lewis A., 94
Grant, Ulysses S., 1, 26
"grape and canister," 100-101
graves, 135-136
"gray-backs" (see lice)
Green, Johnny *
Griffith, John, 37
Groat, James, W., 72
gum blankets, 51

Hack, N. O., 86
Hamilton's Crossing, VA, 127
Handerson, Henry, 72, 101, 110, 144
Hanover Court House, VA, 141
hardtack, (see rations)
Harlan, Edward T., 21
Harley, Stannard, 110
Harmon, O. F., 124
Harpers Ferry, 21, 73, 114
hats and caps, 44-45, 80
haversack, 55, 57
Hay, Charles C., 7
Hendrick, Gus, 134
High Bridge, VA, v
Hilton Head, SC
hoe-cakes, 29, 30
Holmes, James, 103, 107, 125, 140
Holt, John L., 36, 37, 48
Hood, John Bell, 41
Hosmer, James, 66
hospitals, field
    description of, 141-144

horrors of, 142-143
Hough, Alfred, 86-87, 94
House, Eli W., 44
"housewife" or needle case, 60
Hughes, William A., 69
Hulbert, Simon *

Illinois troops
    10th Cavalry, 7
    34th, 100
    55th, 92
    59th, 38, 66, 74
    61st, 51, 119
    81st, 113
    86th, 92, 123
    95th, 113
    104th, 40
    105th, 115, 134
    123rd, 121
Indiana troops
    10th, 43, 122, 132
    26th, 121
    52nd, 44
    75th, 38
    82nd, 115
    100th, 36, 45, 54, 75, 79
infantryman
    ages, 7
    appearance, 77
    characteristics, 6
    hardening of, 79-80
    physical characteristics, 7, 80
    veteran status, 77-79
    what they carried, 77, 127
Iowa troops
    19th, 93
Irish Brigade, 139
Isham, A. B., 44, 140
Issermoyer, Charles, 89
Issermoyer, William, 89
Iuka, MS, 86, 118
Ives, Washington *

Jackets, 34
Jackson, H. W., 101
Jackson, MS, 109, 125
Jackson, Thomas J., v, 63, 83, 116, 138
Jefferson, Thomas, 5
Jennings, Frank, 105
Johnson, Andrew, 1

Johnson, Ed, 113
Jonesborough, GA, 113, 138

Keesy, W. A. *
Kennesaw Mountain, GA, 74, 92, 103, 105, 109
Kentucky troops
    9th, 37, 67, 71, 105-106, 112-113, 128
    10th, 112
kepis, 44
Kernstown, VA, 138
Kilmer, George, 101, 103
Kingman, Eugene, 110
knapsacks, 49-51, 80, 84-85
Knight, T. J., 69
Knoxville, TN, 114

Law, E. M., 29
Lawson, Henry A., 151
Lee, Robert E., 41
Leuschner, Charles, 59, 113, 124
Lewis, James K., 115
Lewis, John, 46, 91, 96
Lewis, Milo, 92
lice, 42, 44
Locust Grove, VA, 73
Logan, Thomas, 111
Longstreet, James, 38, 46
Lookout Mountain, TN, 79
losses
    battle, 11
    disease, 117, 130
Louisiana troops
    3rd, 17
    9th, 101, 110
    19th, 46, 55, 115, 125
Lynch, G., 40

Maine troops
    1st Maine Heavy Artillery, 19
    6th, 153
    12th, 110, 121
    16th, 45, 151
    19th, 100
Malvern Hill, VA, 101, 118
Mann, W. D., 64
Mansura, LA, 91
"March to the Sea," 118
marching, 83
    average distance, 84

breaking camp, 84
  dust and heat of, 77, 86
  forced, 86
  mud and water, 83, 88
  snow, 89
  straggling, 85
Marksville, LA, 113
Mason, W. Roy, 137
Massachusetts troops
  4th, 57
  13th, 15, 31, 44-45, 53, 67, 114, 122, 126, 129, 132, 152
  15th, 90, 108
  19th, 31
  35th, 32, 83, 96, 131
  38th, 50
  52nd, 38, 65
  57th, 104
Mayo, Perry *
McClary, Mike, 128
McClelan, B. G., 132
McCook, Edward, 126
McFarland, J. W., 72, 87, 135
McIlvaine, Samuel, 43, 122, 132
McLaughlin, Pvt., 69
medical treatment, 137-147
Mendall, S., 57
messes, 25
Michigan troops
  2nd, 31, 34, 60, 70, 131
  3rd, 15, 35, 56, 59, 127
  16th, 56
  19th, 94, 133
  22nd, 7
  23rd, 53, 114
Miller, David R., 22
Miller, Mart, 138
Miller, William, 38
Mine Run, VA, 40
minie and musket balls, (see ammunition)
Minie, Claude, 65
Minnesota troops
  1st, 75, 91
Missionary Ridge, TN, 45, 108, 115, 145
Mississippi troops
  1st, 66
  11th, 125
  16th, 134
  37th, 75, 105

39th, 130
43rd, 133
46th, 66, 81, 103, 105, 130, 135
Missouri troops
  21st, 29
Monocacy River, 41
Moon, Thomas, 116
Moore, A. B., 40
Morrill, E. C., 153
Morris Island, SC, 137
Mosman, Chesley A., 38, 66, 74, 101
Murfreesboro, TN, 72, 74
Murphy, Jim, 111
muster-out, 148-152

Nashville, TN, 41, 71, 74
Neal, Andrew, 105
New Hampshire troops
  5th, 11
New Hope Church, GA, 113, 121
New Jersey troops
  4th, 101
New Market Heights, VA, 6
New York troops
  14th New York Cavalry, 7
  4th New York Heavy Artillery, 139
  3rd, 133
  9th, 22, 38
  13th, 103
  15th, 102
  27th, 103
  49th, 126
  60th, 52
  61st, 94
  88th, 74
  91st, 118
  100th, 21, 33, 34, 40, 41, 68, 137
  104th, 47, 64, 71, 148
  107th, 56
  108th, 92
  114th, 91
  117th, 45, 112, 114, 133
  121st, 122
  123rd, 40, 152
  127th, 8, 34, 63, 150
  140th, 51
Nisbet, James C., 30

North Carolina troops
  5th, 7
  16th, 115
  52nd, 32
  55th, 36, 127
Norton, Oliver, 107
Nourse, Henry S., 6, 92
Ny River, 64

Occupations, 8
Ohio troops
  8th, 8, 40, 64, 74, 102, 134
  14th, 112
  15th, 103
  20th, 70, 110
  35th, 100, 103
  50th, 15, 107
  52nd, 33, 51, 103, 107, 125
  54th, 29, 38, 58
  55th, 31, 54, 58
  64th, 71, 127, 130
  65th, 31
  66th, 7
  72nd, 7
  74th, 107
  80th, 105
  82nd, 103
  101st, 25
  104th, 129
  121st, 92
  125th, 71, 125
O'Loughlin, Mike, 129
Orange, VA, 48
Orphan Brigade, 68, 113
Owen, Harry T., 80

Paris, Comte de, 67
Partridge, Samuel S., 103
Patrick's Station, VA, 136
Patterson, Edmund, 93, 103, 119
pay, 13, 34
Peachtree Creek, GA, 125
Pennsylvania troops
  9th, 133
  46th, iv
  47th, 7
  57th, 142
  58th, 7
  62nd, 35, 67, 84, 95, 132, 135
  83rd, 107
  90th, 30, 102, 105, 125, 146

95th, 73
124th, 21
138th, 73
140th, 45, 72, 136
145th, 16
153rd, 89
Pepper, G. W., 105
Perry, Mort, 45
personal items, 60
Petersburg, VA, 26, 81, 90, 100, 104, 126-127, 133, 136
Phelps, Frank, 101
ponchos and gum blankets, 51-53, 80
pone, 29
Pope, Albert A. *
population
   civilian, 1-2
   military, 1, 12
Port Gibson, MS, 130
Port Hudson, LA, 38, 57, 66, 90, 118, 121
Potter, Gilbert J., 40
Prentiss, B. M., 68
Prince, Henry W., 8, 34, 63, 150
prisoners of war, 147

Quinn, John, 139

Raccoon Valley, TN, 128
rate of fire, 19
rations, 24-31
   issuing, 28, 56, 58, 60, 80
Ravenal, Henry W., 5
recruitment, 13-16
Red River, 113
Redwood, Allen, 85
Reed, Thomas, 3
regiment, the
   numbers of, 10
   organization, 9
Regular army, strength of, 1
Reilly, James, 129
Resaca, GA, 106, 115, 129, 134, 139
Rice, Ralsa, 71, 123
Richmond, VA, 26, 47, 67, 78, 95, 133, 136
Ringgold, GA, 115
Robertson, J. B., 43

Robertson, Stephen, 135
Rodgers, J. G., 14, 93, 112
Rogers, Isaac, 107
Ross, W. E., 130
round-about coats, 34, 35, 36
Rowe, Dennis, 131
Rowell, Andrew, 136

Savage Station, VA, 118
Savannah, GA, 135
Sayler's Creek, VA, 110
Schneider, Peter, 125
Schwein, Martin, 153
Scofield, Matthew B., 29
Second Corps (U. S.), 90
Second Manassas, 58, 69, 95, 112, 123
Seminary Ridge, 29,
Seven Days' Battles, 35, 41, 47, 72, 98, 101, 140
Seven Pines, VA, 96, 120, 136
Sharpsburg, MD, 38
sharpshooters, 66, 71, 127
shelter tent, 54
Shenandoah Valley, 86
Shepherd, Henry, 107
Sheppard, Jack, 42
Shiloh, Battle of, 39, 67, 119, 122, 149
shoes and boots, 44, 46-48, 91
shooting
   in combat, 72-73
   killing, 72, 108-111
   rate of fire, 19
   target, 69-72
Silliman, Justus *
Sixteenth Corps (U. S.), 75
Small, Abner *
Smith, Bernard, 137
Smith, Carey, 118
Smith, Edwin, 29, 38, 58
Smith, James, 59
Smith, Judson, 118
South Carolina troops
   1st, 11
   13th, 92
Spencer, William, 94
spider, 28
Spotsylvania, VA, 29, 38, 59, 73-74, 95, 101, 104, 111, 126, 137, 139, 143
Springfield, MA, 67
Stannard, Will, 130

Stearns, Austin C. *
Stevens, John, W. *
Stevens, Thomas, 33, 70
Stewart, Nixon B., 33, 51
Stiles, Robert *
Stillwell, Leander *
Stones River, TN, 111, 128
Stonewall Brigade, 45, 95
Strong, Robert, 134
Stryker, George, 74
Stuckenberg, John, 16
Suffolk, VA, 131
Sykes, Columbus, 133

Tennessee, Army of, 71
Tennessee troops
   1st, 50, 69-70, 109
   2nd, 79
   7th, 127
   10th, 11
   20th, 139
   42nd, 66
   50th, 133
tents, 52-55
Texas troops
   8th Texas Cavalry, 146
   1st, 11
   4th, 37, 41, 46, 69, 105, 125, 128
   5th, 37, 43, 102, 127, 145
   6th, 124
   24th, 108, 121
Theaker, James G., 15
Thomas, George, 74, 111
Thompson, David L. *
Thompson, Tennessee, 50
tin cups, 28, 56, 59
tourniquet, use of, 146
Townsend, Samuel, 118
training, 18-22
Traveler, 41
Tunnard, William, 17
Tunnel Hill, GA, 94, 136
Tuthill, Richard, 99
Tuttle, John, 133

Uniforms
   average type, 38
   captured, 39
   condition of, 79, 81
   C. S., 36, 80
   cost, 31

early war, 37
filth of, 40-41
styles, 78
U.S. cost, 33
washing, 40
United States Infantry
12th, 86
19th, 86
Upson, Theodore F. *
Utoy Creek, GA, 112

Van Buskirk, David, 7
Van Nest, Joseph, 25
Vermont troops
2nd, 8, 15, 17, 84
4th, 52
5th, 94
Vicksburg, MS, 86, 90, 124
Vining, Henry, 88
Virginia troops
9th, 46, 96
12th, 151
13th, 17
18th, 80
19th, 55
21st, 10, 28, 39, 49, 55, 67, 88
33rd, 40, 43, 131, 138
41st, 36, 47
55th, 85
56th, 48

Wade, Edward H., 29
Wafer, Francis, 92
waist belt, 61
war, cost of, 1
Ward, Rowland, 139
Warren, Leander, 69
Washington, D. C., 42

Washington Navy Yard, 70
water, purity and supply of, 87
Watkins, Sam *
Watson, George, 125, 146-147
weapons
accuracy of, 65
Austrian rifle-musket, 65-66
bayonets, 64, 67-68, 109-112,
138
Belgian rifles, 68, 75
bore fouling, 75
captured, 67
cost of, 68
Enfield P1853, iv-v, 64-65,
67-68, 75
Harpers Ferry rifles, 70
Henry repeater, 75
Kerr rifles, 71
loading, 65-66, 68
Mississippi rifles, 67-68, 127
numbers delivered, 67
overheating, 74
personalization of, 69
problems of in battle, 73-74
rate of fire, 19
repeating vs. single shot, 65,
75
Richmond Confederate rifle,
65
Smoothbore, M1842, 65
Spencer, 75
Springfield, M1861 rifle musket, iv, 64-65, 67
Springfield, M1863 rifle musket, 65,
Whitworth rifle musket, 65-
66, 70-71
Welch, Spencer, 92

Weller, Edwin, 56
Wheeler, John, 123
Whitcomb, W. B., 115, 121
White, Amanda, 36
White, George, 31
Whitehorne, James, 151
Widney, 100
Wilderness, Battle of the, 116,
123, 137, 146
Wiley, Bill I., 5
Wilkenson, Frank, 14
Williams, James M., 6, 39, 124
Wilson, Nick, 73
Wilt, Jake, 42, 48, 126
Winchester, VA, 138
Winters, Erastus, 107
Wisconsin troops
5th, 116
7th, 138
25th, 96
28th, 33, 70
38th, 101
Wolford, Aaron, 135
Wood, Richard B., 136
Wood, William, 55
Worsham, John H. *
wounds
feelings of 139, 144
gangrene, 145-146
medical treatment of, 137-147
types, 137-138

Young, James, 52

Zouaves, 35

Gregory A. Coco, a native of Louisiana, was born in 1946. His interest in the Civil War, and especially the role of the common soldier, has led him to write this, his tenth book. By age 22, he had completed a tour in Vietnam where he served as a prisoner of war interrogator and army infantryman. He received the Purple Heart and won the Bronze Star in 1968.

Since college, he has worked as a city policeman, a state trooper, and a park ranger. Greg is currently employed as a seasonal interpreter with the National Park Service and as a licensed battlefield guide at the Gettysburg National Military Park.